Christianity in North America

BLOOMSBURY RELIGION IN NORTH AMERICA

The articles in this book were first published in the digital collection *Bloomsbury Religion in North America*. Covering North America's diverse religious traditions, this digital collection provides reliable and peer-reviewed articles and eBooks for students and instructors of religious studies, anthropology of religion, sociology of religion, and history. Learn more and get access for your library at www.theologyandreligiononline.com/bloomsbury-religion-in-north-america

Also Available:
Islam in North America, edited by Hussein Rashid,
Huma Mohibullah, and Vincent Biondo
Religion, Science and Technology in North America,
edited by Lisa L. Stenmark and Whitney A. Bauman
Religion and Nature in North America,
edited by Laurel D. Kearns and Whitney A. Bauman

Christianity in North America

An Introduction

EDITED BY DYRON B. DAUGHRITY

BLOOMSBURY ACADEMIC
LONDON • NEW YORK • OXFORD • NEW DELHI • SYDNEY

BLOOMSBURY ACADEMIC
Bloomsbury Publishing Plc
50 Bedford Square, London, WC1B 3DP, UK
1385 Broadway, New York, NY 10018, USA
29 Earlsfort Terrace, Dublin 2, Ireland

BLOOMSBURY, BLOOMSBURY ACADEMIC and the Diana logo are
trademarks of Bloomsbury Publishing Plc

First published online 2021
This print edition published in Great Britain 2024

Copyright © Bloomsbury Publishing Plc, 2021, 2024

Dyron B. Daughrity has asserted his right under the Copyright,
Designs and Patents Act, 1988, to be identified as Editor of this work.

Series design by Rebecca Heselton
Cover image: Salvation Mountain, Niland, California, USA © Michael Dwyer/Alamy Stock Photo

All rights reserved. No part of this publication may be reproduced or transmitted
in any form or by any means, electronic or mechanical, including photocopying,
recording, or any information storage or retrieval system, without prior
permission in writing from the publishers.

Bloomsbury Publishing Plc does not have any control over, or responsibility for,
any third-party websites referred to or in this book. All internet addresses given in
this book were correct at the time of going to press. The author and publisher regret
any inconvenience caused if addresses have changed or sites have ceased to
exist, but can accept no responsibility for any such changes.

A catalogue record for this book is available from the British Library.

Names: Daughrity, Dyron B., 1973- editor.
Title: Christianity in North America : an introduction / edited by Dyron B. Daughrity.
Description: London ; New York : Bloomsbury Academic, 2024. |
Series: Bloomsbury religion in North America | First published online in 2021. |
Includes bibliographical references and index.
Identifiers: LCCN 2023040339 | ISBN 9781350406476 (hardback) |
ISBN 9781350406483 (paperback)
Subjects: LCSH: Christianity–North America. | North America–Church history
Classification: LCC BR510 .C38 2024 | DDC 277–dc23/eng/20231004
LC record available at https://lccn.loc.gov/2023040339

ISBN: HB: 978-1-3504-0647-6
          PB: 978-1-3504-0648-3

Series: Bloomsbury Religion in North America

Typeset by Integra Software Services Pvt. Ltd.

To find out more about our authors and books visit www.bloomsbury.com
and sign up for our newsletters

Contents

Illustrations vii

List of Contributors xi

1 Christianity in North America: An Introduction *Dyron B. Daughrity* 1

PART ONE North American Christian Traditions

2 Catholicisms in North America *Chester Gillis* 31

3 Protestantisms in North America *T.J. Tomlin* 47

4 Evangelical Christianities in North America *Emma Rifai* 65

5 Mormonism in North America *Konden Smith Hansen* 81

6 Anabaptism: Mennonites, Amish, and Hutterites *John Sheridan* 105

PART TWO Race and North American Christianity

7 Race and Christianity *Shuma Iwai* 123

8 African American Christianities in North America *Darrius D. Hills* 129

9 Asian Americans and Christianity in North America *Shalon Park* 143

10 Latinx Christianities in North America *Lloyd Barba* 159

11 Native Americans and Christianity in North America
Joseph J. Saggio 177

PART THREE Critical Issues

12 Missionization and Christianity *Thomas E.I. Whittaker* 197

13 Masculinity and Christianity *Seth Dowland* 205

14 Women and Christianity *Emma Rifai* 211

15 Sex, Sexuality, and Christianity *Kristy L. Slominski* 215

CONTENTS

16 On Christians and the Abortion Divide/Debate in North America
Kristy L. Slominski 223

17 Christianity and Politics in North America *Anthony J. Miller* 233

18 Conversion Therapy and the Fight over the First Amendment
Chris Babits 249

Name Index 258

Subject Index 264

Illustrations

1.1 The First Amendment of the US Constitution allowed for unprecedented religious freedom in the United States 2

1.2 *TIME* magazine asked a question that proved to be very controversial 4

1.3 Frenchman Jacques Cartier explores the St. Lawrence River in Canada 6

1.4 A Congolese slave named Renty; a Guinea Coast slave named Jack; and an unidentified slave 9

1.5 John Wesley 12

1.6 Mary Baker Eddy 16

1.7 The Pentecostal movement 18

1.8 The Scopes Trial in 1925 deepened the liberal and conservative divide in the United States 20

1.9 Billy Graham preaching 21

1.10 Pope John Paul II visiting Mexico 25

2.1 St. Francis Xavier Church 32

2.2 The interior of St. Francis Xavier Church 34

2.3 SLU students and healthcare providers gathered in St. Francis Xavier Church to listen to a panel on Jesuit health care 36

2.4 SLUCare Physician Group combines their Catholic traditions with the science of medicine 38

2.5 The candles pictured here very deliberately illuminate only the altar, leaving the rest of the scene in the dark 41

3.1 Anglican priest George Whitefield drew enormous crowds across British North America in the 1730s and 1740s 50

ILLUSTRATIONS

3.2 In 1794, Richard Allen established the African Methodist Episcopal Church, the first independent African American Protestant denomination in the United States 53

3.3 Jarena Lee, a traveling Methodist minister, covered thousands of miles and delivered hundreds of sermons to mixed-race audiences every year 54

3.4 Joseph Smith, the founder and prophet of the Church of Jesus Christ of Latter-Day Saints 55

3.5 Baptist minister Martin Luther King Jr. proclaimed a message of racial and civil equality informed by a prophetic tradition of justice and hope within the African American church 59

3.6 Billy Graham drew huge crowds to his rallies 60

4.1 George Whitefield preaching 68

4.2 Aimee Semple McPherson 73

4.3 Clarence Darrow speaks at the Scopes Trial 74

4.4 Billy Graham 75

4.5 Ronald Reagan speaking with Jerry Falwell 78

5.1 The Angel Moroni delivering the plates of the *Book of Mormon* to Joseph Smith 82

5.2 Facsimile 2 of the Book of Abraham 83

5.3 Youth Handcart Trek, June 10, 2016 87

5.4 Mountain Meadows 89

5.5 "The Real Objection to Smoot" by Joseph Keppler 92

5.6 A woman with two children walking into a store in Colorado City, Arizona, August 13, 2008 94

5.7 The South Temple entrance to the Church Administration Building in downtown Salt Lake City, Utah 97

6.1 A timeline of the three core streams of Anabaptism 107

6.2 An Amish bakery in Kalona, Iowa 111

6.3 Amish children walking on road dressed in traditional Amish attire 112

ILLUSTRATIONS

6.4 Image of Amish horse and buggy 113

6.5 Pie chart of the most recent data collected on Mennonite, Hutterite, and Amish populations in North America 117

7.1 Human hands showing unity 126

8.1 A prayer meeting 132

8.2 George Whitefield preaching 134

8.3 John Wesley 137

8.4 AME congregation holds hands in church 138

8.5 Richard Allen 139

9.1 Asian American students' anti-war protest, Berkley, California, 1972 144

9.2 Indian American demonstrating against the Immigration Legislation, 1968 145

9.3 Chinese section of hunger parade, Sacramento, CA, 1933 148

9.4 French depiction of Yellow Peril in America, 1908 149

9.5 Chinese war brides at religious class, Westminster Presbyterian Church in Minneapolis in 1950 151

10.1 Religious affiliation, by Hispanic origin group 161

10.2 Cesar Chavez and Robert F. Kennedy take Communion 163

10.3 Sister Teresa at a Pentecostal street service 165

10.4 Shrine of Our Lady of Charity in Miami 166

10.5 Nuestra Señora de la Altagracia Catedral Primada de America 168

10.6 Replica of banners at Southside Presbyterian Church, Tucson, Arizona 170

11.1 Bartolomé de Las Casas, "Protector of the Indians" 179

11.2 Statue of St. Kateri Tekakwitha, first Native American Catholic saint in North America 181

11.3 John Eliot of Roxbury, Massachusetts, "Apostle to the Indians" 183

11.4 The 1864 Sand Creek Massacre 184

11.5 The Peyote plant used in Native American religious practices 189

ILLUSTRATIONS

12.1 The Eliot Bible, in Massachusetts, an Algonquian language, was printed in Cambridge, Massachusetts, in 1663 198

12.2 Presbyterian Sabbath school scholars in Caledonia, Columbia County, Wisconsin, in 1900 200

12.3 An image from *The Home Missionary*, the periodical of the American Home Missionary Society, encouraging American Protestants to welcome Italian immigrants in 1905 201

13.1 The YMCA providing rations to American soldiers in Liverpool during the First World War 206

13.2 In October 1997, men from around the country descended on the National Mall in Washington, DC, for the Promise Keepers "Stand in the Gap" rally 208

14.1 Mary Baker Eddy 212

15.1 Mary Steichen Calderone, known as the founder of comprehensive sexuality education 217

15.2 Norma McCorvey ("Jane Roe") and her lawyer on the steps of the Supreme Court in 1989 218

16.1 Norma McCorvey ("Jane Roe") and her lawyer on the steps of the Supreme Court in 1989 225

16.2 A clinic escort outside of a Planned Parenthood clinic 227

16.3 Henry Morgentaler, pro-choice abortion activist in Canada 228

17.1 President Donald Trump with Governor Greg Abbot and Secretary Rick Perry 234

17.2 Bartolomé de Las Casas 236

17.3 Cornel West 240

17.4 Pope Francis visits Mexico 243

17.5 President Barack Obama and Billy Graham 244

18.1 Colorado Two LGBTQ bill signed into law 250

18.2 Sigmund Freud (1856–1939): a conversion therapy skeptic 251

18.3 US states and municipalities banning conversion therapy with minors 255

List of Contributors

Chris Babits is a Postdoctoral Teaching Fellow at Utah State University, USA.

Dyron B. Daughrity is Professor and William S. Banowsky Chair in Religion at Pepperdine University, USA.

Lloyd Barba is Assistant Professor of Religion at Amherst College, USA.

Seth Dowland is Associate Professor of Religion at Pacific Lutheran University, USA.

Chester Gillis is Emeritus Professor at Georgetown University, USA.

Darrius D. Hills is Associate Professor of Race and Religion at Grinnell College, USA.

Shuma Iwai is Assistant Professor at the University of Wisconsin-La Crosse, USA.

Anthony J. Miller is Visiting Assistant Professor of History at Hanover College, USA.

Shalon Park is a PhD candidate at Princeton Theological Seminary, USA.

Emma Rifai holds a PhD from the University of Iowa, USA.

Joseph J. Saggio is the Executive Vice-President and Administrative Dean of the College for Southwestern Assemblies of God University, American Indian College Campus in Phoenix, USA.

John Sheridan is a Religious Studies PhD student at the University of Iowa, USA.

Kristy L. Slominski is Assistant Professor of Religious Studies at the University of Arizona, USA.

Konden Smith Hansen is Lecturer of Religious Studies at the University of Arizona, USA.

T.J. Tomlin is Associate Professor of History at the University of Northern Colorado, USA.

Thomas E.I. Whittaker is Assistant Professor of History at LeTourneau University, USA.

1

Christianity in North America:
An Introduction

Dyron B. Daughrity

Introduction

There are more Christians in the United States of America than in any nation on Earth. As the debate rages on about whether the United States is a "Christian nation," statistics indicate that Christianity is firmly entrenched in American culture.

It might seem strange that the United States has so many active Christians when compared to the other Western nations of the world, which tend to be far more secular. However, the United States is unique in one important category: the history of religious freedom. In the year 1791, when the United States was still very young, the First Amendment was passed, giving religious freedom to everyone within its borders. The first sentence of that amendment reads thus:

> Congress shall make no law respecting an establishment of religion, or prohibiting the free exercise thereof.

That rather short directive has made all the difference. Most Western nations kept the church and state linked well into the twentieth century. Scholars have shown that in all likelihood, the First Amendment is what kept Christianity in America vibrant. As state churches in Europe ossified, religion in the United States has remained robust. Religious competition turned American religion into a marketplace, causing churches to compete with each other. In Europe, the state churches led to lax attendance, unenthusiastic leaders, a captive audience, and finances that were refreshed regularly by the government's deposit of funds. Churches did not have to meet the needs of their parishioners because there was no competition.

FIGURE 1.1 *The First Amendment of the US Constitution allowed for unprecedented religious freedom in the United States.* Source: *Photograph by Attila Csaszar / Getty Images.*

The United States was not able to have a state church. In the earliest days of colonial America, several states tried to have a state church, but the project failed as a diverse array of immigrants kept arriving to its shores. The founding fathers, rightly, saw that something new was needed. The old model that they all knew from England and Europe would not suffice in this grand experiment of cultural and religious diversity. Thus, after only a few years, the government realized something that many nations have instituted ever since: religious freedom. Some people call it the separation of church and state. Religion was decoupled from the state. It was allowed the freedom to experiment, the freedom to adapt to the needs of the people, and the freedom to become extinct if it failed to achieve cultural relevance. Perhaps somewhat surprisingly, the state churches of Europe are the places where religion became irrelevant to its people. Religion in America, however, thrived.

The vast majority of Americans self-identify as Christians. Less than 6 percent of Americans identify with a non-Christian religion. While America is certainly a diverse place in many ways, religiously, it is less so. That being stated, it is important to note that American Christians subdivide into a host of different Christian denominations: Catholic, Baptist, Presbyterian, Mormon, and so many more. Still, what these millions of people share in common is vast: a belief in the God of Israel, a belief in Jesus as

CHRISTIANITY IN NORTH AMERICA: AN INTRODUCTION   3

God's son, a reverence for the Christian scriptures, a Christian ethical sensibility, a sense that God interacts with his creation, and a belief in the afterlife.

While many people have argued, and still argue, that America is no longer a Christian nation, here are some illuminating points:

1   In 2017, the US Congress was 91 percent Christian. This number has remained rather unchanged in the last few decades.

2   The United States has more Christians than any other nation on Earth.

3   The percentage of atheists in the United States has remained steady at around 4 percent since the 1940s.

4   Some scholars point to the millennials (among them the religious "nones") as being far less religious than their older counterparts. But this phenomenon is expected. As millennials mature and start having children, they will likely do what previous generations did—they will return to the religion of their youth.

5   The United States still sends out far more missionaries than any other nation in the world.

If America is not a Christian nation, then it would be difficult to call any nation a Christian nation. It all depends on how one looks at it. Certainly, one could argue that American Christians are less active today than they were a generation or two ago, but that does not necessarily mean that American Christians will remain less active from now on. Religious participation has ebbed and flowed throughout American history.

For example, in 1966, *TIME* magazine featured an ominous cover asking "Is God Dead?" It was their bestselling issue of all time. The late 1960s were certainly a revolutionary time, and to some, it seemed as if religion might be on the way out. But that did not happen. Christianity in America continues on. Catholics keep attending Mass. Pentecostal churches continue to proliferate. Nondenominational churches continue to expand. Every major city in America seems to have numerous megachurches, sometimes with members counted in the thousands. Perhaps the predictions of God's demise have been greatly exaggerated. But they continue, as headlines routinely proclaim the decline of Christianity in America.

For now, at least, Christianity seems to be fully functional in the United States, and thriving. Canadians are usually described as being less religious than Americans, but more religious than Western Europeans. In many ways, Mexico belongs in a study of Latin America rather than in North America, even though its geography is more accurately part of a Central American land mass. Certainly, Mexico is linguistically, politically, and culturally much more Latin American than North American. Indeed, when differentiating themselves, Mexicans usually refer to US inhabitants as *los norteamericanos*, or "North Americans."

FIGURE 1.2 TIME *magazine asked a question that proved to be very controversial.* Source: *Photograph by CBS Photo Archive / Getty Images.*

Beginnings

Scholars are not sure when people started coming to what is now North America. Some suggest 15,000 years ago, while others suggest it was perhaps as many as 35,000 years ago. Native Americans were actually immigrants from Asia who probably traveled over the Bering land bridge. They settled on the American continents and occupied them for thousands of years. Some theorize that others may have come by boats via Southeast Asia, although that theory is far less prominent. Whatever the case, it seems that what we call the Americas was actually settled by people from Asia.

Once these people migrated to this new land, they proliferated into thousands of people groups now known as tribes. Estimates vary about how many of these Asian people were in the Americas when Christopher Columbus arrived, but it was in the millions, perhaps as many as fifty million in North, Central, and South America combined. Some estimate that around five million people lived in what we now call the United States and Canada in 1492 (Taylor 2001: 40).

No one knows exactly what the Indigenous people thought when they saw the European peoples arriving on their shores and expanding all over the continent. The Spanish were the first Europeans to settle, long term, in what is now called the United States. They established Saint Augustine, Florida, in 1565 and held onto it for over two hundred years. The Spanish entered California in the 1540s with the explorations of Juan Cabrillo. The famous Franciscan Father Junipero Serra established several

CHRISTIANITY IN NORTH AMERICA: AN INTRODUCTION

California missions, beginning with San Diego in 1769. Spanish explorers entered Texas in 1520. A Spanish Franciscan priest named Marcos de Niza was the first European to explore the modern state of Arizona, in the 1530s. The Spanish founded Santa Fe, the capital of present-day New Mexico, in 1610.

The English, led by Sir Walter Raleigh, came to what is now North Carolina in 1585, but the experiment failed after a few years. Another wave of English immigrants arrived to present-day Virginia in 1607, with the establishment of Jamestown. In the 1620 and 1630s the English presence became even more fortified with permanent colonies established at Plymouth and Massachusetts Bay. The populations of the Americas surged in both the seventeenth and eighteenth centuries. The Louisiana Purchase of 1803 expanded the land of the United States by nearly around 2.6 million square kilometers, and included the modern American states of Arkansas, Iowa, Missouri, Kansas, Oklahoma, Nebraska, South Dakota, Montana, and parts of Colorado, North Dakota, Minnesota, Louisiana, New Mexico, Texas, and Wyoming. Even portions of the Canadian provinces of Saskatchewan and Alberta were included in the deal.

In 1819, Florida was ceded by Spain to the United States. In 1848, Mexico—which declared independence in 1810—ceded the American Southwest (California, Arizona, Nevada, Utah, and parts of Wyoming, New Mexico, and Colorado) to the United States in the aftermath of the Mexican-American War. This cession was signed at the Treaty of Guadalupe Hidalgo and added around 1.3 million square kilometers to the United States' territory.

The Oregon Territory—which included Idaho and Washington—was ceded by the British to the United States in 1846. Russia ceded Alaska to the United States in 1867, expanding America's land by around 1.3 million square kilometers. Hawaii was annexed by the United States in 1898.

Canada's history is much more linked to Britain and France, and for a much longer time than in the United States. Canada continues its nominal connection to the British monarch, but in reality, the connection between the two countries is today quite insignificant. Beginning with the Canadian Confederation in 1867 and culminating with the Act of 1982, Canada stands today as a sovereign nation.

Canada's great explorers began traversing the Saint Lawrence River in 1534 with the arrival of Frenchman Jacques Cartier. In 1603, under the leadership of Samuel de Champlain, the French established a continuous settlement at Quebec City. French Catholic missionaries worked all around the Great Lakes and especially Quebec, known at that time as "New France." The young Jesuit Jacques Marquette explored the Mississippi River all the way down to Arkansas, but ultimately turned back, fearing he might encounter hostile Spanish forces.

French missionaries had great success converting First Nations peoples to Christianity as they explored and expanded French Catholic influence. They worked in Eastern Canada, the Great Lakes region, and all the way down the Mississippi to New Orleans, which was founded by the French in 1718.

FIGURE 1.3 *Frenchman Jacques Cartier explores the St. Lawrence River in Canada.* Source: *Photograph by Rischgitz / Stringer / Getty Images.*

By the year 1800, North America was well on its way to being Christianized. It had become a living tapestry of Europe's great variety of Christian influence:

- Anglicans established Jamestown, Virginia, in 1607.
- French Roman Catholics established Quebec in 1608.
- Spanish Catholics established Santa Fe, New Mexico, in 1608.
- English Calvinists, also known as "Puritans," arrived to Massachusetts on the Mayflower in 1620 to establish a "purer" form of Protestantism.
- Dutch Reformed Christians established New Amsterdam—later known as New York City—in the 1620s.
- Lord Baltimore (Cecil Calvert) established Maryland in 1632 to help English Catholics escape persecution in their homeland. They were joined by some convicted criminals exiled from England.
- Germans starting arriving in significant numbers in the 1680s, bringing with them Lutheranism and German Catholicism. There were also many smaller groups of Protestant German Christians who came to America for religious freedom, as they were often persecuted in Europe. These included *Anabaptists*, Pietists, Moravians, and Mennonites.

CHRISTIANITY IN NORTH AMERICA: AN INTRODUCTION

- Quakers started coming to America in the 1650s. The most notable Quaker in American history is William Penn, the founder of the state of Pennsylvania, which became known for its religious toleration.

- In 1769, Spanish Franciscan priest Junipero Serra founded the first of many Spanish missions on the coast of California; they had a profound impact on the Indigenous peoples of the era.

- Beginning in the 1790s, Russian Orthodox priests had success converting native Alaskans—specifically the Aleutians—and established a missionary base at Kodiak Island. Saint Herman was part of that mission and is revered in Russian Orthodoxy as the patron saint of North America.

- In the 1840s and 1850s the Irish famines led many Irish Catholics to America, paving the way for an influx of Catholics to arrive en masse.

In just a few centuries, America had become an extension of Europe, yet quite different from Europe in several respects, such as in politics and religion. Politically, America was experimenting with representative democracy. Religiously, America was become a complicated place, as it diversified dramatically. Europe was very different; its nations were largely monolithic in terms of religion. France, Spain, Italy, and Austria were Catholic. England was Anglican. Scandinavian nations were Lutheran. Greeks and Russians were Eastern Orthodox.

English-speaking America was swiftly becoming a "melting pot" of religion. Canadians prefer the term "mosaic," since they tended to divide along Catholic and Protestant lines. The British territories in Canada remained mainly Anglican, while the French regions were decidedly Roman Catholic.

Like New France, Mexico has since its founding maintained a strong connection to the Roman Catholic Church. Protestantism has made very little headway in Mexico until recent times. Only about 10 percent of Mexicans claim to be some form of Protestant. Mexico is the world's second largest Catholic nation, after Brazil.

Indigenous peoples and enslaved Africans joined Christianity in a complex array of ways. Some Christian missionaries had success with Natives, although others failed. Missionaries were often heroic in their efforts, traveling courageously into tribal lands that may or may not prove receptive. Some missionaries developed close relations with First Nations peoples as they moved into their communities and depended upon them for food and shelter.

Historians have shown that missionaries—both collectively and individually—had very mixed motives. On the one hand, they eagerly sought to bring the liberating message of Christ to a people they felt would benefit from it. On the other hand, some missionaries were very much part of the colonial project and could never separate themselves from the colonial mindset that Indigenous peoples needed to, effectively, become like Europeans.

The massive missionary movement of the early centuries of the Americas is too complex to detail here, but suffice it to say that there are ample examples on both sides—disastrous encounters as well as occasions where much good resulted. Some missionaries were able to prepare Indigenous peoples for the swelling tide of European settlers that would prove inevitable. Some missionaries used the Bible to teach Indigenous peoples about European customs and languages in hopes that natives could negotiate more effectively when colonial officers approached them. In all cases, missionaries were utterly dependent upon the First Nations peoples they befriended. Had they not been received and protected by these tribes, they would have lost their lives in all probability due to the bitter cold, the harsh conditions, and the violence that could befall them out on the open frontier.

We conclude this section with a brief discussion of how the Europeanization of America brought with it that hideous institution of slavery. Indentured servanthood of fellow Europeans preceded it, but it paled in comparison to the scale and sordid debasement of chattel slavery that developed. Columbus's expeditions were rife with "that peculiar institution," as Natives were captured routinely and sent back, enslaved, to Spain.

Slavery began in the English colonies in 1619, in Virginia, about a decade after the founding of Jamestown, and a year before the Mayflower landed at Plymouth Rock. British ships seized around twenty Africans from a Portuguese slave ship. In Virginia, these Africans were treated as indentured servants and eventually won their freedom. Part of the reason they were treated more humanely had to do with British law, wherein Christians were not allowed to be enslaved. Thus, it is very likely that some if not most of these earliest enslaved Africans were Roman Catholic Christians from Angola and the Congo. Portugal colonized parts of the present-day nations of Angola and the Congo in the fifteenth century, thus many West Africans had already been Christians for over a century. It was also common for the Portuguese to baptize those they enslaved, after capturing them in the interior of the country prior to loading them onto slave ships. In those cases, they were probably nominal Christians, yet expected to embrace Christianity more deeply over time.

The system of chattel slavery developed throughout the seventeenth century, and eventually morphed into kind of a caste system. The less European blood Africans had—if any—the likelier they were to experience the inhumanity that chattel slavery entailed, including branding, physical violence, and a complete loss of identity. Beginning in Virginia in 1662, children born to enslaved mothers were declared slaves. This was different from British law and custom, which was based on patrimonial law—the status of the father.

The slave population grew dramatically over the eighteenth and nineteenth centuries. By 1860—on the eve of America's civil war—enslaved Africans made up around 13 percent of the US population. The nation's population in that year was thirty-one million, and around four million of them were enslaved. Almost half a million Americans were slave owners when the *American Civil War* broke out, meaning about 8 percent of Americans were slave-owners, and by that time virtually all of them were in the southern states.

Opposition to slavery developed early on as it was clear to many Christians that the system was cruel, unjust, and against God. Richard Baxter (1615–91) was a prolific Puritan scholar and pastor in England who strongly opposed slavery in his writings.

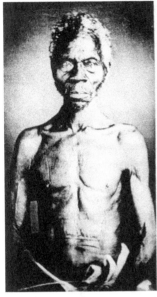 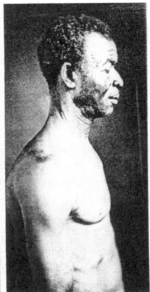 

FIGURE 1.4 *Left to right: A Congolese slave named Renty; a Guinea Coast slave named Jack; and an unidentified slave.* Source: *Photograph by Bettmann / Getty Images.*

He was widely read in English America and no doubt influenced other Puritans. The various Anabaptists groups in America, such as Mennonites—often having experienced punishing conditions themselves—spoke out against slavery with regularity, as did the Quakers who were firmly antislavery from early on.

Why did most of the enslaved Africans adopt Christianity? As discussed earlier, some of them were Christians already. However, the options were very limited for the enslaved. If they practiced their African Indigenous religion, or perhaps even Islam, they could attract unwanted attention by their owners. Thus, some of the enslaved used the system to their advantage. Others, no doubt, were evangelized by other enslaved Africans who drew from the faith to help them cope with the traumas associated with being under another person's complete control. Others were evangelized by their owners, as history attests.

It would be disingenuous, however, to argue that enslaved Africans merely adopted Christianity for superficial reasons. Certainly, some believed in the Gospel and realized the hope it provided. They trusted in Christ, and found the biblical stories to be compelling to them, especially given their plight. The Exodus story makes good sense to the enslaved, promising vindication, justice, and God's eventual freeing of the captive. The story of Jesus, too, appealed to some, as Jesus proclaimed in his first public sermon, recounted in Luke 4:18:

> The Spirit of the Lord is upon me, because He hath anointed me to preach the Gospel to the poor. He hath sent me to heal the brokenhearted, to preach deliverance to the captives, and recovery of sight to the blind, to set at liberty them that are bruised.

Jesus was no friend to the elites. Rather, he was killed by them. This truth would not have been lost on African Americans in a context of profound injustice.

Over time, African Americans began to worship together and nurture leaders among themselves. The first African American denomination—the African Methodist Episcopal Church—was founded by Reverend Richard Allen in 1816. Allen was born into slavery in 1760, but bought his freedom in 1780. He began his ministry a few years later and was ordained by the famous Methodist bishop Francis Asbury in 1799. Allen's ministry thrived, as he proved to be a most capable preacher and church administrator. He spearheaded African American conventions and worked heroically in the Underground Railroad—a network of safe houses for enslaved Africans who had escaped bondage.

Emancipation was a long process in the United States, beginning with the Slave Trade Act of 1794, which forbade American ships to involve themselves in the slave trade. In 1807, Congress passed the Act Prohibiting Importation of Slaves, which made the importation of enslaved Africans a federal crime. The ruling of 1794 had not abolished the importation of slaves; it only made it illegal for American ships to become involved in the slave trade—a law that was not strictly enforced. Nevertheless, enslaved Africans continued to arrive on foreign ships. The law of 1807 made no significant legal impact on the institution of slavery that already existed in the states, however. It continued apace, and enchained Africans continued to arrive via land, such as through Spanish Florida or Spanish Texas.

Maturation

We have noted how American Christianity, from early on, was quite different from European Christianity. It is ironic, therefore, that many of the Puritans policed Christianity in their own colonies, much as it was done in Europe. The Puritans seemed equally convinced as the Europeans were that religion and state went hand in hand. Thus, in the early years of colonial America, we see Puritan infighting and religious persecution that mirrored the European context. In Massachusetts, in the 1690s, over two hundred people were accused of being witches, and nineteen of them were executed at the infamous Salem Witch Trials. Early Americans had not learned the lessons that they themselves, no doubt, should have learned while subjected to religious persecution in Europe.

By the early 1700s, the religious fires were cooling down. The religious flare of earlier generations was not passed on in the DNA of the nation's early settlers. No doubt the religious extremism was off-putting to many. Many Americans had moved further into the interior of the nation to claim their own land. Homesteading, farming, and ranching were lonely enterprises on the frontier. Americans were an extremely self-sufficient people, but they were also very lonely. Church attendance was impossible for many, as the nearest congregation might be many miles away. It was a perfect context for revivalists, itinerant preachers, and religious conventions. And this is precisely what happened.

CHRISTIANITY IN NORTH AMERICA: AN INTRODUCTION

In the 1730s, there arose a series of revivals in the English-speaking world. Beginning in England, it quickly transported to the American colonies. It was an evangelical movement that transcended denominationalism. Protestants of all stripes were swept up in it, and it certainly met a social need on the American frontier.

The American preacher most closely associated with what is now called the First Great Awakening was Jonathan Edwards, the famous preacher who preached one of America's most influential sermons: "Sinners in the Hands of an Angry God." In fact, many who had wandered away from the Gospel were now challenged in the starkest of terms:

> They [wicked men] deserve to be cast into hell [...] justice calls aloud for an infinite punishment of their sins. [...] The sword of divine justice is every moment brandished over their heads ... Every unconverted man properly belongs to hell; that is his place. [...] They are now the objects of that very same anger and wrath of God, that is expressed in the torments of hell. [...] Yea, God is a great deal more angry with great numbers that are now on earth: yea, doubtless, with many that are now *in this congregation*, who it may be are at ease, than he is with many of those who are now in the flames of hell. [...] The devil stands ready to fall upon them, and seize them as his own. [...] They belong to him; he has their souls in his possession. [...] The old serpent is gaping for them; hell opens its mouth wide to receive them.
>
> (Edwards 1741: 6–7)

With threatening sermons like this one, it is no wonder that so many people began to flock back into the churches.

Edwards experienced revival in his own life and touched off a massive movement in the colonies that spread far and wide. His efforts were aided by the incredibly charismatic British Methodist preacher George Whitefield, who along with brothers John and Charles Wesley, established the Methodist movement while they were students at Oxford University. Their ministry was largely aimed at Christians who had been marginalized, especially those in far off places, without access to parish churches. When John Wesley was told he would not receive a parish ministry, he countered with the words, "I look on all the world as my parish."

These religious pioneers believed in lay ministry rather than requiring ordination. They discouraged ostentatious vestments. They were happy to preach in the open fields to anyone who would gather to hear the Gospel. Their sermons were much more focused on the interior of the person rather than the building up of institutional Christianity. Famously, Wesley described his born again experience with the words, "I felt my heart strangely warmed. I felt I did trust in Christ, Christ alone for salvation. And an assurance was given me that he had taken away my sins, even mine, and saved me from the law of sin and death" (Collins 1999: 62). Whitefield and the Wesleys preached to many millions of people as they traversed England and America on horseback. Whitefield in particular became a national icon in America, the first celebrity, due to his spectacular oratory.

FIGURE 1.5 *John Wesley, the father of Methodism, felt his heart "strangely warmed" and traveled England and America to spread his enlivened approach to Christianity.* Source: Photograph by Bettmann / Getty Images.

One of the most important impacts of the First Great Awakening was that it further established an ecumenical, nondenominational ethos in America that has persisted to the present day. Americans began to realize that they were part of *Christianity* rather than simply part of a denominational structure. In the Old World, people were Anglicans, Catholics, Reformed, Lutherans. In the New World, they might be connected to a denomination, but it was not necessarily a life commitment.

CHRISTIANITY IN NORTH AMERICA: AN INTRODUCTION   **13**

In addition, so many Americans lived on the frontier, where denominations hardly existed. The only taste of corporate worship that they ever had was a revivalist preacher who preached to thousands of people coming from all manner of religious and cultural background. American Christianity is almost inherently ecumenical. Even in the present day, Americans switch denominations with regularity. They join "nondenominational" churches that encompass the pluralistic zeitgeist found in the First Great Awakening. And in many ways we have George Whitefield's nondenominational preaching campaigns to thank for that. For example, looking back on his ministry, he commented:

> I saw regenerate souls among the Baptists, among the Presbyterians, among the Independents, and among the Church [i.e., Anglican] folks—all children of God, and yet all born again in a different way of worship: and who can tell which is the most evangelical?
>
> (Whitefield quoted in Noll 2003: 15)

Americans in the twenty-first century still think like this. Even those within denominations tend to think interdenominationally. As denominations continue to decline in the United States, this ecumenical-yet-evangelical perspective shows no signs of weakening.

The Second Great Awakening was equally significant and influenced the religious zeitgeist of the United States in similar ways. First and foremost, it revitalized Christianity in America. Secondly, it birthed numerous denominations that are still with us. Third, it cemented evangelical, pious, and charismatic Christianity as a major player in American religiosity.

It is always difficult to assign a date to large and long-lasting revivals, but a good estimate would be 1801 to around 1840. In 1801, the Cane Ridge Revival broke out in Kentucky and attracted 20,000 pioneers, farmers, settlers, and other country folk. For those who attended, it was like being drunk on God, similar to when the early church was accused of "having too much wine" (Acts 2:13). It was led by a Presbyterian minister named Barton Stone who—along with Alexander Campbell—founded the denomination known as the Disciples of Christ.

At Cane Ridge, several preachers scattered around the camp and preached sermons at all hours of the day, standing on anything they could find to elevate themselves above the crowds. They would rotate around so people could hear several speakers during their days in the holy camp. It only lasted a week, but it has gone down in history as the second most important revival in American history, after Azusa Street—which lasted several years. (The *Azusa Street Revival* will be discussed later in this chapter.)

The Cane Ridge Revival was led mainly by Presbyterians but there were also Methodists and Baptists there. The most notable aspect of the revival was the charismatic ethos of it. Eyewitnesses remarked on people speaking in tongues, falling down in religious ecstasy, running around in circles, barking, laughing uncontrollably, jerking on the ground, shaking, and repenting of their sins with great emotion. It was

14   **CHRISTIANITY IN NORTH AMERICA**

shocking at first, but then everybody started getting involved in these charismatic "exercises"—which is what they called them.

The Cane Ridge Revival planted seeds in people's minds and gave birth to a new form of exuberance and freedom in worship that really caught on, especially on the American frontier. Rural people were impacted more than city folk. It touched off a movement among the lower socio economic classes rather than the university elites. It was a people's movement, and it set the stage for the massive Pentecostal movement that came onto the world stage in the early twentieth century.

The most important preacher of the Second Great Awakening was Charles Grandison Finney (1792–1875). Finney became famous for his electric preaching and his "altar call," which became an American classic ritual in the realm of Christian revivalism. The preacher would convince his hearers that they needed to repent of their sins, and the people would storm forth to pray and confess at the "anxious bench" up at the front of the church. This "coming forward" became a standard feature of American evangelicalism, especially in the ministry of Billy Graham—probably America's most important preacher in history.

All of this chaos in worship would have horrified the Europeans who prized order in the church. Europeans were used to state churches that had rules. Congregants were governed and overseen by religious authorities who were connected to the state. America had no such connection and no such secular authorities to police religion. Preachers and congregants were free to worship with whomever they wanted. Anyone could preach whatever they wanted and without persecution. This was a grand experiment. It was the unleashing of religious ideas. And sociologists believe this is precisely why Christianity in America became so relevant to the people; it allowed no restrictions to get in the way of people's religious convictions. A poor man could be a somebody in the church. One did not have to have a graduate degree from a prestigious university to lead worship or to preach in the open air or to start a church. It was American-style religion, intoxicating in its openness. It was radically uninhibited. And it was rather shocking to the more establishment-oriented people.

Christianity grew dramatically in such a context as this. Churches mushroomed with astonishing speed. By 1840, the United States had more Methodist churches than post offices (Robert Bruce Mullin cited in Hastings 1999: 429).

Since virtually all restrictions upon religion had been removed with the First Amendment of the Constitution in 1791, new denominations were created to meet the needs of all of the people flooding into the churches. From a socio economic perspective, Christianity was very good business, as demand was at an all-time high. Numerous denominations were started during this exuberant context:

- The *Disciples of Christ* were started by Barton Stone and Alexander Campbell. This movement has split into four denominations today: Disciples of Christ, Christian Churches, Church of Christ, and International Churches of Christ.

CHRISTIANITY IN NORTH AMERICA: AN INTRODUCTION

- The *Church of Jesus Christ of Latter-day Saints* (LDS), also known as Mormons, began in New York in 1830 with the claims of a young man named Joseph Smith (1805–44). Smith published the *Book of Mormon* when he was twenty-four years old and grew his movement to tens of thousands of members in only a decade and a half. His successor, Brigham Young, moved the church to Utah, where the Mormons established a society from virtually nothing. Early on, Mormonism was a polygamous religion, but today only the smaller sects still continue that practice. Their membership is around seventeen million worldwide, and they are considered one of the fastest growing religious communities in the world. One of their most important teachings is celestial marriage—that earthly marriage, and earthly families, will continue throughout eternity if covenanted ("sealed") in the LDS church.

- The *Seventh-Day Adventists* began in the 1830s. They believed the end times were coming soon based on biblical prophecy. They were begun by a Baptist preacher named William Miller, but their most important leader emerged a bit later, and was female—something quite uncommon in that era. Her name was Ellen Gould White (1827–1915), and she had many dreams and visions she claimed were from God. She became known as a great preacher and prophetess among her followers. Today there are over twenty million Adventists in the world.

- *Jehovah's Witnesses* arose a bit later, in the 1870s, but have a global membership of over eight million. They began as a Bible study group in Pittsburgh, Pennsylvania, and still focus much of their teaching on the end times.

- *Church of Christ, Scientist*, is a movement that also began in the 1870s. Like Adventism, their most notable leader was a woman: Mary Baker Eddy (1821–1910). This movement arose in Massachusetts and based itself on the idea that the material world is illusory, and physical illnesses and infirmities can be overcome through spiritual means such as prayer.

All of these Christian movements, as well as several others, rose up in America in the nineteenth century, and owe their existence to the religious context created by the Second Great Awakening. However, it was the events of the early twentieth century—no doubt influenced by the Second Great Awakening—that really catapulted American Christianity to the cutting edge of world Christianity.

America's most important "awakening" happened in 1906 in the city of Los Angeles, California. Known as the *Azusa Street Revival*, it has transformed the landscape of Christianity in profound ways and is considered by many to have stimulated that religious phenomenon known as the modern Pentecostal movement.

FIGURE 1.6 *Mary Baker Eddy led the Church of Christ, Scientist movement, which thrived in the nineteenth and early twentieth centuries.* Source: *Photograph by Library of Congress / Getty Images.*

Pentecostal Christianity has deep roots. In the book of Acts, the apostles had dreams and visions that were striking, and paved the way for the growth of the faith in the aftermath of Jesus' resurrection and ascension to heaven. The apostolic church focused on miracles, signs and wonders, prophecy, and glossolalia (speaking in tongues). Led by Peter, James, Paul, and Barnabas, the church expanded prolifically due to the miracles and signs performed by the early church leaders. The blind became sighted, the lame could walk, and even the dead were raised through prayer and

CHRISTIANITY IN NORTH AMERICA: AN INTRODUCTION

intense faith. All of the credit was due to God's Holy Spirit, which Jesus bequeathed to the apostles before he left the earth.

Similarly, throughout church history, there have always been prophecies, miracles, signs, wonders, and apocalyptic visions. Catholic history is filled with such instances. However, during the Second Great Awakening, these ideas came back with full force, yet among Protestants—who were usually more skeptical of these kinds of ideas. Indeed, many Protestants *critiqued* this aspect of Catholicism, preferring to take the path of rationalism and modern interpretations of faith. The Second Great Awakening set the stage for the modern Pentecostal movement by bucking many of those rationalistic trends, and allowing people to come to God without theological straightjackets. The American context of intoxicating freedom aided and abetted this freethinking trend.

The Azusa Street Revival began in a small, dilapidated church in Los Angeles. The preacher—William Seymour—was an African American man from Louisiana whose parents had been enslaved. He waited tables as a young man, and at some point contracted smallpox, which left him blind in his left eye. He wanted to study for ministry under the well-known evangelist Charles Fox Parham, but "Jim Crow" segregation laws in Texas meant he had to sit outside the classroom and listen through the door's crack. Seymour was a quick study and was invited to pastor a church in Los Angeles in February of 1906. He was promptly removed from the position, however, for teaching "baptism in the Spirit." During a home prayer meeting in April that was organized by Seymour, some of the attendees started speaking in tongues. As if it was contagious, several others joined in. They all thought it was evidence that the Holy Spirit had been poured onto them. They reported other miracles and signs from heaven, and became convinced that God had begun a new dispensation on the earth by unleashing his power, just as he did with the early apostles of the faith.

The members felt they should launch a revival to spread the message and unleash the power of the Holy Spirit to the world. Perhaps it seemed like an exaggerated sense of self-importance at the time, but the fact is that people just kept on coming out to the revival's church services. The *Los Angeles Times* featured the revival on its front page, which caused a stir. Many people opposed the revival, thinking it was outrageous. Some were struck by the interracial component of the revival. Los Angeles was and is a very diverse place, but in 1906 it was uncommon to see Latinos, African Americans, Asians, and whites all praising God together. Others noticed that these were poor, working-class, uneducated people. Some people were shocked by the prominent role that women played in the revival. Azusa worshipers were strikingly egalitarian in their understanding of women's leadership. In fact, when William Seymour died, his wife Jennie took over the revival and led the church. Whatever the criticisms were, the movement kept growing.

In time, many Americans came to Azusa with the belief that something special was happening there, and they could benefit by attending the revival. Visitors came from all over the country to witness the events taking place. Numerous visitors, after participating in it, decided to spread the Pentecostal message globally, and thus went

FIGURE 1.7 *The Pentecostal movement began as a humble revival among the economically marginalized but has grown to become the largest form of Protestantism in the world.* Source: Photograph by Francis Miller / Getty Images.

abroad as missionaries. In Brazil, Korea, and South Africa, Azusa missionaries planted the Pentecostal Gospel and it expanded. Today, the largest church in the world—with 800,000 members—is an Assemblies of God church located in Seoul, South Korea. The largest national Pentecostal population in the world is in Brazil. Sub-Saharan Africa has more Christians than any continent on Earth today, and many of them are connected to the Pentecostal movement. Tens of thousands of Pentecostal churches have been established, and estimates are that over half a billion people are members of a Pentecostal church. In the United States, the Pentecostal movement has thrived. In 1907, Charles Harrison Mason, a Black clergyman, was appointed in 1907 as Chief Apostle of the Church of God in Christ—currently America's largest Pentecostal denomination. The Assemblies of God—a global Pentecostal denomination that began in 1914—has become one of the largest Christian denominations in the world. Many of the world's great megachurches are Pentecostal, or began as Pentecostal churches, such as Joel Osteen's Lakewood Church, in Houston, Texas. No one could ever have imagined that a little church on a sleepy street in Los Angeles, led by a poor, half-blind son of enslaved Africans, would impact world Christianity to such an extent. Perhaps the members of Azusa Street Mission were not so delusional after all.

Today

American Christianity is diverse, complex, and thriving. While European Christianity continues to ossify, American Christianity is as vibrant today as it ever has been. The great revivals of American Christianity—the First and Second Great Awakenings along with the Azusa Street Revival—served to strengthen and revitalize American Christianity over the course of its history. And while European Christianity has always been tied to the state, this does not apply to America, and that is precisely what has freed American Christianity to diversify, proliferate, and ultimate meet the needs of its people over the course of three centuries.

The decoupling of church and state in America has created a marketplace for Christian faith where people can pursue the kind of Christianity that best suits their needs. American Christians "church shop" in ways completely unknown to most Europeans. Americans are very individualistic in their choice of religion. They have been called "free agents" due to their reluctance to overly commit to one denomination. It is common for Americans to "switch" churches several times in their lives (Putnam and Campbell 2010: ch. 5). They want the freedom to follow the church that offers the best children's program or the most magnetic speaker or even the best worship band. Just like with any other sector in the market—such as the restaurant industry—Americans like to have choices. Some prefer the Catholic Church with its more solemn and liturgical approach. Some prefer the Pentecostal traditions with its open belief in the power of God to work in the lives of believers today. Some prefer niche churches, such as the Metropolitan Community Church, a denomination begun in Los Angeles in 1968 to meet the needs of lesbian, gay, bisexual, and transgender (LGBT) Christians.

Christianity in America is not all about innovation and experimentation, however. After all, it is the third most populated nation in the world, and with 350 million people comes a lot of diversity. It should be noted that America has a very conservative strain within its DNA as well. The Fundamentalist movement has had a massive influence on American Christians across the board. It is a very similar concept to the great political divide in America between progressives and conservatives. For instance, there are conservative Presbyterians as well as progressive Presbyterians; conservative Baptists, and more progressive Baptists; conservative Methodists, and progressive Methodists. Even within the Catholic Church there is a divide today, with some members preferring to uphold the traditional approach to faith, and others wanting to push ahead with the reforms that were unleashed at the Second Vatican Council in the 1960s.

The conservative/progressive divide in America goes back to theological controversies in the nineteenth century; however, it was in the 1920s that it really became manifest to the nation. In the year 1925 the *Scopes Trial* (also known as the Monkey Trial) occurred, pitting religious conservatives against the progressives. The issue had to do with the teaching of evolution in the public schools. In 1925, it was illegal to teach the theory of evolution in Tennessee's public schools, and the court upheld a legal challenge from the American Civil Liberties Union (ACLU). While the conservatives won that particular case, they eventually lost the war, and evolution eventually became compulsory in American public school curricula. This decision stimulated the growth of a massive network of private, Christian schools throughout the nation. It also drew a line in the sand between two major theological strands in the United States: (1) Fundamentalists (or conservatives): those who take the Bible very seriously, even literally; and (2) liberals (or progressives): those who think the Bible is best interpreted in light of modern science and culture. These two forces continue to battle for the hearts and minds of Americans across the nation.

The heartland for the conservative Christian movement is in the American South and Midwest, whereas the Northeast and the West Coast are thought by some scholars to be moving in a secular direction. There is also the issue of urban versus rural. City folk are far more prone to be liberal, while country people are far more likely to be

FIGURE 1.8 *The Scopes Trial in 1925 deepened the liberal and conservative divide in the United States.* Source: *Photograph by Bettmann / Getty Images.*

conservative. The liberal/conservative divide is perhaps the most important topic—surely the most polarizing and divisive—in American Christianity today.

The twentieth century saw some of the great developments in American Christian history. The century began with the Pentecostal movement, a movement that not only unleashed a zeal rarely witnessed in Christian history but also a healthy dose of egalitarianism. For instance, in the 1920s and 1930s, America's most famous pastor was Aimee Semple McPherson, a pioneer in the megachurch movement as well as in radio ministry. Based in Los Angeles, she built up a huge congregation, and built a massive church building that stands to the present day—Angeles Temple. She was constantly in the headlines, not always for good reasons, and proved to many that women could take center stage in American Christianity. In 1923 she started a Pentecostal denomination called the Foursquare Church that claims nine million members worldwide.

A short history of American Christianity would be remiss without mentioning perhaps the two most iconic preachers of the twentieth century: Billy Graham (1918–2018) and Martin Luther King Jr. (1929–68). It is very possible that Billy Graham preached to more people than any other preacher in history. He lived a long life and had excellent

FIGURE 1.9 *Billy Graham may have preached the Gospel to more people than anyone in history.* Source: *Photograph by Bettmann / Getty Images.*

health, which enabled him to travel the world many times over to preach in his "gospel crusades." He was a Southern Baptist, yet people on both sides of the theological spectrum admired his commitment to Christ and his pious lifestyle. He explicitly avoided political controversy and often defended the marginalized. He spoke out against racism, counseled America's presidents, led the American evangelical movement for decades, and encouraged hundreds of millions to make a decision to follow Jesus, and to realize that their sins were forgiven if they would put their trust in him.

Martin Luther King Jr. did more than any American in history to break the racial barriers separating people on the basis of race, although, as he famously noted, Sunday at eleven o'clock was, and remains, the most segregated hour in American public life. King was a progressive Baptist preacher from the American South. He rose to prominence as a young man, and served the Ebenezer Baptist Church in Atlanta, Georgia. King rose to national prominence in 1955 during the bus boycotts, which strove for seating equality on public transportation vehicles. King's speeches on equal rights were sermons, and he often invoked biblical imagery, such as in his famous "Mountaintop" speech delivered on April 3, 1968, at Mason Temple, a Pentecostal church in Memphis, Tennessee. In that powerful sermon, he drew inspiration from the story of Moses, where the old patriarch was able to see the Promised Land, but was not permitted to enter into it.

> Well, I don't know what will happen now. We've got some difficult days ahead. But it really doesn't matter with me now, because I've been to the mountaintop. And I don't mind. Like anybody, I would like to live—a long life; longevity has its place. But I'm not concerned about that now. I just want to do God's will. And He's allowed me to go up to the mountain. And I've looked over. And I've seen the Promised Land. I may not get there with you. But I want you to know tonight, that we, as a people, will get to the Promised Land. So I'm happy, tonight. I'm not worried about anything. I'm not fearing any man. Mine eyes have seen the glory of the coming of the Lord.
>
> (King 1968)

It would be King's last sermon, as he was assassinated at the Lorraine Motel on the morning of April 4.

In 1983, President Ronald Reagan signed a bill that made Martin Luther King Jr. Day a national holiday. It became official in 1986, bringing national attention to the man who served tirelessly the cause of civil rights in America. He is today considered a national icon, and his great legacy is bringing many Christians into a more deliberate conversation with people of color, low-wage workers, and others out on the margins of the American dream. King was not only one of the most charismatic and powerful preachers America has produced, but he was also the most effective. His ministry of preaching created a revival, but not in the same sense as happened with Billy Graham. King's message was less about the individual coming to repentance and turning over her or his life to Christ. King indeed made an individualistic impact as he pricked the hearts of Americans—especially those in

CHRISTIANITY IN NORTH AMERICA: AN INTRODUCTION

the secure classes. However, his greatest impact was on the social conscience. His impact was on the American collective soul. He caused Americans, collectively, to repent and to look around at the have-nots. He inspired Americans to work hard to address the concerns of those who had not received the same chance that others had received. This he did more effectively than perhaps any American in history. His work in social justice and Christian activism continues today with great vigor, as it impacts new generations of powerful Black preachers such as Vashti McKenzie, Charles Blake, and T.D. Jakes.

Christianity in the United States is going through changes once again. Some are even using the word "revival" to describe what is happening, although it is surely too early to compare today's events with Azusa Street or either of the Great Awakenings. Certainly Christianity in America is going through notable developments, especially among younger people.

For example, California is in the midst of a revival, which is perhaps surprising considering many Americans associate the state with liberalism and secularism. Several ministries have popped up in recent years that have made a significant impact on Christianity in the state. Rick Warren, founding pastor of Saddleback, wrote *The Purpose Driven Life*, which has been called the bestselling nonfiction book of all time outside the Bible. Kanye West, one of the greatest rap/pop stars of our time, recently returned to his Christian roots and hosts Sunday worship gatherings to accompany his hit albums that are thoroughly gospel, attracting huge media attention. In addition, several hipster churches have been launched in California in recent years that attract a young audience, particularly college students and young professionals. A few of these churches are: Mosaic, Reality LA, and Hillsong—a ministry that rose out of the Assemblies of God in Australia. Another is the Zoe Church, founded in 2015 by Pentecostal minister Chad Veach. Justin Bieber—a fervent supporter of Zoe Church—has been associated with several evangelical pastors for years such as Veach, Carl Lentz, Rich Wilkerson Jr., and Judah Smith.

Bethel ministries is another important California Christian movement that, like the Hillsong network, sprung out of the Assemblies of God. Bethel is unabashedly Pentecostal, with its belief in supernatural healing in Christ's name. The Bethel School of Supernatural Ministry, based in Redding, has over two thousand students from fifty-seven countries and nearly all of the fifty US states. It has a music ministry that has even topped the *secular* Billboard charts.

The Roman Catholic Church should not be forgotten here, despite the painful challenges the denomination is going through regarding sexual abuse scandals and the hundreds of resultant lawsuits. Nearly a quarter of America's citizens are Roman Catholic, as opposed to around half of Americans who are connected to Protestantism. The Catholic Church is still the largest single denomination in the United States, and its future in America seems secure, considering America's top source of immigrants is Latin America—which is almost thoroughly Catholic.

Canada has always had a larger percentage of Catholics than the United States, due to the strong French influence on the nation's history. Today, the Roman Catholic

CHRISTIANITY IN NORTH AMERICA

Church is the largest denomination in the nation, with over a third of the population claiming adherence. However, Canada's population is apparently secularizing faster than in America. In the 1960s, Canada's Roman Catholic population—most notably in Quebec—underwent a rapid process of secularization, similar to what happened in France. Canada's largest mainline Protestant churches—the United Church of Canada and the Anglican Church—are going through extremely challenging times as their numbers plummet. The evangelical churches in Canada are faring better than other forms of Christianity as the nation secularizes, but overall the evangelical movement has never been nearly as strong in Canada as in the United States. The big question for Canada, and Western Europe for that matter, is whether secularization is here to stay or whether Christianity in the land is latent—and will arise at a future moment in time.

Mexico's population is strongly Catholic today, around 80–90 percent. However, like in much of the Western world, the rates of attendance are in decline. Protestantism seems to be growing in Mexico, particularly the Mormon Church and La Luz del Mundo (Light of the World). As in much of the world, the Pentecostal and evangelical movements are the styles of Christianity that are growing in Mexico. It should be noted that religious freedom is somewhat recent in Mexico, with the passing of the federal Act on Religious Associations and Public Worship of 1992. This Act emphasized religious freedom in Mexico, and reinstated religious rights in the nation after 130 years of limitations, particularly against the Roman Catholic Church. Since 1992, Mexico's religious groups can own property, conduct religious education, and are entitled to legal status.

For much of its history, though, Mexico had a fraught relationship with the Roman Catholic Church, despite the fact that nearly the entire population held membership in the church. In the *Mexican Revolution* of 1910, many people spoke out against the church, notably Pancho Villa. Relations between the nation and the church began to warm in the 1970s, particularly when Pope John Paul II visited in 1979—the first Pope to do so. Relations have been in a state of repair ever since, and Mexico now receives papal visits on a somewhat regular basis. Pope John Paul II visited Mexico several times and made it clear that the Roman Catholic Church would be more sensitive toward its second largest nation (after Brazil).

Conclusion

Christianity in North America is a fascinating history that continues to unfold in profound ways. No one could have guessed that the United States would blaze the trail for the separation of religion from the state, which had the concomitant effect of energizing religion for two and a half centuries. The United States is home to more Christians than any other nation in the world, and that is unlikely to change any time soon. In addition, the revivals birthed in the United States have had a global impact, particularly the Azusa Street Revival in 1906—perhaps the most important revival in Christian history, period. At around 500 million Christians and counting, the Pentecostal movement that

FIGURE 1.10 *Pope John Paul II made several trips to Mexico, which resulted in dramatically improved relations.* Source: *Photograph by Pool LOCHON / SIMON / Getty Images.*

arose out of Azusa Street has transformed global Christianity in ways unthinkable a century ago. Nobody expected a small, mainly African American, socio economically challenged little church would go on to plant charismatic Christianity all over the world.

Canadians are certainly closer to the secularization thesis that arose out of the 1960s revolutions, but it is not clear whether a return to Christianity is imminent. One thing is clear, however, the established churches of Canada, namely the United Church and the Anglican Church, are struggling. Some have urged the Anglican Church in Canada to close, partly because of its complicity in the residential schools fiasco. The church was sued all across the nation for pulling Indigenous children from their homes and sometimes abusing them in horrific ways. Many lawsuits against the Anglican Church emptied Anglican coffers, and churchgoers became tired of making offerings simply to pay off court-ordered debts. Similar trends have occurred in the Roman Catholic Church, both in the United States and Canada.

Mexicans are only beginning to feel the pressure of Protestantism's growth in a Catholic stronghold. Only time will tell whether the Pentecostal movement will have the success in Mexico that it has enjoyed in Guatemala and El Salvador. One important issue that will impact the future of Christianity in Mexico has to do with US–Mexican political relations. The border wall has signified that the once free-flowing relationship between the two countries may be coming to an end—or at least a trickle. But as many Mexicans move back to Mexico in the face of political pressure, it is possible that they will bring Protestant Christianity with them. But it is also the case that the sixty million Hispanic population in the United States might revitalize the Roman Catholic Church in unpredictable ways, leading to revival.

Canada's Prime Minister Pierre Trudeau said in 1969 that living next to the United States is like sleeping next to an elephant, "No matter how friendly and even-tempered the beast, one is affected by every twitch and grunt." This may well be true, considering the United States is ten times more populated than Canada, and two and a half times the population of Mexico. However, the two countries blend together in more ways than can be counted, and their future, like their past, will be forever linked.

Further Reading and Online Resources

Daughrity D. (2019), *The History of Christianity: Facts and Fictions*, Santa Barbara, CA: ABC-CLIO.

God in America (2010), [TV Program] PBS, October 11. Available online: https://www.pbs. org/godinamerica/view/ (accessed November 14, 2020).

Hastings A., ed. (1999), *A World History of Christianity*, Grand Rapids, MI: William B. Eerdmans.

Kidd T. (2019), *America's Religious History: Faith, Politics, and the Shaping of a Nation*, Grand Rapids, MI: Zondervan.

References

Collins K.J. (1999), *A Real Christian: The Life of John Wesley*, Nashville, TN: Abingdon Press.

Edwards J. (1741), "Sinners in the Hands of an Angry God. A Sermon Preached at Enfield, July 8th, 1741," ed. R. Smolinski. Electronic Texts in American Studies. 54. Available online: https://digitalcommons.unl.edu/etas/54 (accessed January 28, 2021).

The Foursquare Church (2020), "History." Available online: https://www.foursquare.org/ about/history/ (accessed November 14, 2020).

Hastings A., ed. (1999), *A World History of Christianity*, Grand Rapids, MI: William B. Eerdmans.

The Holy Bible, New International Version (1984), Grand Rapids, MI: Zondervan Publishing House.

Jones A. (2018), "A Guide to the Evangelical Celebrities and Pastors Dominating Hollywood," *The Cut*, August 6. Available online: https://www.thecut.com/2018/08/ justin-bieber-hailey-baldwin-hillsong-evangelicals-hollywood.html (accessed November 14, 2020).

Jones M.W. (2016), "Inside the Popular, Controversial Bethel Church," *Christianity Today*, April 24. Available online: https://www.christianitytoday.com/ct/2016/may/cover-story-inside-popular-controversial-bethel-church.html (accessed November 14, 2020).

King M.L. Jr. (1968), "'I've Been to the Mountaintop,' Address Delivered at Bishop Charles Mason Temple," April 3, 1968, Memphis Tennessee. Available online: https:// kinginstitute.stanford.edu/king-papers/documents/ive-been-mountaintop-address-delivered-bishop-charles-mason-temple (accessed January 28, 2021).

CHRISTIANITY IN NORTH AMERICA: AN INTRODUCTION

Marikar S. (2015), "Los Angeles Churches Make Worship … Hip?," *New York Times*, December 12. Available online: https://www.nytimes.com/2015/12/13/fashion/mosaic-oasis-hillsong-churches-los-angeles.html (accessed November 14, 2020).

Noll M. (2003), *The Rise of Evangelicalism: The Age of Edwards, Whitefield and the Wesleys*, Downers Grove, IL: InterVarsity Press.

Putnam R.D. and D.E. Campbell (2010), *American Grace: How Religion Divides and Unites Us*, New York: Simon & Schuster.

Stein J. (2019), "Hollywood's Holy Hipster Scene," *Vanity Fair*, July 12. Available online: https://www.vanityfair.com/style/2019/07/hollywood-and-religion (accessed November 14, 2020).

Taylor A. (2001), *American Colonies: The Settling of North America*, New York: Penguin.

Wacker G. (2019), *One Soul at a Time: The Story of Billy Graham*, Grand Rapids, MI: William B. Eerdmans.

Glossary Terms

American Civil War Lasted from 1861 to 1865. The war ended slavery in the United States, however, it soured relations between Northerners and Southerners for many decades to come. Many American Christian denominations split during the Civil War era, paving the way for long-standing debates in Christian theology, between progressives and conservatives.

Anabaptists Literally, the word means "rebaptizers," as they held that people who were baptized as infants should be rebaptized as adults. They were a small, persecuted group during the Protestant Reformation but eventually morphed into many sects such as Quakers, Mennonites, and the hugely significant Baptist movement—America's largest Protestant denomination.

Azusa Street Revival A charismatic, Christian revival that began in 1906 on Azusa Street in Los Angeles. It was begun by a partially blind African American preacher, but quickly attracted people from several races and grew to become a global phenomenon known as Pentecostalism. The Pentecostal movement today has perhaps has many as 350 million members and is considered the fastest growing form of Christianity. The world's largest churches tend to be Pentecostal.

First Amendment The first part reads, "Congress shall make no law respecting an establishment of religion, or prohibiting the free exercise thereof." This amendment to the US Constitution has made a major difference historically in how Americans understand the relationship between religion and the state. It was a departure from European standards.

Mexican Revolution Lasted from about 1910 to 1917 and had a major impact on Mexican politics and religion. The Roman Catholic Church's institutional power was dramatically curtailed as a result of the conflict, and it was not until the 1990s that restrictions against it began to loosen. Around two million Mexicans lost their lives, while many immigrated to the United States for refuge.

Scopes Trial An American trial that occurred in Tennessee in 1925 over the issue of whether teachers could support Darwin's theory of evolution for understanding human origins. The trial captivated the American population and contributed greatly to America's liberal and conservative divide. Scholars generally hold that while the conservatives won the trial, the liberals won the larger war, since a short time later evolution would be standard curriculum in America's public schools.

PART ONE

North American Christian Traditions

2

Catholicisms in North America

Chester Gillis

Catholics Are Not All Alike

If you live in North America, you know someone who is Catholic. As of 2020, 20 percent of the United States population is Catholic. Mexico, where 83 percent of the people are Catholic, has the second largest Catholic population in the world. The Canadian population is 39 percent Catholic. The American Congress is 32 percent Catholic and the US Senate is 22 percent Catholic. Many public figures in North America are Catholic, for example, Nancy Pelosi and Joe Biden are Catholics. Stephen Colbert and Mark Wahlberg are Catholics. Canadian Prime Minister Justin Trudeau is a Catholic. Five of the nine US Supreme Court justices are Catholics: John Roberts, Anthony Kennedy, Clarence Thomas, Samuel Alito, and Sonia Sotomayor.

However, it is not only well-known politicians, judges, and celebrities who are Catholic. Catholics are found all over North America. And they are not just American or Canadian or Mexican Catholics; they are *Roman* Catholics, which means that they are connected to a worldwide church headquartered in Rome, or Vatican City to be exact. The roots of their religion can be traced to Jesus and the Apostles.

The title of this chapter, "*Catholicisms* in North America," may seem odd to some readers. However, this title captures the variety of ways that Catholics appropriate their religion. Some go to church every Sunday. Some only go on Christmas and Easter. Some rarely go. Some strictly follow the teachings and practices of the faith. Some ignore the teachings and follow practices that contradict the teachings. Some do not know the teachings and do not participate much in the practices. But they are all Catholics. Here is a typology of Catholics.

1   *By-the-rules Catholics*: These individuals attend Mass weekly and obey the teachings of the church as articulated by the *pope* and *bishops*. While they may have questions about some aspects of church life and teaching, they give the

FIGURE 2.1 *St. Francis Xavier Church, known to students of Saint Louis University (SLU) simply as College Church, serves both as a parish church in the Archdiocese of St. Louis and for the SLU community. The duality exemplifies the different roles the church plays in Catholicism.* Source: *Saint Xavier College Church, Saint Louis University.*

benefit of the doubt to church authorities, cooperate with the mission of the church, and look to the church for direction. These are loyal Catholics whose dedication may be attributed to any number of factors, among which are complete agreement with the institutional church, fear that disagreement will have far-reaching consequences spiritually (may not go to heaven) or socially (unwelcome in family or circle of friends) or, less likely but possible, an inability or unwillingness to think for oneself. These Catholics have declined in number since *Vatican II* (1962–5), although the church continues to count on them to support even unpopular positions.

2 *Bend-and-break-the-rules Catholics*: These individuals attend Mass weekly, but on certain issues they choose to follow their own conscience instead of church teachings or practices. This type represents the good Catholic who identifies with the church, participates regularly, but disagrees with certain practices or beliefs. They may practice birth control, believe in capital punishment, or think that abortion is permissible under certain circumstances. But, still, they go to Mass and Communion regularly. They represent the largest segment of churchgoing Catholics.

3 *Ignore-the-rules Catholics*: The third type attends church irregularly, perhaps once a month. They choose which teachings and practices to follow, and ignore those teachings that either do not seem to make sense or appear inconvenient. These Catholics are weary of church teachings and practices that seem backward, but they do not leave the church. Instead they operate within, yet independent of, the church. They appreciate the ritual the church provides, the sense of community, and the spiritual dimension, but they do not allow the church to dominate their moral or spiritual life.

4 *Rules-don't-pertain-to-me Catholics*: These individuals attend church on Easter and Christmas and perhaps a few other select times such as Ash Wednesday, weddings, and funerals. Sometimes derisively called "Christmas and Easter" Catholics, this group has existed in North America, and elsewhere, for as long as the church. They certainly claim Catholicism as their personal faith choice, but have little formal contact with the Catholic community and do not look to the church to guide their lives on a regular basis. If there is a crisis, such as a death in the family, they turn to the church for assistance, but generally they live their lives unaware, uninterested, or unaffected by the activities and teachings of the church.

5 *Don't-know-the-rules Catholics*: These are baptized Catholics who have virtually abandoned all forms of Catholic religious practice. This group is ill informed about recent church teachings and practices and rather uninterested in what the church says or how it functions. They are, for all intents and purposes, non-Catholic. Only their baptism identifies them as Catholic. They may seek to be married in the church, want their children baptized, and hope to be buried by the church, but aside from these chronological life markers, they have little or nothing to do with Catholicism.

6 *From a Catholic family but no religious identification*: The "nones" are a growing segment of Catholics who no longer identify with any religion. As many as one-third of teens and people in their twenties are "nones." Many of them were raised in Catholic families, and some have had at least part of their education in Catholic schools. Most do not consider themselves atheists, but they want nothing to do with institutional religion. The sociologist Grace Davie described this as "believing without belonging" (1990: 455).

The various generations have tendencies that are exposed when it comes to religion. Older Catholics tend to be more vigilant about practicing their religion. They go to church more often, have remained Catholic since birth, and look to priests, bishops, and the pope for guidance. Many younger North Americans—in particular the millennial generation and later—who were born into the religion and baptized, have left it. In Mexico they have often left it to join evangelical churches. In Canada and the United States, they have not left it for another religion but for no religion. Sociologists have called them "nones," because they have no religious identification. The "nones" now

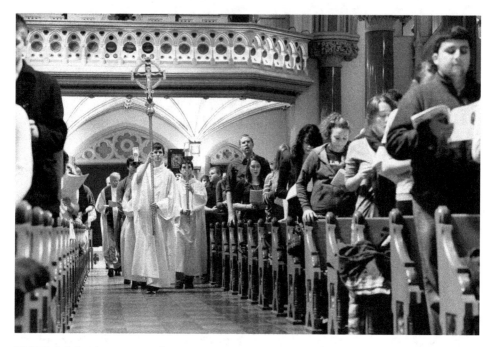

FIGURE 2.2 *The interior of St. Francis Xavier Church is just as beautiful on the inside as it is on the outside. With Mass in session, one can already see differences in the organization of the church.* Source: *College Church, Saint Louis University.*

represent 23 percent of Americans, the same percentage that professes to be Catholic, and many of these "nones" are former Catholics. This does not mean that those who proclaim no religion are not interested in spiritual matters. On the contrary, many of them have spiritual interests. They are not, however, interested in *institutional religion*. They have abandoned the institutions. This is particularly the case with lapsed Catholics and mainline Protestants (Episcopal, Methodists, Presbyterian, Disciples).

Organization(s) of the Church

Those outside of it know, and Catholics know from experience, that the church is not a democracy. It is one of the most hierarchical organizations in the world. While people join, and worship in, the local church, they concurrently become members of a world church. Every Roman Catholic community in North America exists in relation to all other Catholic churches, and all are under the leadership of the Vatican in Rome. The pope is the head of the church. Although the official doctrine of papal infallibility was not promulgated until the First Vatican Council in 1871, historically the pope has always been the leader. In other words, the primacy of the pope is separate from and prior to his infallibility. The church traces this authority to the scriptures, which Catholics believe, record that Peter was appointed the leader of the apostles. The infallibility of the pope only applies when the pope publicly declares a doctrine. This has happened only twice in church history—the Immaculate Conception (that Mary was conceived without sin) in 1871 and the Assumption (that Mary was bodily assumed into heaven) in 1951. On all other matters, the pope is fallible, meaning he could possibly make mistakes. The pope's powers are limited. For example, he cannot tell any better than a weather forecaster if it is going to rain or if the stock market will go up or down.

Parishes

Catholics engage most with the church through their parishes. This is where they gather for Mass, receive the *sacraments*, form a community, and receive information about the church. For many Catholics, the heart of the church is the parish. This is the place where they find a sense of identity and belonging. There are variations of the parish where people worship together on college campuses or in hospitals, monasteries, convents, military bases, and chapels designed to serve a variety of communities. But the parish constitutes one community that is part of the local *diocese* and the universal church.

Many Catholics do not have regular contact with a local parish, which most likely means that they do not participate fully in the life of the church. Recent statistics indicate that one-third of Americans who identify themselves as Catholics—that is, approximately twenty-five million Catholics—do not belong to parishes. Clearly, these Catholics who remain uncommitted to a specific parish can skew statistical results when attempting to ascertain the views of faithful Catholics on a number of issues, because studies indicate that Catholics without parishes have a different, and not as close, relationship to the church. Church leaders question whether this group should be included in national statistical surveys that measure behaviors and attitudes of Catholics.

Parishes differ depending upon the leadership and the community. Some are welcoming of all, others have strict expectations for those who join. Illustrative of the differences in parishes are these two pieces taken from parish bulletins, one on the mission of the parish and the other on what to wear to church.

Old St. Patrick's Church, Archdiocese of Chicago:

We welcome men and women, people of all races and ethnicities, young and old, gay and straight. We welcome rich and poor, searchers and seekers, Catholics and people of other religious traditions. We are gifted by your presence.

St. Joan of Arc Catholic Church, Diocese of Boise:

Women should dress in modest clothing, preferably in a knee-length dress or skirt. Tight-fitting or revealing clothing, including miniskirts, sleeveless and low-cut tops, is not considered appropriate church attire. It is also customary (though not necessary) for women to cover their heads with a veil or similar head covering such as a hat or scarf in the church proper.

FIGURE 2.3 *SLU students and healthcare providers alike have gathered in St. Francis Xavier Church to listen to a panel on Jesuit health care. Catholic education blends a variety of sources together to produce their unique teaching style.* Source: *College Church, Saint Louis University.*

Men whenever possible and especially at Sunday Mass, should wear a collared shirt and long, non-denim pants, preferably with a jacket and tie. T-shirts, shirts with distracting logos or lettering, shorts, and flip-flops are not appropriate.

Catholic Education

One of the most enduring influences by which Catholicism has put its stamp on North American culture has been in education. From elementary schools to universities, Catholic education has helped to shape the lives of millions of Catholics and, more recently, an increasing number of non-Catholics who attend them. One of the major reasons that Catholics developed such an extensive network of schools in the United States is because they initially experienced prejudice. Unwelcome in the private academies and universities catering to Protestants, they needed to create a system of secondary schools, colleges, and universities so that Catholics could receive a quality education at an affordable price. While the public schools were open to them, the curriculum in these schools tended to favor Protestant ways of thinking, including the use of a Protestant version of the Bible that differed from the Catholic edition. So Catholic bishops and pastors decided to create a parallel school

CATHOLICISMS IN NORTH AMERICA

system in which Catholics would feel comfortable and that would teach Catholic doctrine without state interference.

In Canada, where the government supports religious education, Catholic schools are the largest system in the country. This has not been without controversy. Some object that the state is paying for Catholic schools. Others worry that when Catholic schools opened their doors to non-Catholics in 1984, they were diluting their Catholic identity. The 1917 Constitution in Mexico separated education into private (meaning religious) schools that do not receive state support and public schools supported by the state.

Today, millions of school children attend Catholic schools. The alumni of these schools are even more numerous. Thus, many Catholics either presently have or have had an education that unites them with their church. These schools teach religious instruction as part of the curriculum and they reinforce the values and doctrines of the church. Many of these schools, especially at the elementary school level, are associated with parishes and can be found serving neighborhoods where the parish is located. Catholic high schools often serve a broader geographical area, bringing teenagers from several parishes together. Catholic colleges and universities exist across North America, educating Catholics and non-Catholics alike.

In the past, the church recruited nuns to staff the schools and tens of thousands of dedicated, hard-working sisters spent their lives teaching and forming the spiritual and moral character of hundreds of thousands of Catholic children. In the United States, parishes kept tuition rates low so that immigrant families could afford to educate their children in a Catholic setting. This helped to create Catholic communities that enjoyed a certain stability and familiarity. The Catholic reach then extended beyond the school into the family, and the church enjoyed a privileged position that united families and gave the Catholic community identity and visibility.

Religious orders, large groups of sisters, brothers, or priests, played a key role in the development and maintenance of Catholic education. Each religious order exercised a particular type of ministry in the church depending upon the charism (special talents) of its founder. Many orders of sisters were founded specifically to be involved with education. Also, orders of brethren, such as the Christian Brothers, and priests, such as the Jesuits, have dedicated much of their efforts to education. Many of these orders founded colleges and universities to serve the need for higher education for Catholics. As a result, today, hundreds of Catholic colleges and universities enroll a religiously diverse student body to educate them to be doctors, lawyers, engineers, teachers, business executives, and any number of other careers.

The numbers of nuns, priests, and brothers have declined dramatically in recent decades so most personnel in Catholic schools are laypeople who continue the mission of Catholic education. They continue to teach the values of Catholicism and to carry on the important work of educating the next generation.

In the United States, Catholic education peaked at a population of 5.5 million in the mid-1960s. At its peak in 1965, the Catholic system accounted for 12 percent of all US elementary and secondary students. However, since this peak, the overall

FIGURE 2.4 *Like all Catholic healthcare practices, SLUCare Physician Group combines their Catholic traditions with the science of medicine. They emphasize treating patients holistically and respectfully.* Source: *Saint Louis University Medical School and Hospital.*

number of students attending Catholic schools has declined. There seem to be many explanatory factors, including demographics, economics, personnel changes, and a paucity of resources. The population shift from cities to suburbs has deeply affected Catholic schools, many of which were built in the heyday of "brick-and-mortar" bishops who oversaw the construction of thousands of schools in the nineteenth and early twentieth centuries to accommodate the burgeoning immigrant Catholic population. Schools are increasingly expensive to operate, and in some cases, it is impossible to pass the costs along to students' families, especially when they are not from the upper classes.

Catholic Health Care

Even a cursory reading of the Gospels informs the reader that an essential part of Jesus' ministry involved curing the sick. Jesus' cures were occasional and often involved restoration of the soul as much as the body.

Following in his footsteps, the church has developed an elaborate system of hospitals, nursing homes, hospices, and other healthcare facilities. Every day Catholic hospitals and nursing homes serve millions of patients in North America. If the church's only concern were the body, its task would be easier. The church's belief that each person has a God-given soul created at the time of conception, and the costs and complexity of contemporary medicine, has made its attempt to deliver state-of-the-art quality health care immensely complicated. Catholic hospitals, medical schools, and healthcare facilities operate under internal ethical constraints. The church believes that every living person, from the moment of conception until natural death, is a child of God whose life must be respected in all stages. In practice, this means no abortions, no fetal-tissue research, and no assisted suicide. The church's prohibition of artificial birth control means no pill, condoms, or diaphragms. This differentiates Catholic hospitals from public and other private hospitals.

The church is certainly within its rights to prohibit such procedures and to refrain from distributing certain drugs or appliances. However, the healthcare system in North America, from medical schools to outpatient clinics, relies on government funds to accomplish its mission. Government regulation accompanies government assistance.

Catholic hospitals reflect the religious pluralism of North America, particularly in large cities and in places where the Catholic hospital is the sole healthcare facility. These facilities, like all hospitals, rely heavily on government programs for payment, which sometimes complicates their Catholic mission. Nevertheless, the church continues to train doctors and nurses at its medical and nursing schools, to operate hospitals that serve a diverse population, and crucially, to uphold Catholic moral principles in the health care they provide.

Catholic Social Services

Jesus preached, "Blessed are the poor, for theirs is the kingdom of heaven." Christians have an obligation to care for the poor, orphans, and the dispossessed. As a result of this commitment, the church has built an extensive system of social services for the needy. Local parishes provide these services through a variety of mechanisms. Parish funds provide for various needs both within and beyond the parish. When Catholics face economic hardship, they can turn to their local parish for help. Pastors have at their discretion the ability to provide limited emergency aid to individuals and families. Usually they carry out this ministry quietly and without fanfare, but it represents a necessary lifeline for those who may need immediate assistance.

Beyond this personal assistance, parishes provide structured assistance through social action committees. These parish programs support everything from soup kitchens to refugee relocation. Often their generosity extends beyond the geographical boundaries of the parish, and even beyond the Catholic community.

Diocesan agencies support and complement local parish operations. Usually known by the name Catholic Charities, these agencies serve various social needs, including health care, legal aid, counseling, foster care, adoption services, food, and shelter, among others. Sometimes these services specifically reflect Catholic principles such as pregnancy counseling for women who might otherwise consider abortion. Often, funding is supplied almost exclusively by human compassion and Christian generosity. The Roman Catholic Church distributes hundreds of millions of dollars annually to its organizations that care for those in need. North American society benefits immensely from the financial contribution and the investment made by millions of Catholics who staff these efforts, some paid but mostly volunteers.

The church cares for the material as well as the spiritual needs of millions each year, many of whom are not Catholic. For example, in caring for the poor and the homeless, the church does not discriminate between Catholics and others, or even between believers and non-believers. A hungry person is a hungry person, whether or not they are Catholic.

Challenges

The tradition and organization that has developed within Roman Catholicism sometimes puts North American Catholics at odds with the culture and society in which they live. For example, the church opposes same-sex marriage, the death penalty, abortion, and divorce. Many North Americans accept some of these practices. The church is not a democracy, but North Americans live in democracies. As a result, some Catholics struggle to reconcile the teachings of the church with the practices of their society. Some obediently follow the church's teachings and oppose cultural and societal patterns. Others follow the culture in which they live and ignore or oppose the church's mandates. Most find themselves somewhere in the middle, sometimes agreeing with and following the church, and other times disagreeing and taking their cues from North American culture.

The church faces significant challenges that, if ignored or left unresolved, could result in deeper divisions, irreconcilable fragmentation, and costly defections. Is the Roman Catholic Church in North America up to the challenge of secularism? The answer is both yes and no. On the positive side, North American Catholicism is deeply rooted in culture; it has a sizable constituency and continues to grow, though at a slower pace than in the past; it has significant assets, despite the cost of the sexual abuse crisis; and it is more diverse than at any time in its history. On the negative side, the church continues to struggle with a number of long-standing intractable problems, and it faces new and sometimes more complicated challenges in the twenty-first century.

Some of the more troubling problems are: the rise of the "nones"; the continued decline in the number of clergy and religious; the role of women in the church; the ethical and sexual conduct of clergy; the number of inactive Catholics and Catholics who are leaving the Roman Church for other Christian communions or, to a lesser degree, other religions; secularism; sexual and reproductive ethics, including but not limited to birth control, premarital sex, abortion, homosexuality, and same-sex marriage; democratization of structures; church–state relations; ecumenical relations; meeting the needs of the changing ethnic composition of the church, especially the growth in the Hispanic community; the roles and identities of Catholic schools and universities; relations with non-Christian religions; and bioethics.

FIGURE 2.5 *The candles pictured here very deliberately illuminate only the altar, leaving the rest of the scene in the dark.* Source: *College Church, Saint Louis University.*

Priests and Nuns: Decline in Numbers

In the United States, statistics help to tell the story. At the time of Vatican II, there were 180,000 nuns in America. Today there are 44,000, a 75 percent loss. In 1966, there were 35,070 active diocesan priests; in 2017, there were 25,757. Church membership in 1965 was 44,790,000; in 2017, it was 72 million. The ratio of priests to parishioners in 1975 was 1:1,100; in 2017, it was almost double that. Most dioceses in the United States have at least one parish headed by a non-priest, and many dioceses have multiple parishes without clerical leadership. In 2015, there were 3,448 parishes without a resident pastor in the United States.

Sexual Abuse Scandal

No one knows for certain exactly when sexual abuse by priests began, but it came to light in the 1990s. The abuse had been going on for decades, as well as the cover-up by bishops. As a result of this scandal, the Roman Catholic Church in North America suffered the most painful, disturbing, and publicly embarrassing chapter in its history. At the same time that the church was making its presence felt in the arena of public policy, it was attracting unwanted attention because of the private behavior of some of its clergy. In the 1980s and 1990s, a significant number of cases of sexual misconduct involving priests was uncovered. All of the reasons for why it came to light during this period may never be known, but some are apparent. From Vatican II on, among Catholics, the pre–Vatican II reverence toward priests had been slowly eroding. The general cultural shift that made many North Americans become increasingly suspicious of authority in all forms, was undoubtedly a contributing factor. Legal concerns played a role as well. Liability changed from a climate in which people thought it dangerous to disclose knowledge of such matters to one in which it was dangerous not to disclose what one knew. Also, after Vatican II, priests stepped down from the pedestals where generations of reverential awe had placed them. Interacting differently with the community, priests and sisters revealed themselves as human and vulnerable—and, yes, sinful—to those to whom they ministered. Some laity and clergy, however, deplored the newly introduced informality and pined for earlier customs that distanced clergy from the laity whom they served.

However, many of the victims of this abuse were now adults, and as painful as it was, they no longer maintained their silence. They went to therapists, lawyers, district attorneys, and newspapers. The negative publicity was devastating to the image of the church, and the lawsuits were financially debilitating. Settling out of court—which the church generally preferred to avoid further public embarrassment—required millions of dollars, but it did not expose the church on a large scale. However, that strategy collapsed as victims and their lawyers wanted to expose this cancer in the church. Some dioceses declared bankruptcy. The prestige of the priesthood was deeply tarnished by these cases. Although they represented a small fraction of the clergy, the fact that priests were involved shocked and disappointed many Catholics and non-Catholics alike. The fact that the church had denied or mishandled numerous cases early on infuriated many. Lingering questions among the laity about trustworthiness, sexual dysfunction, and institutional accountability are part of the legacy of these tragic events.

Acknowledging the problem of clergy sexual abuse, the Canadian bishops issued a document in 2018: *Protecting Minors from Sexual Abuse: A Call to the Catholic Faithful in Canada for Healing, Reconciliation, and Transformation.* The document called for bishops and others in church leadership, to have

> 1) accountability to victims and their families; 2) accountability to the people whom they serve directly and to wider society; 3) accountability to one another—as members of the Church and as members of the College of Bishops or of one's institute; and 4) accountability both to the demands of the laws of the Church and the laws of the land.
>
> (Canadian Conference of Catholic Bishops 2018)

Similarly, on March 5, 2018, the Mexican bishops issued a plan that stated five objectives: diagnosis, prevention, justice and response, support for victims, and promoting respect for the law (Agren 2019). Between 2010 and 2019 at least 152 Catholic priests in Mexico were suspended for sexual abuse against minors (Diaz 2019).

Pope Francis

After two conservative popes (John Paul II and Benedict XVI), Pope Francis exhibited a pastoral sense that, while not changing doctrine, is certainly changing the church. If Pope Francis is to succeed in changing the church from one that focuses internally on self-preservation to one that looks outwardly to the poor and disenfranchised, he needs time to do so. Elected at age seventy-six and with a compromised lung, his vibrant years are likely numbered. If his energy wanes and his health declines, he may follow his predecessor's example and resign. Even he has said that his papacy would be short.

Austen Inveigh, a biographer of Pope Francis, has called this pope the great reformer. Part of Francis's agenda includes restructuring the Vatican bureaucracy—a Herculean task that frustrated Pope Benedict XVI. Benedict tried but was unable to change the culture of the byzantine Vatican structure. Rome is known as the Eternal City. That moniker could not be truer of the Vatican City State. Vatican officials are not fond of change, especially change that may disrupt the comforts of their jobs. While Benedict, a German, was not Italian, he was a long-time Vatican insider, having lived there for twenty-five years before assuming the papacy. He was a part of the bureaucracy. Francis came to Rome as an outsider from the "New World" of Latin America. He was not beholden to personalities or offices of the Vatican. He rode the subway in Buenos Aires and, as pope, insisted on riding in a modest Fiat rather than a luxurious limousine. He expected something similar from Vatican officials. But not all of them were convinced that this more Spartan lifestyle was better than the conveniences that they enjoyed.

Pope Francis visited the United States in September 2015, going to Washington, New York, and Philadelphia, and was the first pope to address a joint session of Congress. His visit created a media frenzy as he was greeted by huge crowds at every venue he visited, and on every road on which he traveled. With a subtle allusion to immigration policy, he told Congress, and the American people, "We, the people of this continent, are not fearful of foreigners, because most of us were once foreigners." He acknowledged that America had mistreated the Native American population, and he warned: "When the stranger in our midst appeals to us, we must not repeat the sins and the errors of the past. We must resolve now to live as nobly and as justly as possible, as we educate new generations not to turn their back on our 'neighbors.'" After citing the crisis of immigrants globally, he said more directly:

On this continent, too, thousands of persons are led to travel north in search of a better life for themselves and for their loved ones, in search of greater opportunities. Is this not what we want for our own children? We must not be taken aback by their numbers, but rather view them as persons, seeing their faces and listening to their stories, trying to respond as best we can to their situation. To respond in a way which is always humane, just and fraternal.

The Many Cultures of North American Catholicism

In all likelihood, North American Catholics will continue to form a community that is bound by a core of central beliefs and divided by a multiplicity of practices, moral stances, and theological differences. One parish that advertises "God's People in Great Variety" captures the essence of North American Catholicism. No procrustean bed suits them; no single characterization describes them; they are not circumscribed by any one definition. They boast a rich tradition that binds them but is continually developing and changing. They identify with Rome, but often think and act as if their national church, or their own parish for that matter, is the whole of Catholicism. The Catholic subculture so prominent in the 1950s has evolved into less homogeneous manifestations. For some, it signifies spirituality; for others, sacramental life; for others, moral guidelines; and for still others, social bonds. For many other North American Catholics, the church holds little attraction or relevance.

There is no single answer to the question "What does it mean to be a Catholic in North America in the twenty-first century?" But that question had no *single* answer in any previous century either. The portrait offered in this chapter testifies to the variety of expressions that North American Catholicism manifests.

Further Reading and Online Resources

Allen J.L., Jr. (2014), *The Catholic Church: What Everyone Needs to Know*, New York: Oxford University Press.

Center for Applied Research in the Apostolate (CARA) (2020). Available online: https://cara.georgetown.edu (accessed November 5, 2020).

Faggioli M. (2017), *Catholicism and Citizenship: Political Cultures of the Church in the Twenty-First Century*, Collegeville, MN: Liturgical.

Gillis C. (2020), *Roman Catholicism in America*. New York: Columbia University Press.

Holy See (n.d.). Available online: http://www.vatican.va/content/vatican/en.html (accessed November 5, 2020).

References

Agren D. (2019), "Mexican Bishops Present Five Objectives for Action on Clergy Abuse," *National Catholic Reporter*, March 6. Available online: https://www.ncronline.org/news/quick-reads/mexican-bishops-present-five-objectives-action-clergy-abuse (accessed November 5, 2020).

Canadian Conference of Catholic Bishops (2018), "Protecting Minors from Sexual Abuse." Available online: https://www.cccb.ca/wp-content/uploads/2019/04/Protecting_Minors_2018.pdf (accessed November 5, 2020).

Davie G. (1990), "Believing Without Belonging: Is This the Future of Religion in Britain?," *Social Compass*, 37 (4): 455–69. https://doi.org/10.1177/003776890037004004.

Diaz L. (2019), "Mexican Church Suspended 152 Priests across 9 Years for Alleged Abuse: Bishop," *Reuters*, February 12. Available online: https://www.reuters.com/article/us-mexico-church/mexican-church-suspended-152-priests-across-9-years-for-alleged-abuse-bishop-idUSKCN1Q10BJ (accessed November 5, 2020).

Old St. Patrick's Church (n.d.), "Membership." Available online: https://www.oldstpats.org/membership/ (accessed August 28, 2019).

St. Joan of Arc Catholic Church (n.d.), "Newcomers." Available online: https://www.stjoanarc.com/about-us/newcomers/ (accessed August 28, 2019).

Glossary Terms

Bishop A priest selected by the pope who is ordained a second time to lead a diocese.

Diocese A geographical region that is led by a bishop. Catholics who live in that region are members of the diocese.

Pope The head of the Roman Catholic Church worldwide. Popes are considered successors of Saint Peter, the Apostle whom Jesus designated leader of the Apostles.

Sacraments Seven central rites that connect the faithful to God, Christ, and the Holy Spirit. The sacraments are baptism, Eucharist, confirmation, reconciliation, matrimony, anointing of the sick, and Holy Orders (priesthood). They are key markers in the life of a Catholic. Baptism, confirmation, and Holy Orders (for men who receive it) are only received once.

Vatican II A Council of the entire church leadership held in Rome with four sessions from 1962 to 1965. These gatherings determined the pastoral direction of the church going forward.

3

Protestantisms in North America

T.J. Tomlin

Protestant churches represent an extraordinarily diverse constellation of beliefs and practices. Unlike the Roman Catholic Church—which despite its own remarkable diversity is held together by a clearly organized hierarchical structure of religious authority—there is no one "Protestant Church." Perhaps most simply, Protestants are among those Christians who do not believe in the spiritual authority of the Roman Catholic Church. After rejecting Catholic understandings of how people received *salvation*, in particular, Protestants reconfigured their churches around new understandings of the *sacraments*, the Bible, and the proper way to organize the institutional church. Every Protestant expression is an outgrowth of long-standing debates over the nature of religious authority and how people can encounter, worship, obey, and even know God.

Protestantism emerged during an intense period of religious and political upheaval known as the Reformation, which began in Germany during the early sixteenth century and spread across Europe. The name Protestant reflects the "protests" its earliest leaders made against what they perceived to be the abuses and corruption of the Catholic Church. In 1517, a Roman Catholic priest named Martin Luther produced a document known as the Ninety-Five Theses, explaining his conviction that the Catholic Church had strayed from what he believed the Bible taught about salvation. Although Luther initially intended to reform and improve the Catholic Church, he was eventually excommunicated for his ideas and took the reins of leadership in the Protestant advance. A key tenet of Luther's theology was that God would forgive a person's sins and offer salvation solely on the basis of faith in the atoning work of Jesus, whose sacrificial death on the cross made salvation possible (Collinson 2003: 47–64). This was at odds with Catholicism's understanding of salvation, which emphasized the centrality of the church's sacraments in conveying Christ's grace and forgiveness. In the Catholic sacrament of confession, for example, the priest plays a key role in mediating between God and those seeking God's forgiveness.

While Protestants shared these broad convictions, they disagreed over how to interpret the Bible and reform the church. Protestants agreed, for example, that the *New Testament* sanctioned only two sacraments, baptism and the Lord's Supper. In contrast, the Catholic Church taught (and teaches) that there are seven sacraments. But Protestants failed to reach a consensus on what the Bible taught about either baptism or the Lord's Supper. Regarding baptism, for example, most Protestants agreed that the sacrament was appropriate for young children but disagreed about whether it was an essential rite through which God began to draw a soul toward salvation or rather a symbolic ritual communicating the mysterious work of cleansing and forgiveness in Christ. Baptists, meanwhile, maintained that baptism was appropriate only for adult believers. Protestants took a similar range of positions on the meaning and significance of their second sacrament: the Lord's Supper. While Protestants were united in rejecting Catholicism's understanding of the Eucharist, which contends that the elements of bread and wine become the actual body and blood of Jesus during the Mass, they formulated a variety of doctrinal positions on what happened during the Lord's Supper and who should be allowed to partake.

In England, the Reformation generated two influential Protestant groups who would eventually immigrate to British North America: Anglicans and Puritans. When King Henry VIII (1491–1547) was unable to get Pope Clement VII to annul his first marriage, he broke with the Catholic Church and declared that the Church of England (COE) would now be England's official state-sponsored church. Over the ensuing decades, a rancorous debate took place between two parties: (1) those who wanted the COE (whose members were known as Anglicans) to retain the look and feel of a Catholic Mass and (2) those who believed the COE should undergo a more radical shift away from Catholicism. Over time, the latter group became known as "Puritans" (Erie 2016: 318–65).

The debate between Anglicans and Puritans had far-reaching ramifications for the history of Protestantism in North America. Puritans placed special emphasis on the Bible as the ultimate source of religious authority. Because Puritans challenged the COE, criticizing its priests and their authority, they were persecuted throughout England and many fled to British colonies in North America. Beginning with the Plymouth Colony in 1620, the Puritans colonized *New England*, which they believed God had ordained to be a model of holiness and proper religious worship. Though they had experienced and fled religious persecution in England, Puritans imposed their own standards across New England, harshly punishing and even banishing those who challenged Puritan norms. Other Puritans fled England and settled widely throughout British North America, including the American South and the Caribbean. By the eighteenth century, the Anglican Church was the official state-sponsored church across the American South (including Virginia, North Carolina, and South Carolina), while the Puritans' Congregational Church was the state-sponsored church across New England (Noll 1992: 30–53). Both groups undertook missionary efforts to convert Native peoples and African Americans, who when they adopted Protestantism, remade it by creatively merging and integrating Christian worship with traditional Native and African religious practices (Fisher 2012; Frey and Wood 1998).

The region in-between these two strongholds of state-sponsored Protestantism was known as the middle colonies. In New York, Pennsylvania, New Jersey, and Delaware, a far more diverse and inclusive religious culture took shape with Catholics, Jews, and an array of other Protestant denominations living together (Bonomi 1986: 24–6). Pennsylvania was established by the Quaker William Penn as a refuge for persecuted religious groups of all kinds. Quakerism, which emerged in seventeenth-century England, proclaimed that the "inner light" of Christ dwelled in and could speak directly to every individual irrespective of race, gender, age, or social status. As a result, Quakers challenged England's strict social hierarchy, refusing to tip their hats to elites or use formal titles. For this and because of their radical beliefs, Quakers were harshly persecuted in England, spurring the desire for a safe haven in North America (Dandelion 2008: 1–36).

Beginning in the 1730s and 1740s, a provocative strand of Protestantism emphasizing the centrality of the "new birth" arrived in North America, splintering established churches and creating a new fault line in American religious history. Led primarily by a British Anglican priest named George Whitefield, a group of "new light" or "Whitefieldarian" preachers electrified audiences with riveting, dramatic sermons. They preached an incendiary message: that the "new birth"—an intense, personal encounter with God in which an individual confessed sin, repented, placed trust in Jesus, and experienced God's grace, acceptance, and forgiveness—was essential to authentic Protestantism. This strand of Protestantism, particularly its emphasis on religious experience over formal doctrine, was appealing to a significant number of native and African Americans throughout British North America (Fisher 2012; Frey and Wood 1998). New light preachers railed against established Congregational ministers and Anglican priests who had not experienced the new birth, claiming that they were not true Christians. Those who opposed the Whitefieldarians argued that God worked and spoke through the institutional structures of established churches (church services, baptism, the Lord's Supper) and individual and corporate acts of piety (Bible reading, prayer, worship) to draw faithful Protestants into divine love, grace, and acceptance apart from a "new birth" experience (Winiarski 2017). This basic disagreement between those who did and did not proclaim the "new birth" to be essential to authentic Christianity reverberated through the rest of Protestantism's history in North America.

The seventeenth-century arrival of the French to what is now Canada propelled the establishment of Catholicism both among the French and the Indians they attempted to convert. Jesuit missionaries, who learned Indigenous languages, experienced limited success in convincing Indigenous peoples to add Catholic rituals and prayers to their spiritual practices and, in some cases, formally adopt Christianity. At the same time, when relations soured between the French and the far more numerous Indigenous peoples they were attempting to reach, Indians

FIGURE 3.1 *Anglican priest George Whitefield drew enormous crowds across British North America in the 1730s and 1740s. His incendiary, dramatic sermons centered on the claim that true believers would experience the "new birth."* Source: Francis G. Mayer / Getty Images.

executed priests, pointing their fury at efforts to eradicate Indigenous spirituality (Anderson 2010). In the eighteenth century, the British expanded their efforts to overtake parts of Canada, including a colony in Halifax, Nova Scotia. An influx of Protestants from throughout New England, Pennsylvania, and Northern Ireland made Nova Scotia an early example of broad Protestant pluralism and toleration (Noll 1992: 72–3).

PROTESTANTISMS IN NORTH AMERICA

While established, state-sponsored Protestant churches were the norm for most of British North America in the seventeenth and eighteenth centuries, the American Revolution (1776–83) initiated the process of *disestablishment*. Eventually, this movement severed the link between church and state across the young United States, proclaiming instead that religious toleration and diversity best reflected and implemented the revolution's core claims about liberty (Beneke 2006). This new push toward "religious freedom" became an essential portion of American public lore and memory in the nineteenth century, evidence for its supporters, of the emerging greatness of the American republic. At the same time, the move toward disestablishment and the reality of religious freedom were slowly implemented—Massachusetts, for example, did not drop its support for the Congregational Church establishment until 1833—and in many ways the United States continued to support an unofficial Protestant establishment. Blasphemy, for example, remained a state-level crime throughout the nineteenth century (Sehat 2011).

In the Canadian provinces, which came under British control after 1763, Protestants lived alongside Catholics, often with deep, mutual suspicion and mistrust but united by a shared loyalty to the British crown and a rejection of what they viewed as out of control democratic individualism in the United States. After the American Revolution, thousands of "Loyalists" who did not support American independence, fled the United States for Canada. This included Anglicans, Presbyterians, Methodists, and Baptists. Halifax, Nova Scotia, became home to half of the Black Canadian population, who usually worshipped in Baptist churches, by the middle of the nineteenth century. Methodism was especially prominent in Upper Canada, where more than half of Protestant residents claimed it as their preference by 1812. During the War of 1812, Canadians rejected American efforts to entice (and force) them to abandon the British and join the United States. This ensured that Canada's religious landscape would not be characterized by the divisive populism unfolding in the nineteenth-century United States. Instead, nineteenth-century Canadian Protestantism was characterized by orderliness, political conservatism, and respect for the state (Deming and Hamilton 1993: 134–5). The remarkable population growth of Ontario, a province in Canada's western interior, in the early nineteenth century made it home to a diverse collection of Protestant denominations who sought to balance order and stability with revivalistic fervor (Noll 1992: 256–68).

The decline of state-sponsored churches in the United States coincided with or, some scholars contend, caused a dramatic efflorescence of Protestantism in the first half of the nineteenth century. The number of Protestant *denominations*, or religious options, doubled between 1775 and 1845 (Hatch 1989: 4). While the older, formerly established churches, including Congregationalism in New England and Anglicanism across the South diminished in influence and numerical presence during these years, Methodists, Baptists, and Presbyterians achieved marked success in recruiting new members. Historians have disagreed sharply over whether these fast-growing denominations were successful because they modeled and appealed to the young nation's democratic impulses or because they reasserted patriarchy and white supremacy (Hatch 1989; Heyrman 1998; Porterfield 2012; Wigger 1998).

Methodism, which skyrocketed numerically between 1780 and 1830, illustrates the new tenor of American Protestantism and its connection to debates over race and gender in the nineteenth-century United States. Throughout these years, African American and white Methodists often worshipped together (Wigger 1998: 131). At the same time, Black Methodists frequently felt the sting of racism among their Methodist brethren. Frustrated by a requirement that they participate in the Lord's Supper only after white Methodists, Black Methodists in Philadelphia, led by Richard Allen, split from the white Methodist church and formed the African Methodist Episcopal (AME) Church in 1794 (Wigger 1998: 145–6). Inspired both by Methodism's openness to the possibility that God could speak through dreams and visions and by Richard Allen's willingness to challenge customary expectations for African Americans, Jarena Lee, an African American woman, felt the call to preach in the early 1800s. As she put it, "For as unseemly as it may appear now-a-days for a woman to preach, it should be remembered that nothing is impossible with God" (Gaustad, Noll, and Carter 2018: 140). These examples illustrate how early nineteenth-century Protestant churches could become spaces in which racial and gender norms were challenged by those denied equality. The rise of independent Black churches among both the Methodists and the Baptists took place because bold, innovative African American leaders demanded equality and asserted their independence from white churches. This laid a critical foundation for the centrality of African American churches to Black community life in the United States (Lincoln and Mamiya [1990] 2003). Enslaved African Americans embraced a variety of Protestant practices, most often outside the oversight and without the consent of those who enslaved them, to express their sorrow and proclaim their hope that God would free them. Jesus, who was himself acquainted with suffering, became a particularly meaningful figure to enslaved Protestants in the early decades of the nineteenth century (Blum and Harvey 2012: 93–101; Raboteau [1978] 2004).

The Church of Jesus Christ of Latter-day Saints (LDS) is one of the most enduring and influential of the new Protestant churches that came into being in the nineteenth century. The LDS is among a select handful of "home grown" Protestant churches without European roots. After experiencing a series of divine revelations in the 1820s, Joseph Smith, the founder and prophet of the LDS, claimed that God had instructed him to uncover a set of ancient golden plates buried in Palmyra, New York. Smith translated these plates into the Book of Mormon, published in 1830 (Butler, Wacker, and Balmer 2011: 204–11). Offering a sweeping, gripping tale according to which ancient Hebrews sailed to and settled in North America and were visited by Jesus after his resurrection, the Book of Mormon was nothing less than an unprecedented reorientation of Christian history (Givens 2002). Smith attracted a group of followers who believed him to be a prophet tasked with reinstating the *Hebrew Bible* and early Christianity's patriarchal and religious order, including the construction of a temple unto which God would return. Smith and his followers traveled from New York to Ohio, eventually settling in Navoo, Illinois, and moving to Missouri in 1838.

FIGURE 3.2 *In 1794, Richard Allen established the African Methodist Episcopal Church, the first independent African American Protestant denomination in the United States. Born into slavery, Allen purchased his freedom at the age of twenty and was an outspoken opponent of slavery for the rest of his life. His church became a stop on the underground railroad, where enslaved men and women seeking freedom could hide. Source: Kean Collection / Getty Images.*

Throughout this journey, Smith continued receiving revelatory messages from God, most notably the revelation—first written down in 1843—that the LDS should reinstate the Hebrew Bible practice of polygamy or plural marriage. LDS members were viewed with great suspicion wherever they settled. Smith was murdered by a mob after being arrested in 1844. The Saints splintered into numerous groups after Smith's death, with around half following Brigham Young to Salt Lake City, Utah. There, the LDS built an impressive, thriving church. In early 1896, Utah was admitted as the 45th state, which set forth a fresh round of mudslinging and suspicion about

FIGURE 3.3 *Jarena Lee felt a call to preach and eventually convinced Richard Allen to authorize her to do so in 1819. Lee became a traveling Methodist minister, covering thousands of miles and delivering hundreds of sermons to mixed-race audiences every year. Though she often faced racist and sexist hostility, Lee was unwavering in her belief that God could use women as well as men to proclaim the truth. Like Allen, she too preached against the sin of slavery. Source: Fotosearch / Stringer / Getty Images.*

the LDS, centered particularly on the ongoing practice of polygamy. The majority of American politicians viewed plural marriage as a threat to the traditional nuclear family structure and sexual ethics (Talbot 2013: 83–104). By 1907, after a contentious hearing in the US Senate over whether to seat Utah's first Senator, the LDS officially discontinued plural marriage (Flake 2004). This development paved the way for a slow withering of anti-Mormon hostility, although many conservative Protestants continued to view the LDS as a dangerously misguided "cult" throughout the twentieth and into the twenty-first centuries. Mitt Romney's run for the White House in 2012, in which his Mormon faith was largely viewed favorably or at least neutrally, symbolizes how far the LDS has come in its efforts to be seen as a respectable branch of Christianity.

FIGURE 3.4 *Joseph Smith, the founder and prophet of the Church of Jesus Christ of Latter-Day Saints, arguably the most enduring and influential religious movement to have begun in North America.* Source: *Fine Art / Getty Images.*

Beginning in the 1820s, American Protestants played a central role in a variety of efforts to reform and, in their eyes, improve American society throughout the decades preceding the Civil War (1861–5). Protestant Reformers targeted an array of issues. Temperance activists urged Americans to abstain from alcohol consumption. Sabbatarians organized to oppose individuals, businesses, and the US government from working on Sundays. By the 1830s, the abolition movement demanded an immediate end to the institution of slavery, which had been gradually abolished in the northern states after the American Revolution (1776–83). Fueled by a coalition of African American and white activists, abolitionists proclaimed slavery an unchristian, inhumane, and deplorable sin. Formerly enslaved Sojourner Truth, for example, spoke throughout the north proclaiming that God had spoken to her about slavery's wickedness (Gaustad, Noll, and Carter 2018: 222–4). After being introduced to and convinced by Quaker literature opposing slavery, two sisters from a slaveholding southern family, Sarah and Angelina Grimke, became outspoken abolitionists, giving speaking tours in the North. Although they represented the views of a small minority of Northerners, abolitionists vocalized a version of Protestant theology in which God opposed slavery and wanted it to end. Frustrated by their unequal treatment by some male abolitionists, an influential group of women, including Catherine Beecher, Lydia Maria Child, and the Grimke sisters, began organizing in support for the equal rights of women in the United States (Abzug 1994: 190–203). Despite the remarkable diversity of reform efforts in the antebellum years, each strand of reform relied on a Protestant moral imperative to bring lasting, fundamental changes to American society.

The Civil War was a traumatic event for the United States and a reckoning for American Protestants. In the decades preceding the war, northern and southern Protestants argued vigorously over whether or not slavery was compatible with Christianity. Proslavery southern Protestants relied on biblical passages such as "slaves obey your earthly masters" (Eph. 6:5) to support their claim that the Bible sanctioned slavery. African American Protestants and a small group of white northern allies countered by proclaiming that Jesus' command to "love your neighbor as yourself" (Mk 12:31) made slavery an unchristian institution (Noll [2006] 2015). Enslaved African American Protestants placed their hope in Jesus, who like them, was acquainted with suffering (Blum and Harvey 2012). Unable to come to a consensus about whether God supported or opposed slavery, northern and southern Protestants became complicit in making war the only way to find out. After the Civil War, northern and southern white Protestants played a central role in linking whiteness to moral purity and American nationalism, underwriting systematic segregation laws in the South and the ongoing denial of equality and human rights to African Americans throughout the United States (Blum 2005).

Protestantism was prohibited and largely absent from Mexico until the constitution of 1857 cast off Mexico's remaining colonial institutions and practices, including the Catholic Church's religious monopoly. American Protestants from a variety of denominations began sending missionaries to Mexico, which had long been, and still is, overwhelmingly Catholic. Their efforts between 1857 and the outbreak of the Mexican Revolution (1910–20) appealed mostly to middle-class Mexicans, who were less attached to the Catholic Church than upper- and lower-class residents. Methodist and Baptist missionaries were especially successful in northern Mexico, which was more sparsely populated and closer to the United States. Early Protestant converts never represented more than 2 percent of Mexico's population (Baldwin 1990: 3–6, 11–26). With varying degrees of outspokenness, Protestants both in Mexico and the United States generally supported the Mexican Revolution. Initially aimed at ending the autocratic rule of President Porfirio Díaz, the revolution later took a markedly anticlerical turn, in which Catholic priests were intensely criticized. Protestants interpreted this shift as a possible opening for their missionary efforts. In the aftermath of the revolution, when the new government began enforcing anticlerical laws enshrined in the Constitution of 1917, conservatives in Mexico propagated the notion that the revolution was a US-backed effort to attack Catholicism and thus annex a divided Mexico (Weis 2019: 61–79).

A new fault line, with long-term ramifications, emerged in American Protestantism during the early decades of the twentieth century. The controversy stemmed from a deep division over how new scientific and intellectual developments should inform Protestant theology and practice. Those who believed that scientific insights, perhaps most notably evolutionary biology, were God-given and meant to reshape how Protestants read and interpret the Bible became known as modernists. In essence, they believed that God revealed new truths *through* and *in* history. This implied a refashioning of Protestant belief and biblical interpretation. Those who believed that the Bible contained an unchanging core of infallible, essential doctrinal truths became known as Fundamentalists. This name came from a series of books published between 1910 and 1915 titled *The Fundamentals: A Testimony to the Truth*, which offered a spirited defense of what conservative Protestants believed to be "fundamental" doctrines threatened by contemporary intellectual trends. These included the infallibility of the Bible, the *virgin birth*, the miracles Jesus performed while on Earth, and the physical resurrection of Jesus from the dead (Marsden 2006). Although initially focused on protecting and defending a collection of doctrines, Fundamentalists also stood against a variety of cultural shifts in the early twentieth century yielding new roles for women in the labor force, looser sexual norms, and the celebration of freedom and innovation in American popular culture (Bendroth 1993). While modernists relied on and learned from leading intellectual and cultural institutions, Fundamentalists built an impressive system of alternative, conservative radio and print network to disseminate their ideas (Carpenter 1999). Standing against what they viewed as a heretical loss of true religion, the Fundamentalists sustained a unique and deeply influential subculture characterized by traditional gender norms, a mistrust of intellectual elites, a passionate defense of "fundamental" Protestant doctrines, and close-knit church communities.

The birth and rapid spread of Pentecostalism was another monumental development of the early twentieth century. The movement's most renowned event was a series of religious revivals beginning in 1906 led by an African American preacher named William J. Seymour. Influenced by the ministry of Charles Fox Parham, a white Methodist in Texas and Kansas who taught that true believers would experience a baptism of the Holy Spirit—accompanied by *"speaking in tongues"* and, in some cases, miraculous healing—Seymour began preaching in an abandoned Methodist church on Azusa street in Los Angeles. As hundreds and eventually thousands of participants from around the country experienced the baptism of the Holy Spirit, the gift of tongues, healing, and other miraculous signs, local newspapers provided steady coverage of the unprecedented event (Noll 1992: 386–8). According to early Pentecostals, the Holy Spirit united all believers, erasing divisions based on race, class, and gender. As a result, women, African American, Mexican American, and Indigenous peoples played a prominent role in the Azusa revivals. Attendees from outside California returned home proclaiming the necessity for a baptism of the Holy Spirit. Mexican Americans in the American southwest and Mexican Protestants established far-reaching networks to build, grow, and sustain Pentecostalism among Protestants, and eventually many Catholics who embraced the idea of an immediate encounter with the Holy Spirit and physically expressive forms of worship, in Mexico and among Latinos throughout the United States (Ramírez 2015).

In Canada, two issues defined and shaped Protestant history during the first half of the twentieth century: rapid immigration and a spirited effort to merge disparate denominations into a Protestant United Church for all Canada. Before 1900, most immigrants to Canada had come from Great Britain. After 1900, mirroring patterns in the United States, a majority of immigrants arrived from southern or eastern Europe. And they came to Canada in proportionally much larger numbers than they came to the United States. The majority of the new immigrant groups went to Ontario or the western provinces, where they diversified the Protestant landscape. Lutherans and Mennonites as well as a variety of Catholics now called Canada home. Established Protestant groups sought to "Christianize" the newcomers by drawing them into their churches, revealing the boundaries of Protestant inclusivity. At the same time, Methodists, Baptists, Presbyterians, and Anglicans sought to unify their denominations into one united Protestant Church. While the most energetic efforts to promote unification took place before the First World War, the United Church was officially formed in 1925. Of course, not every Protestant agreed to join and intense divisions remained within Canadian Protestantism (Noll 1992: 280–4). But the move toward Protestant unity paved the way for the steady growth of the "mainline" (Presbyterian, Methodist, and Baptist churches) in the middle decades of the century. By the 1940s and 1950s, 65 percent of Canadians over the age of twenty reported attending church in the three-week period following Easter Sunday. In the same poll given in the United States at that time, only 58 percent of participants had done so (Bibby 2017: 12).

Between the First World War (1914–18) and the Second World War (1941–5), African Americans in the United States moved in mass numbers from the South to northern cities, including St. Louis, Detroit, Cleveland, and Denver, where they could find better jobs and, in some cases, less severe racial discrimination than they faced in the American South. The majority of African Americans regularly attended Protestant services in the North, usually in predominantly African American churches. The "black church" remained a crucial institution in African American community life throughout the North and South (Lincoln and Mamiya 2003). The phonograph played a key role in the spiritual lives of African American migrants to the North from the South during these years. On records in their homes, they could listen to preachers whose style and cadence reminded them of Southern African American churches (Martin 2014).

Protestant church membership rates in the United States reached their highest levels ever during the middle decades of the twentieth century. These churches were particularly prominent and influential in the growing suburban areas occupied by middle-class whites. Liberal-minded Methodist, Presbyterian, and Baptist churches became known as "mainline" Protestant groups. They embraced modern psychology, intellectual trends, and centered their spiritual lives on meaningful personal, even mystical, spiritual experiences (Hedstrom 2012). In the 1930s and 1940s, the phrase "Judeo-Christian" entered the mainstream American vocabulary. The term reflected a new willingness among Protestants to acknowledge the shared history and values they had with Jews and Catholics. The term was both inclusive and exclusive, welcoming Jews and Catholics into the "Judeo-Christian" camp while not so subtly indicating that Muslims, Hindus, and other groups outside the Protestant/Catholic/Jew camp were somehow less fully American (Butler, Wacker, and Balmer 2011: 345–7; Schultz

2011). In the 1950s, however, the harmonious proclamations of shared spirituality among liberal white Protestants met the prophetic cries for equality and justice being increasingly voiced by African Americans.

African American Protestant churches provided the civil rights movement's spiritual engine and organizational apparatus. During the 1956 Montgomery Bus Boycott, Martin Luther King Jr. had a profound religious experience. While he had grown up in the church and was an ordained Baptist minister, he described his faith before this 1956 moment as an "inherited religion." As King prayed through his fears, stirred by numerous threats of violence against him and his family, he heard the voice of Jesus telling him to "stand up for righteousness, stand up for justice. Stand up for truth." The experience curtailed King's fear and uncertainty. He would go on to lead a series of nonviolent protests, inspired by Jesus' universal love and sacrificial death (Blum and Harvey 2012: 211–14). King's vision was realized only because of the courageous willingness of African Americans to march, protest, and sacrifice to demand equality in the United States. While liberal white Protestants were generally supportive of civil rights, white Jews, who had experienced persecution and injustice themselves, joined the civil rights movement in much higher percentages than their Protestant counterparts.

FIGURE 3.5 *Baptist minister Martin Luther King Jr. proclaimed a message of racial and civil equality informed by a prophetic tradition of justice and hope within the African American church.* Source: *Agence France Presse / Getty Images.*

Beginning in the 1950 and 1960s, embodied by the huge crowds who flocked to hear Billy Graham's sermons, Protestant evangelicalism surged in the United States. Evangelicalism, whose leaders traced their roots to the "Whitefieldarian" revivals of the early eighteenth century, emphasized the atoning work of Jesus on the cross, the reliability and centrality of the Bible, the need for a personal conversion, an intimate "relationship with God," and the importance of preaching this message to others. The movement spanned many different Protestant denominations and was especially effective at building "para-church" organizations, including Campus Crusade for Christ, Young Life, and the Navigators, all of which focused on bringing the evangelical message to young people. In the 1970s and 1980s, evangelicals became a prominent and important political base for the Republican Party, which began to emphasize "family values," including an emphasis on traditional gender roles and opposition to abortion. Evangelicals have remained steadily committed to the Republican Party ever since. In the 1970s, an influential segment of evangelical leaders began preaching what became known as the "prosperity gospel." Claiming that God intended to bless

FIGURE 3.6 *Beginning in the 1950s, Billy Graham drew huge crowds to his rallies, at which he urged people to accept Jesus as their savior and be "born again." Graham was a key architect of evangelical Christianity's growth after the Second World War.* Source: *Ralph Morse / Getty Images.*

believers with health and wealth, prosperity preachers built enormous churches, raised millions of dollars in donations, and embodied the lives of luxury and wealth that they proclaimed (Bowler 2013). Jim and Tammy Faye Bakker were among the most notable and successful example of this movement, but contemporary celebrity preachers such as T.D. Jakes, Paula White, and Joel Osteen have continued preaching the message of prosperity (Wigger 2017). Other evangelical leaders built enormous "megachurches," characterized by a casual dress code and everyday conveniences such as coffee, rock-style worship music, and relatable sermons, beginning in the 1980s.

In all its forms, Protestantism has thrived in North America, reflecting its diversity, adaptability, and ongoing significance in the lives of its practitioners. While no one strand of Protestantism dominates North American life, its fingerprints touch almost every aspect of the past and present.

Further Reading and Online Resources

Frey S. and B. Wood (1998), *Come Shouting to Zion: African-American Protestantism in the American South and British Caribbean to 1830*, Chapel Hill: University of North Carolina Press.

God in America (2010), [TV program] PBS, October 11. Available online: https://www.pbs.org/godinamerica/view/ (accessed November 6, 2020).

Noll M. (1992), *A History of Christianity in the United States and Canada*, Grand Rapids, MI: Eerdmans.

Raboteau A. ([1978] 2004), *Slave Religion: The "Invisible Institution" in Antebellum America*, New York: Oxford University Press.

Winiarski D. (2017), *Darkness Falls on the Land of Light: Experiencing Religious Awakenings in Eighteenth-Century New England*, Chapel Hill: University of North Carolina Press.

References

Abzug R. (1994), *Cosmos Crumbling: American Reform and the Religious Imagination*. New York: Oxford University Press.

Anderson E. (2010), "Blood, Fire, and Baptism: Three Perspectives on the Death of Jean de Brebeuf," in J. Martin and M. Nichols (eds.), *Native Americans, Christianity, and the Reshaping of the American Religious Landscape*, 125–8, Chapel Hill: University of North Carolina Press.

Appold K. (2011), *The Reformation: A Brief History*, Chichester, UK: Blackwell Publishing.

Baldwin D. (1990), *Protestants and the Mexican Revolution: Missionaries, Ministers, and Social Change*, Urbana: University of Illinois Press.

Bendroth M. (1993), *Fundamentalism and Gender, 1875 to the Present*, New Haven, CT: Yale University Press.

Beneke C. (2006), *Beyond Toleration: The Religious Origins of American Pluralism*, New York: Oxford University Press.

Bibby R.W. (2017), *Resilient Gods: Being Pro-Religious, Low Religious, or No Religious in Canada*, Vancouver: University of British Columbia Press.

Blum E. (2005), *Reforging the White Republic: Race, Religion, and American Nationalism, 1865–1898*, Baton Rouge: Louisiana State University Press.

Blum E. and P. Harvey (2012), *The Color of Christ: The Son of God and the Saga of Race in America*, Chapel Hill: University of North Carolina Press.

Bonomi P. (1986), *Under the Cope of Heaven: Religion, Society, and Politics in Colonial America*, New York: Oxford University Press.

Bowler K. (2013), *Blessed: A History of the American Prosperity Gospel*, New York: Oxford University Press.

Butler J., G. Wacker, and R. Balmer (2011), *Religion in American Life: A Short History*, 2nd edn., New York: Oxford University Press.

Carpenter J. (1999), *Revive Us Again: The Reawakening of American Fundamentalism*, New York: Oxford University Press.

Collinson P. (2003), *The Reformation: A History*, New York: Modern Library.

Dandelion P. (2008), *The Quakers: A Very Short Introduction*, New York: Oxford University Press.

Deming J.C. and M.S. Hamilton (1993), "Methodist Revivalism in France, Canada, and the United States," in G.A. Rawlyk and M.A. Noll (eds.), *Amazing Grace: Evangelicalism in Australia, Britain, Canada, and the United States*, 124–53, Grand Rapids, MI: Baker.

Erie C. (2016), *Reformations: The Early Modern World, 1450–1650*, New Haven, CT: Yale University Press.

Fisher L. (2012), *The Indian Great Awakening: Religion and the Shaping of Native Cultures in Early America*, New York: Oxford University Press.

Flake K. (2004), *The Politics of American Religious Identity: The Seating of Senator Reed Smoot, Mormon Apostle*, Chapel Hill: University of North Carolina Press.

Frey S. and B. Wood (1998), *Come Shouting to Zion: African-American Protestantism in the American South and British Caribbean to 1830*, Chapel Hill: University of North Carolina Press.

Gaustad E., M. Noll, and H. Carter, eds. (2018), *A Documentary History of Religion in America*, Grand Rapids, MI: Eerdmans.

Givens T. (2002), *By the Hand of Mormon: The American Scripture that Launched a New World Religion*, New York: Oxford University Press.

Hatch N. (1989), *The Democratization of American Christianity*, New Haven, CT: Yale University Press.

Hedstrom M. (2012), *The Rise of Liberal Religion: Book Culture and American Spirituality in the Twentieth Century*, New York: Oxford University Press.

Heyrman C. (1998), *Southern Cross: The Beginnings of the Bible Belt*, Chapel Hill: University of North Carolina Press.

Lincoln E.C. and L.H. Mamiya ([1990] 2003), *The Black Church in the African- American Experience*, Durham, NC: Duke University Press.

Marsden G. (2006), *Fundamentalism and American Culture*, New York: Oxford University Press.

Martin L. (2014), *Preaching on Wax: The Phonograph and the Shaping of Modern African-American Religion*, New York: New York University Press.

Noll M. (1992), *A History of Christianity in the United States and Canada*, Grand Rapids, MI: Eerdmans.

Noll M. (2015), *The Civil War as a Theological Crisis*, Chapel Hill: University of North Carolina Press.

Porterfield A. (2012), *Conceived in Doubt: Religion and Politics in the New American Nation*, Chicago: University of Chicago Press.

PROTESTANTISMS IN NORTH AMERICA

Raboteau A. ([1978] 2004), *Slave Religion: The "Invisible Institution" in Antebellum America*, New York: Oxford University Press.

Ragosta J. (2010), *Wellspring of Liberty: How Virginia's Religious Dissenters Helped Win the American Revolution and Secured Religious Liberty*, New York: Oxford University Press.

Ramírez D. (2015), *Migrating Faith: Pentecostalism in the United States and Mexico in the Twentieth Century*, Chapel Hill: University of North Carolina Press.

Schultz K. (2011), *Tri-Faith America: How Catholics and Jews Held Postwar America to Its Protestant Promise*, New York: Oxford University Press.

Sehat D. (2011), *The Myth of American Religious Freedom*, New York: Oxford University Press.

Talbot C. (2013), *A Foreign Kingdom: Mormons and Polygamy in American Political Culture, 1852–1890*, Urbana: University of Illinois Press.

Weis R. (2019), *For Christ and Country: Militant Catholic Youth in Post-Revolutionary Mexico*, Cambridge: Cambridge University Press.

Wigger J. (1998), *Taking Heaven by Storm: Methodism and the Rise of Popular Christianity in America*, New York: Oxford University Press.

Wigger J. (2017), *PTL: The Rise and Fall of Jim and Tammy Faye Bakker's Evangelical Empire*, New York: Oxford University Press.

Winiarski D. (2017), *Darkness Falls on the Land of Light: Experiencing Religious Awakenings in Eighteenth-Century New England*, Chapel Hill: University of North Carolina Press.

Glossary Terms

Denomination A term for a specific, organized subset of Protestantism. For example, Baptist, Methodist, Anglican, and Presbyterian churches represent four distinct denominations.

Disestablishment The process by which state-sponsored established churches, such as the Anglican Church in the American South, lost their privileged standing and funding from states. Rather than one "established" church, disestablishment was based on the idea that diversity and religious freedom best reflected the values of liberty and equality in the early nineteenth-century United States.

Hebrew Bible A collection of scriptural books believed to be God-given by Jews, Christians, and Muslims. The Hebrew Bible, which Christians refer to as the Old Testament, opens with an account of the world's creation and then narrates the story of God's special relationship with Jews, who

eventually call themselves Israel. Highly monotheistic, the Hebrew Bible centers on the covenant made between God and Israel, through prophets such as Moses and Abraham, which sealed Israel's place as the chosen people of God. Beyond Israel's history, The Hebrew Bible also contains poetry and prophetic books, which Christians believe foreshadow and validate Jesus as the promised "messiah," sent to bring salvation to the world.

New England A region of British North America, and later the United States, including the states of Massachusetts, Connecticut, Maine, New Hampshire, and Vermont.

New Testament The books added to the Hebrew Bible, which Christians refer to as the Old Testament, to form the Christian scriptural canon. The New Testament contains the four "Gospels," Matthew, Mark, Luke, and John, which tell the story of Jesus' earthly ministry and death, as well as letters from early church leaders to various Christian communities and prophetic predictions about Jesus' "second coming" to Earth.

Sacraments Both Protestants and Catholics believe that sacraments are a ritualistic means through which God offers his grace and presence. For Protestants, the sacraments include baptism and the Lord's Supper. In baptism, a child or an adult is sprinkled with or submerged in water to signify cleansing from sin and a new life in Jesus (who himself was baptized by John the Baptist as he began his ministry). In the Lord's Supper or Communion, Christians consume bread and wine (or juice) to remember Jesus' death and resurrection. At the "Last Supper," the night before his death, Jesus instructed his disciples to consume bread and wine to commemorate the breaking of his body (bread) and the spilling of his blood (wine). Catholics believe there are seven sacraments, including baptism, the Eucharist (what Catholics call the Lord's Supper), confession (in which a person confesses sin to a priest and receives God's forgiveness), Confirmation (in which a person formally joins the Catholic Church), marriage, Holy Orders (ordination to the priesthood), and the anointing of the sick (given when one is gravely ill).

Salvation In Christian theology, salvation refers to being forgiven from sin and being made right with God. The New Testament uses several metaphors to describe the concept of salvation, including the language of being "born anew," being "rescued" from a life of sorrow, and being "adopted" into the family of God.

Speaking in Tongues In the New Testament book of Acts, Jesus visits his disciples after his resurrection and imparts his spirit, the Holy Spirit, to them. As a result, the disciples begin to speak earthly languages with which they had no fluency before receiving the Holy Spirit. The disciples were thus able to spread the message of Jesus among listeners whose languages they did not speak. The New Testament also contains references to the "spiritual gift" of speaking in and interpreting foreign tongues. For Pentecostals in the early twentieth century, speaking in tongues was an undeniable manifestation of God's presence and power and, for some, necessary to salvation. Beyond a recognizable foreign language, Pentecostals also experienced the gift of tongues as a private prayer language whose meaning was known only to God.

Virgin birth The belief that Jesus' mother Mary was miraculously impregnated by the Holy Spirit of God without a human father and remained a virgin before Jesus' birth. The doctrine is taken from two accounts in the New Testament, found in the books of Matthew and Luke, each of which claim that Mary was a virgin when Jesus was born. For those who believe in the virgin birth, it is an essential theological truth because it explains and proves how and why Jesus was both fully God and fully human.

4

Evangelical Christianities in North America

Emma Rifai

Thanks to the 2015 "Religious Landscape Survey" conducted by the Pew Research Center, we know that evangelical Christianity is the single largest religious community in the United States, representing over a quarter of the adult population. Indeed, the United States has the largest concentration of evangelical Christians in the world. Even so, we simply cannot think of "evangelical Christianity" in the singular. Since its origins, the evangelical movement "has always been *diverse*, *flexible*, *adaptable*, and *multiform*" (Noll 2001: 14, emphasis in the original). Because of its remarkable fluidity, evangelical Christianity has been able to respond to and evolve with American culture more broadly. For example, while the majority of evangelical Christians in the United States today are white—around 75 percent—there is a notable and growing number of African American and Latino evangelical Christians as well.

Tracing the history of evangelical Christianities in North America is a complicated task because it is not a unified entity, supported by institutional structures commonly associated with mainline Protestant denominations. This is largely because evangelical Christianity is a transdenominational signifier, meaning it is not explicitly linked with any singular Protestant denomination. As an umbrella term, evangelical Christianity can include various groups such as the Baptists, Mennonites, Methodists, Presbyterians, Congregationalists, Episcopalians, Lutherans, German and Dutch Reformed, Restorationists, Holiness groups, Pentecostals, and any number of so-called "nondenominational" congregations. "Because of its malleability, its populism, and its uncanny knack for speaking the language of the culture," historian Randall Balmer argues, "evangelicalism will continue to be America's folk religion well into the twenty-first century" (2010: 75).

Shared History and Beliefs

Because of its remarkable diversity, it can be challenging to identify what exactly is the glue that holds evangelical Christianity together. Most scholars agree that evangelical Christians share three core commitments: the authority of the Bible as God's revelation to humanity; the centrality of the conversion or "born again" experience; and the need to bring others, far and wide, to the faith through evangelism. "Evangelical" comes from the Greek "evangel" and means "good news," a term that often refers to the biblical Gospels of Matthew, Mark, Luke, and John. The word "evangelical" entered the popular lexicon in the eighteenth and nineteenth centuries when it was first used to refer to the massive revivals that swept across the eastern United States during the First and Second Great Awakenings (1730–50 and 1790–1840, respectively).

North American evangelical Christianity developed from European Protestant Reformation theology in the "New World" context. Indeed, the United States is the first Western nation not historically grounded in Roman Catholicism. Reformation doctrine is, perhaps, best captured in the "Five Solas" that articulate the core tenets of the faith: (1) Sola Gratia, or by grace alone, (2) Sola Fida, or through faith alone, (3) Solus Christus, or in Christ alone, (4) Sola Scriptura, or according to scripture alone, and (5) Soli Deo Gloria, or for God's glory alone. In addition to these five tenets, evangelical Christians embraced, according to historian Thomas Kidd, "increased emphases on *seasons of revival*, or *outpourings of the Holy Spirit*, and on *converted sinners experiencing God's love personally*" (2008: xiv, emphasis in the original).

Writing that "the American strain of evangelicalism is peculiarly, well, American," Balmer argues that evangelical Christianity resulted from the confluence of what he calls the "Three Ps": Puritanism, Presbyterianism, and Pietism (2010: 2). He writes:

From Puritans contemporary evangelicals inherit the penchant for spiritual introspection; just as Puritans in the seventeenth century were charting their religious pilgrimages, so too evangelicals constantly are taking their spiritual "temperatures" to discern whether they are good or godly. From the Presbyterians evangelicals derive their insistence on doctrinal precision, and from the Pietists they insist that mere intellectual assent is insufficient. Evangelicals prize a warmhearted piety.

(Balmer 2016: x)

In addition to weaving together these different Protestant doctrinal orientations, evangelical Christianity simultaneously disrupted what Timothy Gleoge calls the "churchly orientation." That is, evangelical Christians "shifted the primary locus of authentic faith from the communal context of church membership to an individual's personal relationship with God" (Gleoge 2015: 6). We can trace this turn toward a more experiential faith experience to the First Great Awakening.

The First Great Awakening

During the third and fourth decades of the eighteenth century, a series of revivals swept across the American colonies. Led by such figures as George Whitefield, John Wesley, and Jonathan Edwards, colonists were gripped with a renewed sense of individual piety and religious devotion. William McLoughlin defines a revival as "the Protestant ritual [...] in which charismatic evangelists convey 'the Word' of God to large masses of people who, under this influence, experience what Protestants call conversion, salvation, regeneration, or spiritual rebirth" (1978: xiii). Religious conversion and revivalism, according to Amanda Porterfield, "encouraged people to leave their mistakes behind, work hard, and redouble their commitment to the future" (2012: 10).

The American colonies were remarkably diverse in terms of religion. While Congregational churches dominated New England, and Anglican churches dominated the southern colonies, the middle colonies were peppered with Quakers, Dutch Reformed, Anglican, Presbyterian, Lutheran, Congregational, and Baptist churches. During the early eighteenth century, church membership throughout the colonies had declined and many colonists had turned to atheism, Deism, Unitarianism, or Universalism. In response, minsters of various congregational affiliations started calling for a renewal of faith, a recommitment to piety, and a revival of religion. A revivalist spirit took hold of the colonies most notably during the Northampton revival of 1734–5, led by Congregationalist minister Jonathan Edwards. Having preached a series of sermons, grounded in Calvinist theology, and with a strong emphasis on "justification by faith," Edwards witnessed his congregation break into a religious fervor. According to Frances FitzGerald: "People laughed and wept, some saw visions, and many were filled with hope and joy" (2017: 16–17). In a letter, Edwards, whose congregational membership doubled over the course of six months, wrote that this town "never was so full of Love, nor so full of Joy, nor so full of distress as it has lately been ... I never saw the Christian spirit in Love to Enemies so exemplified, in all my Life as I have seen it within this half-year" (quoted in Ahlstrom 1972: 282).

A number of revivalists also took to itinerant preaching during the decades of the First Great Awakening. George Whitefield, for example, traveled up and down the Atlantic seaboard preaching to various communities in colonies such as Rhode Island, Massachusetts, New Hampshire, and Connecticut, to larger and larger crowds. Indeed, on October 12, 1740, he preached to a crowd of over thirty thousand people. Had preachers like Whitefield and the Wesleys not embraced itinerancy, the revivals of places such as Northampton might have remained relatively isolated affairs. Instead, Whitefield, the Wesleys, and others wove together the revivalist tendencies appearing throughout the colonies into a movement we now call the First Great Awakening.

Itinerant ministry during both great awakenings was not the sole domain of men. Indeed, there were over a hundred evangelical women who preached in either the eighteenth or nineteenth centuries. For example, Margaret Meuse Clay was sentenced to a public whipping for "unlicensed preaching" in the mid-1760s; "Old Elizabeth,"

FIGURE 4.1 *George Whitefield preaching.* Source: *Culture Club / Getty Images.*

a woman of color and former slave, advocated against slavery in the south in the early nineteenth century; and Harriet Livermore was invited to speak in the House of Representatives Chamber of the United States Congress in January 1827. These women have mostly been forgotten to history because, Catherine Brekus argues, "revolutionary in their defense of female preaching, yet orthodox in their theology, female preachers had been too conservative to be remembered by women's rights activists, but too radical to be remembered by evangelicals" (2000: 7). After having brought tens of thousands to the faith, preachers such as Clay, Edwards, and Whitefield witnessed the revivalist spirit begin to fade by the middle of the eighteenth century, only to reemerge at the turn of the nineteenth century.

The Second Great Awakening

"Somewhere between 1800 and 1801, in the upper part of Kentucky, at a memorable place called 'Cane Ridge,'" Peter Cartwright writes, "there was appointed a sacramental meeting by some of the Presbyterian ministers," he continues,

> at which meeting, seemingly unexpected by ministers or people, the mighty power of God was displayed in a very extraordinary manner; many were moved

to tears, and bitter and loud crying for mercy. The meeting was protracted for weeks. Ministers of almost all denominations flocked in from far and near. The meeting was kept up by night and day. Thousands heard of the mighty work, and came on foot, on horseback, in carriages, and waggons [*sic*]. It was supposed that there were in attendance at times during the meeting from twelve to twenty-five thousand people. Hundreds fell prostrate under the mighty power of God, as men slain in battle. Stands were erected in the woods from which preachers of different Churches proclaimed repentance toward God and faith in our Lord Jesus Christ, it was supposed, by eye and ear witnesses, that between one and two thousand souls were happily and powerfully converted to God during the meeting. It was not unusual for one, two, three, and four to seven preachers to be addressing the listening thousands at the same time from different stands erected for the purpose. The heavenly fire spread in almost every direction. It was said by truthful witnesses, that, at times, more than one thousand persons broke out into loud shouting all at once, and that the shouts could be heard for miles around.

(1862: 7)

Peter Cartwright (1785–1872) was a Methodist revivalist preacher who, it is believed, was responsible for the baptism of twelve thousand individuals during the Second Great Awakening. He also participated in the great Cane Ridge Revival that took place in Kentucky in early August in 1801, which he recounts in his autobiography. Between ten thousand and twenty-five thousand individuals participated in the Cane Ridge revival, led by various Baptist, Methodist, and Presbyterian evangelical ministers. Cane Ridge was the most famous and most dramatic of the frontier camp meetings of the Second Great Awakening.

The Second Great Awakening marked profound shifts in evangelical Christianity at the turn of the nineteenth century. Over the course of the early decades of the new century millions of new members joined various established evangelical denominations as well as a number of newly formed denominations. Unlike the Calvinist theology of the First Great Awakening, the Second Great Awakening embraced an Armenian philosophy. Calvinism argued that God alone determined whether or not an individual would achieve salvation, while Arminianism embraced the idea that salvation was available to anyone who exercised faith. Indeed, much of the Second Great Awakening was imbued with a sense of optimism. Many, embracing a postmillennial eschatology, believed that the massive revivals of the Second Great Awakening marked the beginning of the millennium as foretold in the book of Revelation. It is important to understand that *postmillennialism* holds that Christ's Second Coming will occur after a thousand years of righteousness brought about by believers working to reform society for an era of peace and happiness. Thanks, in part, to theologies like these, Christians during the Second Great Awakening were inspired to reform their communities in an effort to contribute to the establishment of a society ripe for the return of Jesus Christ.

70   CHRISTIANITY IN NORTH AMERICA

Perhaps the most important of the Second Great Awakening preachers was Charles Finney, a Presbyterian minister who championed social reforms—including abolitionism and women's rights—on theological grounds. In one lecture, Finney argues:

> As on the subject of slavery and temperance, so on this subject, the church must act right or the country will be ruined. God cannot sustain this free and blessed country, which we love and pray for, unless the church will take right ground. Politics are a part of religion in such a country as this, and Christians must do their duty to the country as part of their duty to God. It seems sometimes as if the foundations of the nation were becoming rotten, and Christians seem to act as if they thought God did not see what they do in politics. But I tell you, he does see it, and he will bless or curse the nation, according to the course they take.
>
> (1835: 274)

Finney and others like him ushered in an era of progressive evangelism devoted to various benevolence movements including education, prison reform, advocacy for the poor, rights for women, prohibition, and abolitionism.

Despite a theology that endorsed abolitionism, in practice, Methodists, Presbyterians, and Baptists were split on the issue of slavery. Powerful slave-owners opposed any institutions that challenged their rights to hold slaves, and many evangelical Christian leaders abandoned abolitionist work in fear that it would alienate possible new converts, particularly in the south. At the same time, African slaves were drawn to the movement because, Porterfield argues, evangelical Christianity "provided some of the few opportunities they had to form any kind of organization or gathering for mutual support, remembrance, and resistance to persecution" (2012: 108).

Evangelical Christianity is, perhaps, best thought of as a double-edged sword insofar as it provided African slaves opportunities for organization and catharsis while simultaneously benefiting those who supported slavery by promoting themes of hard work, humility, honesty, and future salvation.

The Postwar Years

The second half of the nineteenth century witnessed a waning of the revivalist spirit of earlier decades and a dampening of the optimism of the prewar years. Early fundamentalist theologies gained traction as premillennialism took hold in evangelical Christian communities. While postmillennialism had been popular during the decades of the Second Great Awakening, *premillennialism*—an eschatology that suggested Jesus would return to his followers *before* the millennium of righteousness—better resonated with the more pessimistic attitudes of the later nineteenth century. Premillennial eschatology is far less optimistic than postmillennial eschatology because it embraces the belief that the millennium of righteousness predicted in the book of

EVANGELICAL CHRISTIANITIES IN NORTH AMERICA

Revelation will only occur *after* the return of Christ leaving little hope for the present. It is from dispensational premillennialism that we get the notion of the *"rapture,"* or the belief that true believers will be taken up by God before the tribulations of the Apocalypse.

John Nelson Darby, an Irish Bible teacher, made seven visits to North America between 1859 and 1874 during which he spread his ideas on dispensationalism. American historian George Marsden writes: "Rejecting the prevailing postmillennialism which taught that Christ's kingdom would grow out of the spiritual and moral progress of this age, dispensational premillennialists said that the churches and the culture were declining and that Christians would see Christ's kingdom only after he personally returned to rule in Jerusalem" (1991: 39). *Dispensationalism* was a particular interpretative approach to the Bible that argued that human history can be divided into identifiable ages—dispensations—during each of which God approaches "his" relationship with humanity differently. Premillennialists embraced the notion that they were living in the final dispensation and that the return of Christ was imminent.

While evangelical Christians were embracing the eschatology of Darby and others like him, they were also embracing the "plain reading" of the Bible promoted by Dwight Lyman Moody. A proponent of evangelical realism, Moody, according to Gleoge, "offered a new source of religious authority: a Bible interpreted in a personal, plain, and practical manner" (2015: 38). Believers need not turn to the learned ministry to interpret the Bible. Rather, according to Moody, they were *already* fully capable of doing interpretive work themselves. This impulse led to the publishing of the *Scofield Reference Bible* in 1909. The annotated *Scofield Reference Bible* brought together the text of the Bible along with extensive commentary promoting Scofield's views. The Scofield Reference Bible became a best seller and ushered dispensationalist premillennialism into the homes of evangelical Christians all over the United States.

Pentecostalism

Dispensationalist premillennialism was later taken up by the early twentieth-century Pentecostal movements, though it was better known as the "latter rain covenant" within these communities. Pentecostalism emerged at the turn of the twentieth century from earlier holiness movements that had embraced the doctrine of Christian perfectionism and personal holiness. Pentecostalism, more than most evangelical Christian communities, emphasized the role of the Holy Spirit in religious life. Historian Grant Wacker argues Pentecostalism emerged at the intersection of four "confluent streams that had been flowing across the American religious landscape" (2001: 1). These streams included an emphasis on heartfelt salvation through faith in Jesus Christ; Holy Ghost baptism; divine healing; and anticipation of the Lord's imminent return (2). The Pentecostal emphasis on "Baptism of the Holy Spirit" led practitioners to embrace *glossolalia*, or the practice of speaking in tongues, and other spiritual gifts like divine healing and prophecy.

Pentecostalism percolated into a boil in 1906, with the outbreak of the Azusa Street Revival. Led by African American holiness preacher William J. Seymour, the Azusa Street Mission in Los Angeles became the center of the burgeoning Pentecostal movement. Within ten years, the revival had spread throughout North America and had reached between 50,000 and 100,000 converts. "Black Christians played a prominent role in the early history of Pentecostalism in America," Molly Worthen writes, "and for many white evangelicals 'holy-roller' worship had carried racial connotations ever since the shocking origins of modern Pentecostalism in the integrated revivals of Azusa Street" (2014: 138). Indeed, while white congregations such as the Assemblies of God flourished, African American Pentecostal communities would continue to outnumber white communities for decades.

Pentecostalism also embraced a certain level of social equality between men and women. Wacker writes that "the most revealing index of female authority in the worship context was men's grudging willingness to subordinate themselves to women in spiritual matters" (2001: 104). Of African American women in the Church of God in Christ, Anthea Butler writes:

By creating new identities based on the Bible, lower- and middle-class African American women gained status for themselves in a society that ascribed to them only sexual or utilitarian identities. As visible "saints," they valued women's spiritual authority and prowess in a system that recognized the power of women's faith but still affirmed patriarchal leadership.

(2007: 180)

Women of various racial and ethnic identities served as pastors and co-pastors of Pentecostal congregations as well as divine healers, missionaries, tract writers, hymn writers, and newspapers editors. The most outstanding example is Aimee Semple McPherson (1890–1944) who founded the Foursquare Church and was likely the most important American evangelist—male or female—in her heyday.

Modern Fundamentalism

Between 1910 and 1915, a series of pamphlets appeared called *The Fundamentals; or, Testimony to the Truth*. Most scholars consider these tracts to be the genesis of the modern Fundamentalist movement, which includes, according to Joel Carpenter:

an intense focus on evangelism as the church's overwhelming priority, the need for a fresh infilling of the Holy Spirit after conversion in order to live a holy and effective Christian life, the imminent, premillennial second coming of Christ, and the divine inspiration and absolute authority of the Bible, whose very words were free from errors.

(1997: 6)

FIGURE 4.2 *Aimee Semple McPherson.* Source: *Underwood Archives / Getty Images.*

This final point took center stage during the 1920s as a coalition of conservative Protestant forces worked to resist what they saw as the liberalization of American culture, culminating in the "Scopes Monkey Trial" of 1925.

The Scopes Trial was a legal case in Tennessee that challenged legislation prohibiting the teaching of evolution in public schools. Substitute teacher John Scopes was found guilty of violating Tennessee's Butler Act, which prohibited the teaching of human evolution in any state-funded school. He was penalized with a fine in the amount

FIGURE 4.3 *Clarence Darrow speaks at the Scopes Trial.* Source: *Bettmann / Getty Images.*

of $100. The trial was intended to be a national public spectacle, and it certainly lived up to the hype like no other trial before. The famed criminal lawyer Clarence Darrow—an agnostic—defended Scopes while three-time presidential candidate William Jennings Bryan represented the prosecution. "Although the outcome of the trial was indecisive and the law stood," Marsden writes, "the rural setting and the press's caricatures of fundamentalists as rubes and hicks discredited fundamentalism and made it difficult to pursue further the serious aspects of the movement" (1991: 60). Indeed, according to Laurence Moore, "it was the last occasion when a man with a long history of involvement in populist-progressive politics spoke, without any sense of contradiction, in behalf of Biblical literalism" (1986: 159–60).

Neo-Evangelicalism

Having decisively lost the Scopes Trial in the "larger courtroom of public opinion," evangelicals withdrew, according to Balmer, forming a subculture around "their own congregations, denominations, missionary societies, publishing houses, Bible institutes, Bible colleges, Bible camps, and seminaries" where they could "insulate themselves from the larger world" (2010: 49). This retreat continued until the

FIGURE 4.4 *Billy Graham*. Source: *Keystone / Stringer / Getty Images*.

emergence of the "neo-evangelical" movement and meteoric rise of Billy Graham (1918–2018). Neo-evangelicalism distanced itself from the contentious attitudes of the 1920s and 1930s to embrace a softer approach to evangelizing the society around it.

Billy Graham, the most famous of the neo-evangelical preachers of the midtwentieth century, was born to a Fundamentalist evangelical family in 1918 near Charlotte, North Carolina. Having had a conversion experience himself at a revival in 1934, Graham would lead over four hundred revivals—what he called "crusades"—in 185 countries and territories over six continents. Of his crusade in Seoul, Korea, Wacker writes:

> A five-day meeting in the spring of 1973 drew three million attendees, with 73,000 decision cards turned in. On the final day, with more than 1,100,000 souls crowded onto a converted airport tarmac, Graham delivered the Good News to what may have been at that time the largest gathering of humans for a religious purpose in history.
>
> (2014: 21)

Graham maintained broad appeal partly because he, on the one hand, embraced more liberal views on ecumenism and inclusivity in the church while, on the other hand, he maintained more conservative social views on issues related to sexuality and women's rights. Graham, who met with thirteen consecutive presidents—from Harry S. Truman to Donald Trump—before his death in 2018, was also heavily involved in politics. He represents an important shift during the mid-twentieth century. "The major divisions in American religion," according to Robert Wuthnow, had now come to "revolve around an axis of liberalism and conservatism rather than the denominational landmarks of the past" (1989: 178).

The Charismatic Movement

The 1960s witnessed the rise of a new branch of evangelical Christianity: the Charismatic movement, which according to Balmer, "brought Pentecostal fervor—including divine healing and speaking in tongues—into mainline denominations" (1999: 114). While very similar, Pentecostals and Charismatics are different insofar as Charismatics tend to maintain membership in more mainstream denominations while Pentecostals tend to join specifically Pentecostal denominations such as the Assemblies of God or the Church of God in Christ. While many Charismatics maintain membership in more mainstream churches, a number of distinct Charismatic congregations have emerged as well, including Calvary Chapel in Santa Ana, California, Cathedral of Praise in South Bend, Indiana, Vineyard Christian Fellowship in Anaheim, California, and Victory Christian Center in Tulsa, Oklahoma.

The movement traces its origins to St. Mark's Episcopal Church in Van Nuys, California. On April 3, 1960, rector Dennis J. Bennett received the Baptism of the Holy Spirit in the form of glossolalia and at least one hundred parishioners followed suit. The Charismatic movement spread among a number of mainstream Protestant denominations throughout the 1960s including the American Lutheran Church, the Lutheran Church in America, the United Presbyterian Church, the American Baptist Church, and the United Methodist Church as well as in various independent congregations. By 1967, even Roman Catholic communities had started to embrace aspects of the Charismatic movement.

The Religious Right

By the end of the 1970s, evangelical Christians were ready to reengage with politics, something that had been mostly avoided since the Scopes Trial of 1925. Instigating this reengagement was not, as many have assumed, the outcome of *Roe v. Wade* handed down by the Supreme Court in 1973. In fact, former president of the Southern Baptist Convention W.A. Criswell affirmed the decision to legalize abortion stating: "I have always felt that it was only after a child was born and had a life separate from

EVANGELICAL CHRISTIANITIES IN NORTH AMERICA

its mother that it became an individual person, and it has always, therefore, seemed to me that what is best for the mother and for the future should be allowed" (quoted in Balmer 2010: 61–2). Indeed, evangelical Christians did not rally around the "pro-life" agenda until later.

The rise of the religious Right is more accurately traced to another court case: *Green v. Connally*, which denied institutions—including churches—tax exempt status if they participated in institutional forms of racial discrimination. As a result of this ruling, Bob Jones University, a Fundamentalist evangelical university in Greenville, South Carolina, started admitting married students of color in 1971 but maintained "inter-racial dating" as cause for expulsion. Refusing to change this policy resulted in the school losing its tax-exemption status. Having taken its case all the way to the Supreme Court, Bob Jones University failed in its efforts to revive its tax-exemption status, and many evangelical Christians took the ruling to be an attack on the American evangelical subculture.

Largely in response to these developments, Southern Baptist preacher Jerry Falwell founded the Moral Majority in 1979. The Moral Majority was a religiopolitical organization that arose at the intersection of the so-called "Christian right" and the Republican Party and played a significant role in mobilizing conservative Christians to participate in modern politics. In a 1980 speech, Falwell urges:

> Listen, America! Our nation is on a perilous path in regard to her political, economic, and military positions. If America continues down the path she is traveling, she will one day find that she is no longer a free nation. Our nation's internal problems are direct results of her spiritual condition. America is desperately in need of a divine healing, which can only come if God's people humble themselves, pray, seek His face, and turn from their wicked ways.
>
> (2009: 175)

The Moral Majority brought together Christian political action committees and worked on issues that it believed were integral in maintaining its Christian conception of moral law. Described as pro-family and pro-American, the Moral Majority opposed abortion, pornography, the Equal Rights Amendment (ERA), and gay rights, while supporting defense sending, an anti-communism foreign policy, and Israel. With members numbering in the millions, the Moral Majority worked to register voters, lobby congress, and raise money and included influential members such as James Dobson, Beverly and Tim LaHaye, and Pat Robertson. The Moral Majority is largely credited with the successful bid for election of Ronald Reagan in 1980. Despite the organization having dissolved by 1989, its impact has been long reaching. Indeed, the Pew Research Center found that 81 percent of white evangelicals voted for Donald Trump in the 2016 election.

FIGURE 4.5 *Ronald Reagan speaking with Jerry Falwell.* Source: *Bettmann / Getty Images.*

Conclusion

In a 2016 op-ed in *The New York Times*, Russell Moore wrote that the "vital core of American evangelicalism today can be found in churches that are multiethnic and increasingly dominated by immigrant communities." "The next Billy Graham," he continues, "probably will speak only Spanish or Arabic or Persian or Mandarin." While the number of evangelical Christians who described themselves as conservative and Republican increased between 2007 and 2014, the number of white evangelicals decreased. Interestingly, the number of immigrants, African Americans, Asians, and Latinos who identified as evangelical also increased. These changing dynamics will certainly impact evangelical Christianities in North America. If, as Randall Balmer predicted, "evangelicalism will continue to be America's folk religion well into the twenty-first century" it will likely have to reengage with its more fluid, adaptable, and flexible roots to address the needs of a changing North American landscape (2010: 75).

Further Reading and Online Resources

Brasher B.E. (1998), *Godly Women: Fundamentalism and Female Power*, New Brunswick, NJ: Rutgers University Press.

Dochuk D. (2012), *From Bible Belt to Sunbelt: Plain-Folk Religion, Grassroots Politics, and the Rise of Evangelical Conservatism*, New York: W.W. Norton.

Griffith R.M. (2000), *God's Daughters: Evangelical Women and the Power of Submission*, Berkeley: University of California Press.

Ingersoll J. (2003), *Evangelical Christian Women: War Stories in the Gender Battles*, New York: New York University Press.

Irons C.F. (2008), *The Origins of Proslavery Christianity: White and Black Christians in Colonial and Antebellum Virginia*, Chapel Hill: University of North Carolina Press.

References

Ahlstrom S. (1972), *A Religious History of the American People*, New Haven, CT: Yale University Press.

Balmer R. (1999), *Blessed Assurance: A History of Evangelicalism in America*, Boston: Beacon Press.

Balmer R. (2010), *The Making of Evangelicalism: From Revivalism to Politics and Beyond*, Waco, TX: Baylor University Press.

Balmer R. (2016), *Evangelicalism in America*, Waco, TX: TX Baylor University Press.

Brekus C.A. (2000), *Strangers and Pilgrims: Female Preaching in America, 1740–1845*, Chapel Hill: University of North Carolina Press.

Butler A. (2007), "Unrespectable Saints: Women of the Church of God in Christ," in C.A. Brekus (ed.), *The Religious History of American Women: Reimagining the Past*, section A, 25, Chapel Hill: University of North Carolina Press.

Carpenter J.A. (1997), *Revive Us Again: The Reawakening of American Fundamentalism*, New York: Oxford University Press.

Cartwright P. (1862), *Autobiography of Peter Cartwright, the Backwoods Preacher: The Birth, Fortunes, and General Experiences of the Oldest American Methodist Travelling Preacher*, London: Arthur Hall, Virtue, and Co.

Finney C.G. (1835), *Lectures on Revivals of Religion*, New York: Leavitt, Lord & Company.

FitzGerald F. (2017), *The Evangelicals: The Struggle to Shape America*, New York: Simon and Schuster.

Gleoge T.E.W. (2015), *Guaranteed Pure: The Moody Bible Institute, Business, and the Making of Modern Evangelicalism*, Chapel Hill: University of North Carolina Press.

Ingalls R.P. and D.K. Johnson (2009), *The United States since 1945: A Documentary Reader*, Chichester, UK: Wiley-Blackwell.

Kidd T.S. (2008), *The Great Awakening: The Roots of Evangelical Christianity in Colonial America*, New Haven, CT: Yale University Press.

Marsden G.M. (1991), *Understanding Fundamentalism and Evangelicalism*, Grand Rapids, MI: William B. Eerdmans.

McLoughlin W.G. (1978), *Revivals, Awakenings, and Reform*, Chicago: University of Chicago Press.

Moore R. (2016), "A White Church No More," *New York Times*, May 6. Available online: https://www.nytimes.com/2016/05/06/opinion/a-white-church-no-more.html (accessed August 30, 2019).

Moore R.L. (1986), *Religious Outsiders and the Making of Americans*, New York: Oxford University Press.

Noll M.A. (2001), *American Evangelical Christianity: An Introduction*, Oxford: Blackwell Publishing.

Porterfield A. (2012), *Conceived in Doubt: Religion and Politics in the New American Nation*, Chicago: University of Chicago Press.

Wacker G. (2001), *Heaven Below: Early Pentecostals and American Culture*, Cambridge, MA: Harvard University Press.

Wacker G. (2014), *America's Pastor: Billy Graham and the Shaping of a Nation*, Cambridge, MA: Harvard University Press.

Whorten M. (2014), *Apostles of Reason: The Crisis of Authority in American Evangelicalism*, Oxford: Oxford University Press.

Wuthnow R. (1989), *The Struggle for America's Soul: Evangelicals, Liberals, and Secularism*, Grand Rapids, MI: William B. Eerdmans.

Glossary Terms

Dispensationalism A particular interpretive approach to the Bible that argues that human history can be divided into identifiable ages—dispensations—during each of which God approaches "his" relationship with humanity differently.

Glossolalia The spiritual gift of speaking in tongues.

Postmillennialism The belief that Christ's Second Coming will occur after a thousand years of righteousness brought about by believers working to reform society for an era of peace and happiness.

Premillennialism The belief that Christ's Second Coming will occur before the millennium of righteousness as foretold in the book of Revelation. This pessimistic eschatology did not inspire believers to engage in social reform, as followers of postmillennialism had, but rather encouraged a withdrawal from mainstream "secular" society.

Rapture The belief that true believers will be taken up by God before the tribulations of the apocalypse.

5

Mormonism in North America

Konden Smith Hansen

Mormonism in North America: The Beginnings

Traditional accounts of the Mormon *restorationist* movement begin with the religious enthusiasm of New York's "burned over district." This "burned over" reference underscores the heavy presence of evangelical revivals in the area, which *Joseph Smith* credits for inspiring his initial confusions concerning God's true church. It was then within this contested context that Smith, a determined and uneducated farm boy, came across a passage of scripture (Jas 1:5) that told him to go directly to God for answers. Untouched by the religious opinions of the day, Joseph received a series of visions where he saw and spoke with God, Jesus, and various angelic messengers who directed him to restore God's true church to Earth, complete with bestowing on him ancient priesthood authority and a set of golden plates written in Reformed Egyptian. The significance of this new set of scriptures was that it linked together the Old and New Testaments, addressed contested doctrines of Joseph's day such as infant baptism and free will, and revealed a broader ministry of Christ that took place on the American continent just after his death.

Published by Joseph under the title *The Book of Mormon* in March 1830, the text focus' on a few small Jewish families who escaped Jerusalem prior to its destruction by Babylon in 589 BCE, thanks to the visions of prophet-patriarch Lehi and the faithfulness of one of his younger sons named Nephi. After having sailed to the Americas, wickedness separated the families into various tribes, which the text simplifies down to the light-skinned and industrious "Nephites," and that of a more wicked nomadic dark-skinned people called "Lamanites."

The *Book of Mormon* charts the role of ancient American prophets who inscribed onto metal plates visions that parallel popular nineteenth-century notions of American exceptionalism, yet adding to it the providential designs of a restoration of Christ's

FIGURE 5.1 *The Angel Moroni delivering the plates of the* Book of Mormon *to Joseph Smith*. Source: *C.C.A. Christensen, 1886. Courtesy of the Library of Congress.*

ancient church in preparation for his coming in the "latter days." Highlighted by Christ's appearance in America just after his resurrection, the epic primarily follows the history of the Nephites up to their eradication by the Lamanites around 400 CE. Initially, the *Book of Mormon* was a literary tool to bring modern decedents of the Lamanites, that is, Native Americans, into this long-promised restoration and the building of the American New Jerusalem.

The idea that Native Americans were of ancient Israelite ancestry had been a popular speculation among Christians at the time of the *Book of Mormon*'s publication, and Mormon missionaries were eager to reveal this new scriptural evidence. Though white immigrants to America were referenced in the *Book of Mormon* as "gentiles," failed missions to the Lamanites brought new revelations by Joseph that Mormon converts of European ancestry were of a superior Israelite tribe through Ephraim, and that Joseph himself was the "Stem of Jesse," or pure descendent of Ephraim upon who would be "laid much power." Consequently, the role and placement of Native Americans in the Mormon worldview shifted in importance and has since remained minimal (Garrett 2016: 14–23).

Beyond the *Book of Mormon*, Joseph produced a number of new revelations that refined Mormon beliefs and helped establish a unique institutional body of faith, which in 1838 became, by way of revelation, renamed the Church of Jesus Christ of Latter Day Saints. Further defining his movement as outside the boundaries of traditional Protestantism and its reliance on ecumenical creeds, Joseph compiled these revelations into a new book of scripture called the *Book of Commandments*, later renamed *Doctrine and Covenants*.

FIGURE 5.2 *Facsimile 2 of the Book of Abraham. Having purchased several Egyptian mummies and scrolls from a traveling mummy exhibition, Joseph claimed to have translated them in 1835, proclaiming them to be the writings of the biblical patriarch Abraham while residing in Egypt. Though Joseph's translation proved unrelated to the scrolls, this new expansion of scripture further aligned his theology with that of the American occult, while furthering the divide with Protestantism. In 1880, the LDS Church grafted the Book of Abraham into their canon of scripture, along with the Bible,* Doctrine and Covenants, *and* Book of Mormon. Source: Courtesy of Getty Images.

Mormonism's Metaphysical Roots

Though traditional narratives of Mormonism point to New York evangelical revivalism, Mormonism's origins and the substance of its theological speculations are not Protestant. Joseph proclaimed a *restoration* of God's ancient truth, which is very different than that of a *reformation*, which Protestants looked to. In his 1820 *First Vision*, Jesus told Joseph that all churches, Protestant and Catholic alike, were "all wrong," and that "all their Creeds were an abomination in his sight." In the words of Christ, these "corrupt" professors of religion drew "near to me with their lips but their hearts are far from me," having a "form of Godliness" but denied "the power thereof" (Joseph Smith Papers). As Catherine Albanese has shown, this emphasis on the "heart" over that of "form" was deeply rooted in what she called America's metaphysical religion, a tradition of esoteric Christian speculation and the utilization of magical objects that experienced a sort of revival in upstate New York in the 1820s (Albanese 2007).

Once limited to a class of elitist European Renaissance intellectuals, metaphysical Christian speculation and its occultic wisdom entered the American colonies and reached a new revival of interest among more rural classes in the early 1800s. Throughout the American colonies, almanacs containing astrological information outsold Bibles, and many Christians looked to the stars and their associated powers for divine guidance. Individual free will, the linkage of spiritual power to intelligence, the tangibility of God, and the divinity of all humanity were all central tenets in a worldview that required the manipulation of material elements on Earth as a means of controlling the invisible power of heaven. This metaphysical worldview did not follow the Protestant Gospel of faith in an unfathomable God, but rather a Gospel of wisdom that contemplated a fathomable God. For the occult, the Garden of Eden was not a story of human depravity but that of partaking of the tree of knowledge that in effect made one "like God."

While not formally educated, Joseph was unusually well read and had generous access to local libraries and borrowed texts, becoming a highly sought out "village seer." Just as the magi of Matthew's Gospel found the baby Jesus by consulting the stars, adepts of the magical arts looked to the stars as a means of accessing heavenly powers on Earth. Under the full moon and just before the autumnal equinox on Sunday September 21, 1823, Joseph was visited by a guardian spirit who charged him three times with returning to a hill near his home, each year on the same night. Carrying his family dagger sealed with the planet Mars and "Holiness to the Lord" magic parchment close to his chest, Joseph arrived on the same night under the new moon in 1827 with his new wife Emma Hale Smith, wearing all black with his palm smeared in black pigment, riding a borrowed switched-tail black horse and carriage (Quinn 1998: 142–4, 165–6, 176). From his initial conjuring and communing with spirits, to the unearthing of the golden plates and their translation, Joseph Smith consistently and carefully drew upon the powers of astrology, nature magic, necromancy, and occultic philosophy as a means of inspiration and insight into what it meant to "restore" God's truth to Earth in the "latter-days."

Latter-Day Divisions

One of Joseph Smith's biographers pointed out that rather than founding a parish or synod, Joseph built a community based on his charismatic leadership (Bushman 2005: 556–8). The assassination of Joseph and his brother Hyrum on June 27, 1844, sent the community into a crisis over succession. On two occasions, Joseph blessed his eldest son Joseph III that he would one day preside over the church, but he was only eleven years old at the time of his father's death. In light of the trauma of Nauvoo, mostly surrounding the secretive practice of plural marriage, Emma remained aloof, raising her children independent of any Mormon movement. Scattered throughout Iowa, Illinois, and Wisconsin however, several Mormon groups anticipated Joseph III's leadership, and in 1859, after years of pleading, Joseph III accepted leadership over "the Mormon Church," which was then officially "reorganized" on April 6, 1860, as the Church of Jesus Christ of Latter Day Saints. The prefix "reorganized" was added in 1872, being the Reorganized Church of Jesus Christ of Latter Day Saints (RLDS) (Avery 1998: 43; Flanders 1975: 312–16; Newell and Avery 1994: 266–8, 284–5).

Weeks prior to Joseph's death, William Law, former counselor in the First Presidency, published on June 7, 1844, in the *Nauvoo Expositor* that Joseph was a fallen prophet and, as such, pushed the idea for Mormons to look to a reformation to renew the church "as originally taught by Joseph Smith." After his death, another counselor to Joseph, Sidney Rigdon, called a meeting on August 4, to discuss the direction of the church. Rejecting both the idea of reformation and succession, Rigdon claimed to have received a vision that no one could follow Joseph, but instead he was to continue to be Joseph's "spokesman," as he had long been (Bushman 2005: 556; Park 2020: 242–3). However, as president of the lower ranking Quorum of the Twelve Apostles, *Brigham Young* argued that Joseph had given him and the Twelve the keys or authority to lead the church, and as such, could rightfully lead *pro tempore* until the church could be properly reorganized, presumably under the leadership of Joseph III. Forced from Nauvoo, Young led the majority of Saints to what soon became the Utah Territory in the American West, with Young retaining the name, as would Joseph III, the Church of Jesus Christ of Latter Day Saints (Flanders 1975: 316). Rigdon rejected the Twelve's authority, claiming his own revelations and secretly ordaining "Prophets, Priests, & Kings," to which the Twelve excommunicated him on September 8. In return, Rigdon excommunicated them and returned to Pittsburgh, where he reorganized the church with a new First Presidency and Twelve Apostles, calling his movement the Church of Christ, which was later renamed the Church of Jesus Christ of the Children of Zion. Rigdon's church faced its own schisms, as William Bickerton reorganized the church in 1862 and renamed it the Church of Jesus Christ. After Rigdon's death in 1876, only a few remained (Newell and Avery 1994: 206).

In part over her disdain for *polygamy*, Joseph's widow Emma Hale Smith supported William Marks, a presiding authority among the Nauvoo High Council and Stake President in Nauvoo, though Marks supported Rigdon before supporting James J. Strang (Newell and Avery 1994: 216–19). There was strong reason, however, to look toward familial succession, which would have landed on Joseph's younger brother Samuel Smith, who died only a month after Joseph and Hyrum. Joseph's youngest brother William Smith claimed succession as well, though not before joining the "Strangites," or the Church of Jesus Christ of Latter Day Saints as led by recent Mormon convert James Strang. Like Joseph, James Strang legitimated himself, not through institutional or familial authority but charisma. Strang claimed to have been ordained to succeed Joseph by an angel, produced scriptures from translating metal plates, and utilized nature magic by way of magic seer stones. Strang produced a letter supposedly written by Joseph that upheld his succession dated June 18, 1844, attracting two thousand followers. Following internal tensions, Strang was assassinated in 1856 (Bushman 2005: 555; Newell and Avery 1994: 231). Though initially rivalling Brigham's leadership in Utah, Strang's movement dwindled after his death, with many joining Joseph III's movement. Today, only a few remain.

Utah and the "Brighamites"

While Joseph Smith's authority had been framed within the charismatic, Brigham Young's was based in the ecclesiastical authority of the Twelve Apostles that he presided over. Young's leadership represented a promise to rebind a broken church on an institutional level—something that brought structure and stability in an important moment of charismatic disarray. After leading the majority of Saints to the intermountain West in July 1847, the Twelve co-opted the First Presidency in December and sustained Young as "prophet, seer, and revelator," establishing a pattern of succession based on seniority in the Twelve (Flanders 1975: 318). Continuing Nauvoo-era practices, such as temple rites and plural marriage, Young established a powerful colonial machine that defied American social customs, political structures, and economic norms. The Church in Utah quickly became more than a denominational church, being instead an ethnic "peoplehood" that had been arranged through shared trauma and geographic isolation, together with highly centralized ecclesiastical control (Shipps 2007).

Though some had hoped the Mormon exodus to Mexico effectively solved the "Mormon problem," the territory was annexed by the United States in 1848, and by 1850 the Mormon movement had grown beyond fifty thousand. These numbers became real as church policy dictated that all new converts and old members gather to the Utah territory, whatever the sacrifice. According to prophet and territorial governor Brigham Young, *gathering* was just as much a religious duty "as it is for sinners to repent and be baptized for the remission of sins." The warning was clear: "Every Saint who does not come home, when he has an opportunity will be afflicted by the Devil" (Clark 1966: 2:49, 82). Young established the Perpetual Emigrating Fund (PEF) Company in 1852, which aided the gathering of approximately eighty thousand converts. By his death in 1877, Young had directed some nearly four hundred settlements in Utah,

FIGURE 5.3 *Youth Handcart Trek, June 10, 2016. For Latter-day Saints, the Mormon pioneer trek has become a sort of faith-promotional pilgrimage as well as a way of connecting to the "pioneer spirit" of the early church, regardless of one's ancestry. As part of this construction of a particular form of Mormon memory, Mormon youth dress up as pioneers, listen to emotional stories, and perform "the trek" by way of pulling readied handcarts.* Source: *Courtesy of Utah's Bureau of Land Management, Hannah Cowan.*

Idaho, Wyoming, Nevada, Arizona, and California (History 2018). As Mormonism's political and geographic presence grew, many began to see, as did Protestant historian Philip Schaff in 1855, that an "armed interference" between Utah and the nation was imminent (Schaff 1855: 115–16, 246–50).

The Utah War and Massacre at Mountain Meadows

On July 5, 1857, ten years following the Saints initial entrance into the Salt Lake valley, Young stood before the Mormon people and spoke of an American Zion that would someday cover the entire American continent. Young rebuffed the idea that new converts "came to Zion," but instead insisted that it was up to them to help build it upon their arrival. After all, if the streets of the New Jerusalem were to be paved in gold, then Young's "practical religion" demanded they get to work. In the same speech, however, Young pointed out that US troops were on their way to Utah (Watt and Long 1858: 5:1–6).

In response to alarming reports coming from territorial officials who had left Utah on bad terms, US President James Buchanan hastily assembled troops to "put down" what he falsely described to be the "first rebellion, which has existed in our Territories" (U.S. Congress 1858: 25). Briefly stated, the Utah War, which sent 2,500 US troops (nearly one-third of the US Army) to Utah to replace Brigham Young as governor in the late summer of 1857, came after several years of smaller Federal-Mormon conflicts and growing rumors of Mormon murder, conspiracy, and treachery. The expedition however was poorly planned and badly executed, with vulnerable troops having to wait out the winter with few supplies in burned-out Fort Bridger sixty-five kilometers from Salt Lake City. Before the winter thaw, Brigham Young surrendered his role as governor, and in April 1858, Buchanan proclaimed the rebellion over and granted amnesty to Utah and the church.

It was amidst this military drama that the infamous *Mountain Meadows Massacre* took place, being the largest white-on-white massacre in American frontier history, followed by its massive cover-up by the LDS Church. As superintendent of Indian affairs, Young attempted to provoke Native tribes to attack emigrant trains passing through Utah, arguing them to be mutual enemies, and on September 1, 1857, reminded church leaders of their responsibility to fight Americans in the impending war against the United States. Even before troops were sent to Utah, animosity toward the United States on the part of the Saints was high, as seen in the 1856 to 1857 *Mormon Reformation* where roaming Mormon preachers excited settlements against local federal officials and emigrants, who they believed to have incited the nation against them. In his visits to southern settlements, Apostle George A. Smith admitted, "In spite of all I could do I found myself preaching a military discourse" that left the people full of "enthusiasm" (Walker, Turley, and Leonard 2008: 127–8).

Consisting of about 140 people, the Arkansas Fancher-Baker emigrant train stopped in southern Utah in September 1857 for supplies on their way to California. Under the direction of Young, however, Mormons refused to sell. After a series of negative encounters and misjudgments, Mormon's plotted to teach the emigrant party a lesson by way of attacking the train disguised as Indians. After a five-day siege with no access to fresh water, the party turned themselves over to the Mormon militia who said they had come to protect them. Believing the party to have seen through their Indian disguises, Mormon priesthood and military leaders held a High Council priesthood meeting where they determined to kill the entire party and blame it on the Paiutes. On September 11, Mormons demanded the party surrender their livestock and supplies to the Paiutes, who they had claimed to have made a treaty with for their safe passage. When transporting the train under such promises, the Mormon militia disarmed the party, and with the aid of recruited Paiutes, killed the entire party, excepting children under the age of seven. In public statements, Young declared the massacre God's judgment and refused to cooperate with federal officials investigating the crime. Under Young's authoritarian leadership and cultivation of a culture of violence and fear, the exaggerations of territorial officials gained credibility (Walker, Turley, and Leonard 2008: 127–8).

FIGURE 5.4 *Mountain Meadows. Drawn by H. Steinegger; Lith. Britton, Rey & Co. Published by the Pacific Art Co., 1877. Library of Congress. This image depicts the Fancher-Baker train traveling through Mountain Meadows in the southern part of Utah territory, while war-painted Indians hide behind rocks ready to attack.* Source: *Courtesy of the Library of Congress.*

Anti-Polygamy Laws and an End of Theocratic Rule

Americans and Mormons remained largely at odds with each other when President Abraham Lincoln signed the Morrill Anti-Bigamy Act in 1862 that banned bigamy in federal territories and limited church ownership to $50,000. Church authorities disregarded the law as unconstitutional, since polygamy was a religious principle and thus protected by the First Amendment. In 1874, Territorial Delegate in Congress and counselor to Young in the First Presidency, George Q. Cannon asked his friend George Reynolds to offer himself up as a "test case" to challenge the law. Reynolds claims of religious liberty however were consistently rebuffed by the courts, which stated the need for "limits to this high constitutional privilege" (Bitton 1999: 218–21). The case went before the US Supreme Court in 1878 that upheld these earlier rulings, thus establishing the Morrill Act constitutional and setting forth new legal precedent that said Mormons were free to believe in polygamy, but not act on it.

Despite this Supreme Court ruling, Mormon authorities continued to practice and encourage the practice of polygamy, and as such, the Edmunds Act was signed into law March 23, 1882. The Edmunds law closed gaps left open from the Morrill Act that made prosecution difficult and imposed heavy punishments for suspected polygamists. Utah's registration and electoral offices were also declared vacant. Mormon leaders went into hiding and church president John Taylor and George Q. Cannon appeared on wanted posters. Fearing that the Mormon hierarchy continued to oppress its members and dictate elections, polygamy was a powerful emotional unifier, and in 1887 congress passed the more draconian Edmund-Tucker Act. This new law disincorporated the church, seized its property and dissolved Utah's military, educational, and emigration structures. Wives were required to testify against their husbands, polygamous children were denied inheritance, Mormon women were disenfranchised and an anti-polygamy oath was required for civic participation, thereby disenfranchising all Mormons, polygamous or not (Firmage and Mangrum 2001: 161–2, 199–201, 235–56, 329). Though Mormons took these and other anti-Mormon laws to the Supreme Court, they were met with hostility, and in 1890 the theocratic Mormon kingdom had effectively fallen. In a complete about face, President Wilford Woodruff stood before the church in 1890 and presented a manifesto that called for the end of the practice of polygamy.

Entering into "America"

Granted amnesty by both President Benjamin Harrison in 1893 and President Grover Cleveland in 1894, church leaders promised the nation that the practice of plural marriage was over, opening up space for Mormon participation on the national stage (Lyman 1986: 191, 206–7; Roberts 1965: 6:288–9). Though initially hesitant, church leaders accepted an invitation for their Mormon Tabernacle Choir to participate in a singing competition in Chicago at the World's Fair in 1893.

In Chicago, the 250-piece Mormon Tabernacle Choir sang before thousands, softening prejudice. According to the *Chicago Sunday Herald:* "Festival Hall has echoed with the music of many famous organizations, but it never witnessed more enthusiasm than followed the Mormon choir's 'Star-Spangled Banner' at the opening of the exercises. The three Mormon leaders glowed with pride as the audience burst into applause when their pet choir finished" ("Mormon and Gentile" 1893: 8). In one account following a performance, the audience "went wild with enthusiasm" and demanded an encore, with some shouting "Three cheers for the Mormons!" ("The Great Contest" 1893: 6; McDaniel 1894: 51). The *Herald* noted that something had changed between the Mormons and their visitors. "Mormons and gentiles came together as friends." Be it the music of the choir or the oratory of Utah's Governor Caleb West, "something made all the people from Utah friends and all their guests happy" (McDaniel 1893: 53–4; "Mormon and Gentile" 1893: 8).

MORMONISM IN NORTH AMERICA

Beyond music, Mormons gained wide favor at the fair by redefining themselves as frontier pioneers over that of polygamous refugees. Utah's governor Caleb West, a veteran of the Civil War and anti-polygamist, argued in a speech that Mormons were "made of sterling stuff" and deserved recognition as American pioneers, while George Q. Cannon reframed Brigham Young as a "noble pioneer" that built a commonwealth that was "consecrated to religious liberty and the rights of man." Though refugees from a nation to "the then unknown and uninhabited, the vast and forbidding West," Mormons now equated themselves, as had Cannon, with "Pilgrim Fathers and all the early colonists who came out from the Old World in search of that freedom of conscience which is the inalienable right of human kind"; "for Utah, too, was founded by men who held to these same views and were actuated by the same high resolves" (McDaniel 1893: 53–7; Woodruff 1985: 9:230, 262). Focusing on frontier hardships and a supposedly shared Christian past, Governor West argued that Mormons were deserving of "the highest honors that can be accorded the first settlers of any country." As the audience listened on, West pointed out that whatever "struggles and differences" there had once been, "I mention these only to say that they exist no more" ("Mormon and Gentile" 1893: 8).

The myth of the American frontier was rough, inspiring a rough response. Ultimately, so the myth went, individuals who worked to cultivate the wild wilderness were transformed into strong and independent freedom-loving democratic Americans. Mormons may have been "rough" in their polygamous marriage, culture of violence, and theocratic structures, but as William "Buffalo Bill" Cody wrote early in the twentieth century, now "the Mormon community meets all the demands of our ever advancing civilization" (Inman and Cody 1914: 111, 131). In 1896, following promises that polygamy had ended, Congress granted Utah statehood—a process that took over half a century. Brigham Young's polygamous autocratic theocracy was over, and Mormons were set on a path to participate in America's capitalist economy and two-party political system.

This inclusion was challenged in 1903 when Reed Smoot of the Twelve Apostles was elected to the United States Senate. Protests rose throughout the nation, charging Smoot with polygamy and that his role as apostle disqualified him from being able to properly serve his constituents. In response, the Senate began hearings on March 1, 1904, recommending his removal from office on June 1, 1906. However, on February 20, 1907, the full Senate with backing of President Theodore Roosevelt, rejected this recommendation and Smoot retained his seat.

It was the Smoot hearings themselves that proved pivotal in transforming Mormonism into a more acceptable form of American faith. At the beginning of the hearings, despite earlier promises, church leaders had no intention of ending polygamy, with most secretly teaching and continuing its practice (Quinn 1993: 241). Drawn-out national scrutiny, however, exposed this duplicity, forcing the church to prove its sincerity under threat of newly drafted anti-polygamy laws. At a height of public outcry, President Joseph F. Smith released a "second manifesto" that dishonestly denied church

FIGURE 5.5 "The Real Objection to Smoot," by Joseph Keppler, Centerfold of Puck magazine, April 27, 1904 (New York: J. Ottmann Lith. Co.). The real fear for many of the protesters against Smoot was that he was merely a pawn of the Mormon hierarchy, which he himself was part of. The stitched-together coat shows how earlier fears of the LDS Church were ever present, including "Mormon Rebellion," "Resistance to Federal Authority," "Blood Atonement," "Murder of Apostates," "Polygamy," and "Mountain Meadow Massacre." The attire of this large figure also mimics that of Uncle Sam, demonstrating the institutional church as a type of American forgery. However "American," however independent, and however against polygamy Smoot claimed to be, he was but a puppet of this larger sinister figure hiding behind the door. Source: Courtesy of the Library of Congress.

MORMONISM IN NORTH AMERICA

93

involvement in new polygamous marriages but now threatened excommunication for any involved. Smoot himself, a supportive, yet publically avowed anti-polygamist, symbolized for Mormons and the nation the new face of a monogamous and politically relevant modern form of Mormonism—a Mormonism that looked and acted more like a Protestant denomination.

Mormon Fundamentalism and the Continuation of Polygamy

This dramatic shift in opposition of Mormon polygamy led to internal division that challenged the authority of church leaders and their new standing in the nation. Lorin C. Wolley, a pivotal figure in *Fundamentalist* Mormonism, opposed the second manifesto, pointing to a revelation by church president John Taylor on September 27, 1886, that emphasized the "everlasting" nature of "celestial marriage" and "those who will enter into my glory must obey the conditions thereof." Excommunicated in 1924, Woolley presided over the Council of Friends in 1928, which Woolley claimed Taylor gave priesthood sealing keys to. Charged with continuing polygamy, this special council, noted Cristina Rosetti, presided over the higher priesthood, and thus God's higher work on Earth. Though some fundamentalist groups saw Lorin's father John Woolley, who initially presided over this council as Taylor's rightful priesthood successor, others claimed that it was not until the 1920s under LDS president Heber J. Grant that this authority moved to Lorin Woolley. Claiming the LDS Church had "lost its way," Woolley ordained new apostles (Rosetti 2019: 121). Troubled by the gains made by Woolley in the early 1930s, the LDS First Presidency issued a "third manifesto" on June 17, 1933, which denounced the council as satanically "misguided," denied the existence of Taylor's 1886 revelation, and proclaimed that Grant alone held the priesthood keys of "sealing" (Clark 1966: 5:316–30; Quinn 2002: 60).

According to historian D. Michael Quinn, it is from Woolley and the Council of Friends that nearly 90 percent of Mormon fundamentalists take root. Though Mormon fundamentalism is often reduced to the practice of polygamy by outside observers, what makes them "fundamentalist" expands into other nineteenth-century Mormon ideas and practices since dropped by the LDS Church, including theocracy, economic cooperation, political hegemony, anti-pluralism, and speculative doctrines such as Adam being God, and Jesus and God being polygamists (Quinn 1993: 243–4). While sharing these roots, each of the various fundamentalist groups have their own history and response to American society, from the clannish Fundamentalist Church of Jesus Christ of Latter-Day Saints (FLDS), to the more culturally integrated Apostolic United Brethren (AUB), best known through the Brown family of the TLC reality television series *Sister Wives*. For most fundamentalists, including the AUB and FLDS, the LDS Church remains God's "one true Church" despite its being "out of order." As Cristina Rosetti explains, "many early fundamentalists were not focused on the foundation of a

FIGURE 5.6 *Colorado City. A woman with two children walking into a store in Colorado City, Arizona, August 13, 2008. The woman's clothing is distinctive of the Fundamentalist Church of Jesus Christ of Latter-Day Saints (FLDS). As shown by the name of this store, "Cooperative Mercantile Corporation," Fundamentalists do not chart polygamy as the only "fundamental" of Mormonism but continue to follow Joseph Smith's earlier economic Law of Consecration, which Brigham Young attempted through his United Orders. Source: Image from Wiki Commons.*

temporal church, but on the continuance of the true priesthood that would oversee the continued practice of the central principles of the gospel" (Rosetti 2019: 121). Woolley was commissioned to keep polygamy alive, not start a new church.

Embracing Christian Nationalism

By the 1930s, the LDS Church had entirely broken off its connections to plural marriage by excommunicating and encouraging overly harsh laws and harassment toward those who continued its practice, even as fundamentalists secretly attended LDS church services and temple rituals (Quinn 1993: 245). Aside from these efforts to distance the church from the stigma of polygamy, LDS leaders feared the spread of communism among its own, due in part to the church's own anti-capitalist communal roots. Though Mormons leaned Democrat in the 1930s and overwhelmingly voted for Democratic candidates in 1932, President Heber J. Grant and his counselor J. Reuben Clark, both Republicans, charged President Franklin D. Roosevelt and his

New Deal policies with advocating communism (Quinn 2002: 73, 79–81, 85, 94). In 1936, both men issued a First Presidency statement, warning that communism bore no resemblance to the United Order, being more of a clumsy Satanic counterfeit. For any Latter-day Saint contemplating its support, the letter warned that "no loyal American citizen and no faithful Church member can be a Communist" (Clark 1966: 6:151–2; Improvement Era 1936: 488).

In the 1930s and throughout the rest of the century, church leaders rearticulated the Mormon Gospel through a more conservative branch of American Christian nationalism and its sacralization of capitalist enterprise. Citing a Supreme Court decision from 1892 that declared the United States a "Christian nation," Apostle Richard L. Evans celebrated this earlier Protestant hegemony within American politics and law. As he argued, "the America of today," in "all of its better and more stable aspects," is the product of this earlier Protestant prominence and privilege in American society. Helping establish a Latter-day Saint approach to American public life, Evans argued that the country could not afford to exclude from the schools and government "a due consideration of Christian philosophy, ideals, and practices." Indeed, "the teaching and observance of Christian truth and practice in any institution within the land, private or public, is not only justifiable but essential—in a Christian nation" (Improvement Era 1937: 96–7). Apostle Joseph Fielding Smith similarly helped enshrine Mormonism within the folds of Christian nationalism, proclaiming that the United States "was founded as a Christian nation, with the acceptance of Jesus Christ as the Redeemer of the world." Perhaps unaware of the prominent role religiously infused nationalism played in nineteenth-century anti-Mormonism, Smith now lamented its loss. If the nation would once again adopt Christianity as its nationalist impulse, then God would "help us fight our battles to cleanse the world of despotism and make it a fit abode for all who love the principles of truth and righteousness" (Improvement Era 1937: 274–5, 313).

Though Mormon leaders in Utah linked their religious identity to that of an unqualifiedly conservative vision of white Protestant America, they were frustrated when rejected from the Temple of Religion at the New York World's Fair in 1939. According to fair officials, the temple had room only for groups "decidedly American," which had just recently expanded to include Catholics and Jews (Todd 2010: 216). At the overtly materialistic New York World's Fair of 1964 to 1965, however, anyone with sufficient financial means were allowed to participate in its more competitive religious marketplace. Though pricey, the fair's "Mormon Pavilion" proved a success as it brought in five million visitors, revealing a new level of popular acceptance and national interest in the LDS Church and its projection of white, Victorian suburban values, which were then being challenged. As George H. Mortimer, New Jersey Stake President explained, "During the World's Fair, we found out what it was that appealed to people about the Church, and these features have been put into the new visitors centers" ("Dr. Peale Lauds Religious Exhibits at Fair" 1964: 15). During the decades when the civil rights movement and second-wave feminism upset the perceived stability of these racially defined patriarchal values, Mormonism represented an appealing option that idealized them (Mason and Turner 2016: 88–92). In the 1960s, the Mormon growth rate ballooned to 5.7 percent, remaining above 4 percent until 1991 (Statistical Report 2019).

The structure of the LDS Church dramatically shifted in 1960 with the creation of the Correlation Committee, which was headed by apostle Harold B. Lee. *Correlation* has reference to the structural changes overseen by this committee that mimicked the corporate business model of the 1950s. Emphasizing a simplistic and repetitive message for global consumers around a single spiritual product, correlation brought a new level of top-down uniformity that minimized and even discouraged cultural expression and theological speculation. As part of correlation, church offices in Salt Lake City, under the leadership of the Twelve, established intellectual and financial oversight over all church auxiliaries, including the female Relief Society and Sunday School, two organizations that had until then enjoyed a certain level of independence. Recognizable today, the uniform architectural designs of church buildings and their internal art hangings and furniture are a product of decisions in Salt Lake City, who also decide church lessons, teaching materials, music as well as dress attire for men and women. Throughout the world, LDS missionaries, numbering 85,000 in 2015, embody this American-style formal dress code and attitude, further defining a particularly American image of global Mormonism (Howlett and Duffy 2016: 156–62).

Statistics of the Latter-Day Saint Movement Today

Making up 1.7 percent of the United States population, 96 percent of "Mormons" identify with the Church of Jesus Christ of Latter-day Saints, with a reported membership of over 16.5 million in 2019. The second largest, the Community of Christ, reports approximately 250,000 members, making up 1 percent of Mormons in the United States. Though overwhelmingly the largest Latter-Day Saint restorationist movement, the growth rate of the LDS Church since 1991 has decelerated on a consistent scale, reaching 1.5 percent in 2019 (0.6 percent in the United States), just above the overall 1 percent world growth rate (Community of Christ and Consolidated Affiliates 2018: 10; Statistical Report 2019; US Census Bureau 2007). Mirroring national trends of religious disaffiliation, internal research suggests that only 30 percent of young single adults in North America (20 percent internationally) can be considered active churchgoers, while other research shows a retention rate of 50–60 percent among young adults more generally (Riess 2019: 7). The Community of Christ has suffered from slow growth rates, being 0.09 percent in 2018. Projections of Mormon fundamentalists are at 37,000, about half of which are "independent," meaning they don't affiliate with any particular group. As fundamentalist groups don't normally missionize, growth is dependent upon birth rate; though youth disaffection among the AUB and other orders such as the Davis County Cooperative have been noted to be as high as 50 percent (Quinn 1993: 250–1, 271).

FIGURE 5.7 *The South Temple entrance to the Church Administration Building in downtown Salt Lake City, Utah. This building serves as headquarters for the Church of Jesus Christ of Latter-day Saints, housing offices of the First Presidency and Quorum of the Twelve Apostles, as well as other general authorities and their staff. It is from here that the Twelve Apostles oversee the correlation of church curriculum that shapes Mormon theology throughout the world. It is also from here that a particular image of what it means to be "Mormon" has been defined, as a means of unifying the Latter-day Saint community in response to the pressing needs of an expanding global religion. In the background is the imposing 28-story Church Office Building, housing offices of church authorities and administrators. Also serving as part of the church's headquarters, much of the inner workings of the church take shape here, including the regulation of missionary efforts and the production of churchwide educational materials.* Source: *Courtesy of Wikimedia Commons.*

Politically, Mormons are overwhelmingly white, socially conservative, and Republican, though studies point to important shifts. While 93 percent of baby boomers (those born before 1964) are white and seven in ten identify as Republican, millennials (those born before 1996) are 83 percent white and only 46 percent Republican. According to Newsweek, however, "Mormons were the only religious group to overwhelmingly approve [61 percent] of the president [Donald Trump] in

2017," while being the least supportive for President Barack Obama (18 percent) in 2014 (Guarnieri 2018; Jones 2014). Millennial Mormons have, in some ways, demonstrated more openness than their elders toward social issues, such as four in ten who support the legalization of gay marriage (only 28 percent of baby boomers do). In other ways, however, they have mirrored their parents and grandparents. Until 1978, the LDS Church upheld a policy of racial exclusion, which meant that anyone of Black African ancestry were considered cursed and thus designated a second-class status in the church, denied both leadership roles and saving ordinances. Regardless of age, gender, and race, roughly eight in ten Mormons support the ban as inspired, while four in ten resist the idea that racial and ethnic pluralism in the United States is a positive thing (Riess 2019: 111–25, 138–45). In similar ways, when gay marriage was ruled constitutional in 2015 by the Supreme Court, the church enacted a policy a few months later, dubbed the "November 5th policy," that labeled same-sex couples "apostates," and barred their children from church membership (Prince 2019: 242–5, 257). Seven out of ten Mormons, regardless of age, supported the "apostate" label, while six out of ten supported the barring of their children (Riess 2019: 138–45).

With deep roots in the American environment, the Latter Day Saint restorationist movement highlights a profound element of American religious history, from a past that dissented from Protestant American norms and values, to a present that identifies with them. At the same time, the LDS Church, though the largest, is not the only expression of Mormonism in North America, representing instead a rich American millennialist tapestry that cannot be reduced to any single faction. Mormonism then is many, with each responding in its own way to its American environment, be it the assimilationist Community of Christ's ordination of women and acceptance of gay marriage, the rejectionist tendencies of polygamist fundamentalists, or the socially conservative accommodations of the LDS Church that idealizes a type of 1950s American patriarchal order. Steven Shields has projected there to be over four hundred expressions of Latter Day Saint restorationist movements, all who trace their spiritual heritage to Joseph Smith, with over a hundred of which remain active in the twenty-first century (Bringhurst and Hamer 2007: iv).

Further Reading and Online Resources

Bowman M. (2012), *The Mormon People: The Making of an American Faith*, New York: Random House.

Flake K. (2004), *The Politics of American Religious Identity: The Seating of Senator Reed Smoot, Mormon Apostle*, Chapel Hill: University of North Carolina Press.

Fluhman J.S. (2012), *"Peculiar People": Anti-Mormonism and the Making of Religion in Nineteenth-Century America*, Chapel Hill: University of North Carolina Press.

Howlett D.J. and J.-C. Duffy (2016), *Mormonism the Basics*, New York: Routledge.

Reeve W.P. (2015), *Religion of a Different Color: Race and the Mormon Struggle for Whiteness*, New York: Oxford University Press.

References

Books and articles

Albanese C.L. (2007), *A Republic of Mind & Spirit: A Cultural History of American Metaphysical Religion*, New Haven, CT: Yale University Press.

Avery V.T. (1998), *From Mission to Madness: Last Son of the Mormon Prophet*, Urbana: University of Illinois Press.

Bitton D. (1999), *George Q. Cannon: A Biography*, Salt Lake City, UT: Deseret Book.

Bringhurst N.G. and J.C. Hamer, eds. (2007), *Scattering of the Saints: Schism within Mormonism*, Independence, MO: John Whitmer Books.

Bushman R.L. (2005), *Joseph Smith, Rough Stone Rolling: A Cultural Biography of Mormonism's Founder*, New York: Knopf.

Clark J.R., ed. (1966), *Messages of the First Presidency*, Salt Lake City, UT: Bookcraft Publishers.

Firmage E.B. and R.C. Mangrum (2001), *Zion in the Courts: A Legal History of the Church of Jesus Christ of Latter-Day Saints*, Chicago: University of Illinois Press.

Flanders R.B. (1975), *Nauvoo: Kingdom on the Mississippi*, Urbana: University of Illinois Press.

Garrett M. (2016), *Making Lamanites: Mormons, Native Americans, and the Indian Student Placement Program, 1947–2000*, Salt Lake City: University of Utah Press.

Gordon S.B. and J. Shipps (2017), "Fatal Convergence in the Kingdom of God: The Mountain Meadows Massacre in American History," *Journal of the Early Republic*, 37 (Summer): 307–47.

Howlett D.J. and J-C. Duffy (2016), *Mormonism the Basics*, New York: Routledge.

Inman H. and W.F. Cody (1914), *The Great Salt Lake Trail*, Topeka, KS: Crane & Company.

Lyman E.L. (1986), *Political Deliverance: The Mormon Quest for Utah Statehood*, Chicago: University of Illinois Press.

Lyman E.L., ed. (2010), *Candid Insights of a Mormon Apostle: The Diaries of Abraham H. Cannon, 1889–1895*, Salt Lake City, UT: Signature Books.

MacKinnon W., ed. (2008), *At Sword's Point, Part I: A Documentary History of the Utah War to 1858*, Norman, OK: Arthur H. Clark Company.

Mason P.Q. and J.G. Turner, eds. (2016), *Out of Obscurity, Mormonism Since 1942*, New York: Oxford University Press.

McDaniel E.A. (1894), *Utah at the World's Columbian Exposition*, Salt Lake City, UT: Salt Lake Lithographing Co.

Newell L.K. and V. Tippetts Avery (1994), *Mormon Enigma: Emma Hale Smith*, Urbana: University of Illinois Press.

Park B.E. (2020), *Kingdom of Nauvoo: The Rise and Fall of a Religious Empire on the American Frontier*, New York: Liveright Publishing.

Prince G.A. (2019), *Gay Rights and the Mormon Church: Intended Actions, Unintended Consequences*, Salt Lake City: University of Utah Press.

Quinn D.M. (1993), "Plural Marriage and Mormon Fundamentalism," in M.E. Marty and R.S. Appleby (eds.), *Fundamentalisms and Society: Reclaiming the Sciences, the Family, and Education*, Chicago: University of Chicago Press.

Quinn D.M. (1998), *Mormonism and the Magic World View*, 2nd edn., Salt Lake City, UT: Signature Books.

Quinn D.M. (2002), *Elder Statesman: A Biography of J. Reuben Clark*, Salt Lake City, UT: Signature Books.

Riess J. (2019), *The Next Mormons: How Millennials are Changing the LDS Church*, New York: Oxford University Press.

Roberts B.H. (1965), *A Comprehensive History of the Church of Jesus Christ of Latter-Day Saint, Century I*, 6 vols., Provo, UT: Brigham Young University Press.

Rosetti C. (2019), "'Further Light Pertaining to Celestial Marriage': The Law of Purity and Twentieth-Century Mormon Fundamentalist Discourse on Sexuality," *Journal of Mormon History*, 45 (3) (July): 111–32.

Schaff P. (1855), *America. A Sketch of the Political, Social, and Religious Character of the United States of North America*, New York: C. Scribner.

Shipps J. (2007), "From Peoplehood to Church Membership: Mormonism's Trajectory since World War II," *Church History: Studies in Christianity and Culture*, 76 (2) (June): 241–61.

Todd J.T. (2010), "The Temple of Religion and the Politics of Religious Pluralism: Judeo-Christian America at the 1939–1940 New York World's Fair," in C. Bender and P.E. Klassen (eds.), *After Pluralism: Reimagining Religious Engagement*, 201–22, New York: Columbia University Press.

US Congress (1857), *Message of the President of the United States to the Two Houses of Congress at the Commencement of the First Session of the Thirty-Fifth Congress of Territory of Utah*, Vol. 2, 35th Cong., 1st session. Cong. Doc. 2 Washington, DC: William A. Harris, Printer.

Walker R.W., R.E. Turley Jr., and G.M. Leonard (2008), *Massacre at Mountain Meadows*, New York: Oxford University Press.

Watt G.D. and J.V. Long (1858), *Journal of Discourses, by Brigham Young, President of the Church of Jesus Christ of Latter-Day Saints, His Two Counsellors, the Twelve Apostles, and Others*, London: Latter Day Saints' Book Depot.

Woodruff W. (1985), *Wilford Woodruff's Journal, 1833–1898: Typescript*, 9 vols., ed. S.G. Kenney, Midvale, UT: Signature Books.

Magazine and newspaper articles

"Dr. Peale Lauds Religious Exhibits at Fair" (1964), *Confident Living Chicago Tribune*, July 18: 15.

Evans R.L. (1937), "A Christian Nation," *The Improvement Era*, 40 (2) (February): 96–7.

"The Great Contest" (1893), *Deseret Semi-Weekly News*, September 12: 6.

The Improvement Era (1936), Editorial, 39 (August 8): 488.

"In Jackson County!" (1893), *Deseret Semi-Weekly News*, September 5.

"Mormon and Gentile: Join Hands Heartily on Utah Day" (1893), *Sunday Herald* (Chicago), September 10: 8.

One-Hundred and First Annual Conference of the Church of Jesus Christ of Latter-Day Saints (1931), Salt Lake City.

Riess J. (2016), "Worldwide, only 25 percent of Young Single Mormons Are Active in the LDS Church," *Religion News*, October 5. Available online: https://religionnews.com/2016/10/05/leaked-worldwide-only-25-of-young-single-mormons-are-active-in-the-lds-church/ (accessed January 7, 2020).

Seventy-Fourth Annual Conference of the Church of Jesus Christ of Latter-Day Saints (1904), Salt Lake City, UT: The Deseret News.

Websites

The Church of Jesus Christ of Latter-Day Saints (2018), "2018 Statistical Report for 2019 April Conference." Available online: https://newsroom.churchofjesuschrist.org/article/2018-statistical-report (accessed November 7, 2019).

Community of Christ and Consolidated Affiliates (2018), *Consolidated Financial Report*, June 30. Available online: https://www.cofchrist.org/common/cms/resources/Documents/FY18-CofC-Audit-Report.pdf (accessed November 7, 2019).

FLDS Truth (2008), "1886 Revelation." Available online: https://web.archive.org/web/20080914104710/http://www.fldstruth.org/sysmenu.php?MParent=HISTORY&MIndex=0 (accessed December 7, 2019).

Guarnieri G. (2018), "Mormon Approval of Trump's Job Performance Was More than Any Other Religious Group in 2017," *Newsweek*, January 14. Available online: https://www.newsweek.com/mormons-donald-trump-approval-religion-781134 (accessed June 8, 2019).

History (2018), "Brigham Young," updated August 21. Available online: https://www.history.com/topics/religion/brigham-young (accessed February 8, 2019).

Jones J.M. (2014), "U.S. Muslims Most Approving of Obama, Mormons Least," Gallup, July 11. Available online: https://news.gallup.com/poll/172442/muslims-approving-obama-mormons-least.aspx?g_source=link_newsv9&g_campaign=item_225380&g_medium=copy (accessed June 8, 2019).

US Census Bureau (2007), "Census 2007." Available online: https://www.census.gov/data/tables/time-series/demo/popest/pre-1980-national.html (accessed December 1, 2020).

Wilde A. (2007), "Polygamist Numbers Broken Down by Group," *Deseret News*, August 11. Available online: https://www.deseretnews.com/article/695199792/Polygamist-numbers-broken-down-by-group.html (accessed December 7, 2019).

Glossary Terms

Brigham Young (1801 to 1877) President of Joseph Smith's Council of Twelve Apostles at the time of Smith's death in 1844, allowing him to lead the main body of Saints to the Salt Lake valley in the American West. Not all followed, in part to his continuation of plural marriage and esoteric temple rituals, together with the claims of succession by others. Later in Utah, Brigham Young was sustained as Joseph's successor, and in 1851, Young was appointed Territorial Governor and Superintendent of Indian Affairs, governing the Utah territory as an autocratic theocracy, which he described as a "theo-democracy." From his public teachings that revealed a more violent and speculative theology, this husband of fifty-five wives provoked national controversy but local loyalty. Aside from tragedies such as Mountain Meadows, Young's legacy resides in his oversight and settlement of nearly four hundred colonies throughout the intermountain west.

Correlation Beginning in the 1960s with the LDS Church, the Correlation Committee as led by Apostle Harold B. Lee, was a response to the needs of a growing global church, as a means of simplifying and unifying acceptable ideas and practices within an increasingly diverse church. Under the direction of the Twelve Apostles, this committee centralized all teachings, leadership manuals, financial holdings and spending, magazines, architectural designs, and acceptable styles of dress for Mormons throughout the world. The term "correlation" became shorthand for this dramatic restructuring of the LDS Church toward that which mimicked the 1950s American corporate business model, informing a particular and easily recognized "American style" of being Mormon. This trend toward correlation also reinforced a powerful top-down structure of apostolic authority that church members were expected to be uncritically supportive of, informing both group thought and action.

First Vision While not well known among early followers of Joseph Smith, nor unique in his own family and locality at the time, the First Vision became in the twentieth century a central theme for some Latter-day Saint movements, particularly the LDS Church whose missionaries often memorized portions of the account as a means of heightening truth claims of the church. While there are multiple accounts with different details, basic themes are that in 1820, Joseph prayed in a grove of trees in response to personal concerns regarding his youthful sins, as well as to settle confusions he had with what church to join. Taking all accounts together, Joseph was visited by God the Father, his son Jesus, as well as a host of angels. In one account, Joseph was told to join none of the churches, since God had rejected all of Christendom, while in another Jesus assured Joseph that his sins were forgiven. The experience taken by Joseph was that God and Jesus were separate physical entities, though looked nearly identical, and that God's ultimate truth was yet to be restored to Earth through him as a medium.

Fundamentalism As the LDS Church moved away from the Principle of plural marriage by way of excommunication and the encouragement of legal and social persecution, individuals within the LDS Church, such as Lorin Woolley,

continued to advocate the practice as a "fundamental" and "everlasting" component of the Latter-day Saint restoration. Most fundamentalists today point back to Woolley and his authority with the special priesthood organization the Council of Friends, believed to have been given the higher "sealing" authority by church president John Taylor. The LDS Church denies this. Other fundamental principles advocated by these LDS offshoots are that of economic cooperation, theocratic rule, political hegemony, anti-pluralism, patriarchal rule, and speculative doctrines such as Blood Atonement and the polygamous marriages of God and Jesus Christ. Not all fundamentalists are polygamous, and many do not belong to any specific organization.

Gathering In the early years of the LDS Church in Utah, Brigham Young established the policy of "gathering," which required all saints to gather to the Salt Lake valley. Brigham upheld this requirement as just as important as other religious obligations, such as repentance and baptism. Believing that part of the "restoration" was the restoration of scattered Israel, both spiritually and geographically, converts were charged with gathering with the main body of the Saints. This gathering was all part of building Zion (the New Jerusalem) in preparation of Christ reign and the transformation of Earth into a millennial paradise. As it was understood, only among the Saints could one receive the "fullness" of ordinances necessary for salvation, as given temples. As LDS temples began to be built around the globe, church policy shifted to emphasize the building up of the "stakes of Zion" by way of gathering throughout the world.

Joseph Smith (1805–44) Founder of the restorationist movement largely known as "Mormonism." While a youth, Joseph Smith was known and sought out for his knowledge and skill in the

MORMONISM IN NORTH AMERICA

occult, publishing in 1830 a new work of scripture called the *Book of Mormon* by way of a magic stone used to find lost or buried items. Following this publication, Joseph Smith founded the Church of Christ, later renamed the Church of Jesus Christ of Latter Day Saints. Joseph's movement quickly gathered tens of thousands of followers, but was racked in controversy and violence in New York, Ohio, Missouri, and Illinois. Hundreds of religious movements sprung up with roots pointing back to Joseph Smith, the most successful being the Church of Jesus Christ of Latter-day Saints, headquartered in Salt Lake City, Utah.

Mormon Reformation Largely isolated in the Rocky Mountain, LDS leaders anticipated a unified religious society that could usher in Christ's millennial reign on Earth. Affected by several years of drought and worried over the lack of sufficient zeal among members, Brigham Young and his counselors initiated a top-down revivalism by way of enthusiastic preaching in 1856 to 1857 throughout the Mormon settlements, calling members to recommit by way of being rebaptized and to embrace the practice of polygamy. Home missionaries were assigned to each congregation with a 27-question checklist that provided accountability of righteous living, inclusive of hygiene and the fulfilling of church obligations. As a controversial side of the Reformation, church leaders utilized violent rhetoric against Americans and the noncommitted, threatening spiritual and at times physical harm. Brigham Young's doctrine of Blood Atonement for example, which claimed that some sins were beyond the bounds of Christ's sacrifice, thereby necessitating the sinner's own blood to be shed, was emphasized during this era. It was also partly a result of this enthusiasm and violent rhetoric that established the context for the massacre at Mountain Meadows to take place.

Mountain Meadows Massacre On September 11, after a four-day siege that began on September 7, members of the Utah Territorial Militia, equipped by Mormon settlers and local church leaders, massacred nearly the entire Baker-Fancher emigrant train of around 140 people at Mountain Meadows, with the aid of recruited Paiutes. Seventeen children, considered young enough not to recount the event, were adopted into Mormon homes. Brigham Young dismissed the massacre as well deserved and committed by Native Americans, while federal investigations demonstrated Mormon involvement and cover up. Only Indian agent John D. Lee was ever convicted for the atrocity, being executed by firing squad in 1877. Historians of the tragedy point to the violent enthusiasms of the Mormon Reformation, war hysteria, and a wholesale culture of violence inspired by Brigham Young's theocratic leadership.

Polygamy A broad term with reference to the marriage of one person with multiple spouses, often used as shorthand to refer to the Mormon practice of "The Principle" or "Celestial Marriage." Though Joseph Smith practiced polyandry, meaning the marriage of one woman with multiple husbands, polygyny has specific reference to what was practiced by the LDS Church in Utah and other offshoot groups, where one man married multiple women. Best known, the LDS Church openly practiced polygyny from 1852 to 1890, when it announced its cessation with the Woodruff Manifesto. Though continuing to uphold the belief, the church released two more manifestos denouncing the practice in 1904 and 1933. Today, many fundamentalist groups continue the practice.

Restorationism Emerging within America during the early nineteenth century, the restorationist movement rejects the Protestant Reformation's embrace of ecumenical Creeds, and instead focuses on the original source of Christian truth—the New Testament. One particular restorationist group, the Disciples of Christ, led by Alexander Campbell, rejected Christian Creeds and traditions, emphasized a united Christian church, and looked to the New Testament to restore Christ's "ancient order of things." While also rejecting earlier Christian Creeds as part of a general Christian apostasy, Joseph Smith restored lost Christian truth by way of revealing new scriptures and receiving lost authorities and spiritual powers from angelic visitations. The restoration then included the bringing forth of lost teachings, lost authorities, and lost rituals that were considered necessary in creating the New Jerusalem and preparing Earth for its restored paradisiacal status. Other restorationist movements, such as the Jehovah's Witnesses, similarly reject Christian Creeds and look directly to their reading of the Bible to restore God's lost ancient truth as a means of establishing a theocratic kingdom on Earth prior to its transformation into an earthly paradise.

6

Anabaptism: Mennonites, Amish, and Hutterites

John Sheridan

Introduction

Anabaptism originated in the 1520s in Europe during the time of the *Protestant Reformation (1517–1648)*, a period of radical religious change and discontentment with perceived corruption in the Roman Catholic Church. The Anabaptists received their name from those who opposed and persecuted them, branding them as "rebaptizers," which was a capital offense. These men and women were some of the many emerging *radical reformers* who were being persecuted due to their religious beliefs and practices. Three main streams of Anabaptism emerged from these early movements— the Mennonites, the Hutterites, and the Amish. Hostetler, a major contributor to Anabaptist studies, articulates early Anabaptists' core beliefs in a succinct summary:

> Central to their beliefs were the reconstruction of the church according to the New Testament pattern and entirely separate from the state; adult baptism following repentance and confession of faith; the "priesthood of all believers," referring not only to man's relation to God but also to the equality of all men in Christian community; a disciplined way of life incorporating only persons who are Christian by free decision and excluding those who became apostate; and the practice of nonconformity to the world. They refused to participate in war or to swear oaths of any kind, since these acts violated the new life in Christ and the injunctions of the New Testament. Anabaptists admitted that the state was a necessary institution for mankind, but they themselves felt unable to assume any responsibilities for functions of the state involving coercion.
>
> (1997: 7–8)

It was for these beliefs that Anabaptists were tortured and put to death, and it is these core beliefs that we see lived out in contemporary Anabaptist communities in North America. The *Martyrs Mirror*, originally written in 1660, recounts the gruesome and horrific violence that befell Anabaptists who were captured, tortured, and executed for refusing to renounce their religious convictions. This lengthy book continues to be an important reminder to Hutterite, Amish, and Mennonite communities of the spiritual conviction and strength of their ancestors. You will find a copy of the *Martyrs Mirror* in the homes of contemporary Amish, Mennonites, and even some Hutterites, most likely in High German, the language that makes up much of Anabaptists' literature, liturgy, and hymns.

Religious persecution had a major role in developing the identities of early Anabaptist communities and continues to play a role in shaping the identities of Anabaptists today. However, disagreements among Anabaptists also worked toward identity formation. A paradigmatic example of this is the schism that brought about the Amish. To escape persecution in Switzerland, a staunch Anabaptist by the name of Jakob Ammann (1644–1730) made his way to an Anabaptist refuge in Alsace (present-day France). One might think that Ammann would have been pleased to arrive at a place where his people could be free from death and torture. However, it was quite the opposite. Ammann saw that a peaceful existence had made his fellow Anabaptists spiritually soft and worldly. Ammann proposed swift changes to reinvigorate his spiritual community—ritual observance of Communion (the Eucharist or Lord's Supper) twice a year, which would involve the washing of feet in reverence for Jesus; the implementation of the practice of shunning wayward members; improvement of the overall strictness and separation from the world within the community; and the utilization of hooks instead of buttons on members' garments. Ammann's forceful and inflammatory requests did not go over well, leading to the 1693 schism that brought about the formation of the Amish.

Due to the intense persecution that the Anabaptists experienced in Europe as well as their desire for fertile farmland, the United States had a strong appeal to them. Thus, Mennonites and Amish immigrated to Pennsylvania in the eighteenth century. The Mennonites settled in the southern area of Pennsylvania and expanded into other states and into Canada. With them, they brought over a German dialect that stems from the Rhineland-Palatinate region in Germany—still spoken by regional natives—this has since been designated in North America as *Pennsylvania German*. Though a misnomer, this dialect is sometimes referred to as Pennsylvania Dutch, and is still spoken by Mennonites and Amish in religious ceremonies and daily life.

The Hutterites emerged in 1528 in Austerlitz, Moravia; the historic location where the first *Gütergemeinschaft* (community of goods in which all members surrendered their private property) was established (Hutterian Brethren 1987: 80–1). Hutterites developed separately from the other two streams of Anabaptists that became the Amish and Mennonites. It was not until 1533 when Jacob Hutter, after whom the Hutterites are named, became the leader of the religious community. Only after his rise to leadership did Hutterites truly begin to solidify and organize their religion and

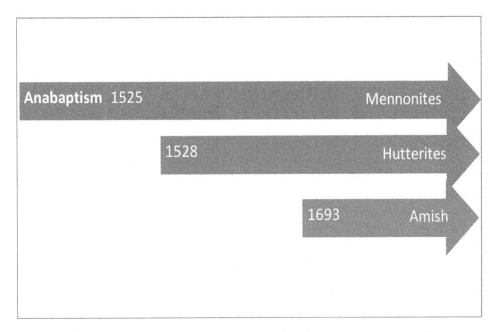

FIGURE 6.1 *A timeline of the three core streams of Anabaptism.* Source: By author.

community. Hutter emphasized the suffering of the temporal world and the need for Hutterites to band together in Christian community to withstand the evils of the world. Hutterites took the book of Acts and Jesus' command to live in Christian community a step further than Mennonites and Amish Anabaptists. Community members held that to be a good Christian it is necessary to surrender all worldly possessions to the community and hold all goods in common. Those who were drawn to this particular strain of Anabaptism entered the community with diverse skill sets and areas of specialization, such as blacksmiths, carpenters, farmers, butchers, and seamstresses, providing an ideal scenario for developing a Christian community that could exist separately and independently from the world. However, Hutter's time as a leader was short-lived. He was captured, beaten, tortured, and burned at the stake. The Hutterites immigrated all over Europe seeking freedom and relief from persecution. This caused them to refrain from immigrating to the United States until much later than the Mennonites and Amish did. It was between 1874 and 1880 that 1,200 Hutterites emigrated from Russian to the Dakota Territory and began their life in North America.

Hutterites

The Hutterites today number around 49,000 members, the vast majority possessing one of the original fourteen family names, and live in 480 colonies in the United States and Canada. Out of the 1,200 Hutterites that emigrated to North America, only 400 remained Hutterites. Upon arrival to the Dakota Territory, the 1,200 Hutterites divided into four groups: the Dariusleut (*Leut*, meaning people and Darius being the name of the leader of the *Dariusleut*), Schmiedeleut (*Schmied,* meaning blacksmith, which was the profession of their leader, Michael Waldner), the Lehrerleut (*Lehrer*, meaning teacher, which was the profession of their leader, Jacob Wipf), and the Prairieleut (prairie people). The Prairieleut abandoned communal living and soon became part of the broader US society. The Hutterites have grown from the three initial Dariusleut, Schmiedeleut, and Lehrerleut colonies to the nearly 500 colonies by splitting colonies in half once they reach roughly 150 members. During a split, the old colony supports the new colony financially, ideally building the necessary homes and purchasing the necessary equipment. Typically, half of the families remain in the old colony with one minister while the other half of the families move to the new colony with another minister. Hutterite colonies function like small towns. The land, buildings, homes, and equipment are owned by the colony, not by individual members. Everyone on a colony works for free for the betterment of the community as a whole. The majority of colonies have carpenter shops, mechanic shops, colony gardens, kitchens, communal dining halls, churches, laundry rooms, schools, individual family homes, and cemeteries. Hutterites also have livestock on the colony that they raise to feed everyone and, in some cases, sell commercially, such as chickens, geese, ducks, milk cows, beef cows, and pigs. Some colonies butcher and freeze 500–600 ducks per year, which serves as their traditional Sunday meal for the entire year. If you have a meal on a colony, it is likely that everything on the table came from the colony, including the butter, milk, and cheese.

The colonies are hierarchal and *patriarchal* with gendered divisions of labor. Baptized Hutterite men have a vote on colony decisions, but women do not, nor can they hold major power positions on the colony, such as farm manager, financial manager, first minister, second minister, and deacon. However, women are eligible to be elected to the colony head cook position, which is considered to be a prestigious position of power. Furthermore, being the wife of men in positions of authority affords women certain powers and privileges. It would be a mistake to write Hutterite women off as disenfranchised and oppressed individuals in need of rescue. Hutterite women fill colony life with their presence and influence. They discuss economic, religious, and social matters and are not afraid to speak their minds. Women who are aged fifteen to forty-five belong to complex organizational systems that order their daily lives and arrange them into work groups. Hutterite women keep colony life running smoothly.

In 1992 a dispute caused the Schmiedeleut, the largest Hutterite group at the time, to split into two groups: Schmiedeleut 1 and Schmiedeleut 2. In August 2017 Jake Kleinsasser, the elder (bishop) of Schmiedeleut 1 and the alleged cause of the split and its continuation, passed away. However, a new bishop was elected in September 2017, bringing Schmiedeleut 1 and Schmiedeleut 2 closer than ever before—since the 1992 split—to reconciliation (Kirkby 2017). Each *Leut* (group) has one bishop; there are currently four *Leut* (Dariusleut, Lehrerleut, Schmiedeleut 1, and Schmiedeleut 2). Thus,

ANABAPTISM: MENNONITES, AMISH, AND HUTTERITES

there are a total of four bishops presiding over all the Hutterites in North America. The only authority above a bishop is God, the supreme authority. The bishop has two main duties: ordain ministers and resolve disputes between or within colonies. He also serves as the guiding spiritual force for the whole *Leut*. However, he is not necessarily revered as holy or more spiritual than any other Hutterite member. Below his position is a committee of ministers who can be called upon by the bishop to resolve member disputes. Next in line is the first minister in a Hutterite colony, then the second minister, then the financial manager, and finally the farm manager. This makes up the executive committee on each Hutterite colony, which meets every morning to discuss colony matters. In church they sit on the front bench facing the rest of the community.

There are multiple texts that make up the Hutterite canon:

Peter Riedemann's Hutterite Confession of Faith (articulates the traditional Hutterite worldview);
the Hutterite Chronicles One and Two (recounts Hutterite persecution and history);
the *Ordnungen* (church rules);
the *Lehren* (church sermons);
the *Lieder* (historical hymns); and
the Bible (typically the seventeenth-century King James translation).

There are two types of Hutterite worship services. First, the daily *Gebet* (prayer). This is a thirty-minute worship service that occurs every day. The second worship service is the *Lehr* (ninety-minute weekly Sunday service). The Hutterite Sabbath begins after the Saturday *Gebet* and ends after the Sunday *Gebet*. The worship service consists of a song from one of the song books and a prewritten sermon. The entire service is in High German. Young Hutterites learn three languages: *Hutterisch*, English, and High German. Hutterites typically receive up to an eighth-grade education and also go to German school, but some go on to get a GED and some even receive college degrees, though this is rare. Many colonies utilize online Christian curriculums and even online Mennonite curriculums.

The spiritual realm is structured as a hierarchy. The chain of spiritual authority is God, husband, wife, and children. Hutterite wedding sermons discuss Peter's Epistles and the reasoning behind this religious hierarchy. Much has changed about Hutterite religious beliefs from fifty years ago, not to mention from the time of Jacob Hutter. Most Hutterites would not say that you must live in a Hutterite colony to be saved and receive eternal life. Hutterites read the New Testament as literal truth and attempt to live as Jesus commanded. There are two commitments that are of utmost importance to Hutterites: (1) love God with all your heart, soul, and mind; (2) love your neighbor as yourself; Hutterites follow the teachings in the book of Acts that tell them to live in a community where no one owns major private property. Hutterites understand God, as well as the devil, as a real force acting in the world. Contemporary Hutterites may be unsure about the importance of the community. However, they believe strongly in selflessness and humility. They are strongly opposed to the sin of pride.

Hutterites dress in plain clothes. Men wear black pants, a button up shirt, and suspenders. Women wear a dress, black-and-white-polka-dotted head scarfs (*Kupftiechle*), and braid their hair. These disciplines keep Hutterites humble, and protect them from pride and vanity. Generally, Hutterite women do not cut their hair, which makes braiding it a bit more practical. Hutterites tend to understand braiding hair and covering it with a scarf as consistent with the requirements from passages in the New Testament such as 1 Peter 3:3–4, which instruct women to not focus on their outer appearance and specifically denounces the braiding of hair. Each Hutterite you ask about why they dress the way they do may give you a slightly different answer and their reasoning is more dependent on the socioreligious climate of each particular colony. However, dressing in Hutterite attire is generally considered to be a sign of respect for one's self, the community, and God.

Hutterites embrace technology. This is very different from the Old Order Amish and Mennonites. Some Hutterite colonies make millions of dollars each year on farming and on colony factories. Technology for business and the betterment of the community is welcome. Technology for entertainment or selfish reasons is strongly discouraged. That said, this varies from colony to colony and some Hutterites have iPhones, iPads, computers, and musical instruments.

It is important to understand the diversity of Hutterites. There are four *Leut*, which exist on a spectrum of liberal to conservative. However, within each *Leut* there is a spectrum of liberal to conservative. Once more, each colony and each individual Hutterite has its or their own character. For each declarative statement scholars can make about Hutterites, there is an exception. There are differing social, political, and religious perspectives from colony to colony and Hutterite to Hutterite. For instance, some colonies have been influenced by evangelical worldviews and emphasize having Jesus in your heart as the most important aspect of a good Christian life.

Amish

The Amish consist of two main groups: the Old Order Amish and the New Order Amish. About 95 percent of the Amish are Old Order Amish, and just 5 percent are New Order Amish. Due to a schism in 1693, the Amish split away from the Mennonites. By 1937, all Amish had either immigrated to North America or disbanded. Scholars are not sure when Amish first began immigrating to the United States; however, 1736–1770 was a major time period in which large numbers of Amish made their way to North America. The first Amish settlement was established in Pennsylvania, in 1737. Pennsylvania was particularly enticing to the Amish because it was founded by William Penn who promoted freedom of conscience—as long as you were willing to pledge your allegiance to the one true God—and a version of separation between church and state. Furthermore, Pennsylvania was fertile land on which Amish could build their settlements and farms, a dream compared to the persecution they had experienced in

Europe. From Pennsylvania, the Amish branched out to Ohio, Indiana, and Wisconsin, eventually settling in twenty-five states and in Ontario, Canada.

The Amish, unlike the Hutterites, have private property owned by individual family units. They live in communities called settlements, which consist of twenty to forty Amish families. A husband and wife will typically have a large number of children, which provides the labor necessary to support their familial economic endeavors. Amish families are structured hierarchically and patriarchally, with the husband being the highest religious authority in his family unit, under the ultimate authority of God. It is the wife's duty to support her husband and respect his authority. At the same time, the husband and wife may work and make decisions together. Variations are dependent on individual characteristics and familial dynamics. Like the Hutterites, official community positions of power and privilege are only available to male community members. However, unlike Hutterite women, Amish women can vote for community business decisions and nominate ministers. In even sharper contrast to Hutterites, some Amish women run their own side businesses, such as food or craft stores.

Bishops hold the highest authority within Amish settlements. Their duties include baptism of members, ordaining ministers, officiating weddings and Communions, upholding the unwritten *Ordnung* (church rules), and shunning and excommunicating

FIGURE 6.2 *An Amish bakery in Kalona, Iowa.* Source: *Author.*

members. They serve as spiritual leaders guiding their flock. Below the bishop are the community ministers. Ministers give extemporaneous sermons every other Sunday in a member's barn, basement, or other large building in which people can gather. The location rotates through each family unit, which is not necessarily the easiest duty because the host family has to clean their home and feed the entire attendance of Amish members. The deacon's role is to read a chapter out of the New Testament and the minister will expound. The three-hour Sunday services, in which men and women sit separately, are mostly void of physical images, objects, or any type of sensorial stimuli.

Amish do not cast lots to elect their ministers but rather any male member can be called upon to give a sermon, once he has been baptized. Some Hutterite colonies have had to contend with issues related to members having difficulty understanding the archaic High German in the *Lehren* (formal sermon), which traditionally is not to be reinterpreted or expounded upon by the minister. It is important to note that the majority of these sermons were written centuries ago. Thus, in contrast, Amish services are conducted in two languages, Pennsylvania German and High German. The songs are sung in High German and the extemporaneous sermons are spoken in Pennsylvania German.

The Dordrecht Confession of Faith was written in 1632 by Anabaptists. The eighteen articles of faith contained in this document are taught to members going through baptism. This is the same confession of faith to which Old Order Mennonites adhere. Parts of the *Ausbund* (a sixteenth-century German hymnal) is sung during Sunday worship ceremonies.

FIGURE 6.3 *Amish children walking on road dressed in traditional Amish attire.* Source: *Stocktrek / Getty Images.*

Similarly to Hutterites, the Amish sing these songs without official written music notes. The music, for instance the *Ordnung*, is passed down culturally through rote memorization. Another worship service that is very important to the Amish is Communion, which takes place in the fall and spring. Kraybill explains that the ritual "emphasizes self-examination and spiritual rejuvenation. Sins are confessed, and each member in turn reaffirms his or her willingness to uphold the rules of the *Ordnung*." Members wash each other's feet in pairs, and commemorate the death of Jesus (2001: 108–9).

Amish children receive a private eighth-grade education that is curated and managed by fathers in the community. Teachers are typically unmarried women in their late teens or early twenties. However, they do not have a college or high school degree, only an eight-grade Amish education. Amish are not required to, and do not, teach science and sex education. Thus, there is no discussion of evolution or other aspects of science that might call a literalist interpretation of the Bible into question. Instead, each day of school begins with prayer and teachers are careful to emphasize Amish values and worldviews. This was made possible by an important 1972 US Supreme Court decision, *Wisconsin v. Yoder*, in which the judge ruled that forcing Amish to adhere to broader societal conventions would be discriminatory and unjust.

FIGURE 6.4 *Image of Amish horse and buggy.* Source: *Author.*

Amish dress plainly, and it is their distinctive garb and renunciation of certain technologies that set them apart from the broader society. Amish men who are married have a beard, wear a hat, don black pants, and use hooks and eyes rather than buttons to fasten their clothes. Amish women are not to wear jewelry or anything else that would demonstrate excessive pride. Old Order Amish drive horse drawn buggies, not cars. In our contemporary mechanized age, it can be hardest to imagine that Amish use horses or mules to conduct farm work. The Amish are well known for their rejection of modern technologies, which is underlined by their iconic use of a horse and buggy. However, Amish may utilize and interact with some aspects of technology in indirect ways. They are prohibited from owning or operating a car, but they can rent a car and hire a driver for long trips, which they do. Furthermore, they utilize telephones on a regular basis and occasionally use technology. Members may have telephones in their barns or workshops, but not in their homes. Of course, computers, radios, and televisions are prohibited, but that does not mean that gas-powered chainsaws, gas grills, and steam-powered industrial equipment are prohibited. The Amish, like most members of the broader society, see the efficiency of modern technology and compromise where they can—compromises that do not erode the Amish way of life.

Mennonites

Menno Simons (1496–1561), a highly influential Anabaptist leader for whom the Mennonites are named, wrote *Foundation of Christian Doctrine*, an influential text written in Dutch in 1539. As early as 1545, Simons's followers were referred to as Mennists, which eventually led to the name Mennonites. The Mennonites are the largest Anabaptist group in North America and the world. Their estimated population in North America is 700,000. They are in eighty countries, numbering over 1.6 million worldwide. They also have the greatest diversity with over 150 different Mennonite communities in North America. Mennonites are also ethnically diverse with significant portions of members being Asian, Hispanic, Native America, African American, and Latino. Mennonites essentially divide into two groups: assimilated and traditional. Assimilated Mennonites may be supportive of lesbian, gay, bisexual, transexual, and queer/questioning (LGBTQ) communities, and accept modern technology, dress, values, and ideologies. Traditional Mennonites would be much more conservative and wary of outsiders and worldly influences. It is not possible to do justice to the vast Mennonite diversity here. Thus, this section is geared toward Old Order Mennonites, a traditional group of Mennonites who dress plainly, speak Pennsylvania German and English, and resist modern technology.

According to Kraybill, there are two types of Old Order Mennonites: those who drive cars and those who drive horse and buggies (2010: 137). The latter became known as team Mennonites, in reference to the team of horses that pull a buggy, which make up less than 10 percent of US Mennonites. After the Civil War, a heavy Protestant influence led the Old Order Mennonites to form themselves as a distinct

ANABAPTISM: MENNONITES, AMISH, AND HUTTERITES

Mennonite category. It was by way of Old Order Mennonites attempting to resist certain Protestant practices and beliefs that schisms began to occur, and groups began to separate. Another divisive issue was accepting cars into daily life, which divided Old Order communities in 1907 (Indiana), 1927 (Pennsylvania), and 1939 (Ontario). Old Order team Mennonites use tractors for farming, have telephones and electricity in their homes, but they do not have televisions, radios, computers, or travel on airplanes. Additionally, they can hire taxies, but they cannot drive a car.

Similar to the Amish, Old Order Mennonites hold private property and live dispersed, in family units. Their family units consist of a husband and wife and eight to nine children on average; the man is considered to be the head of the household. Like the Amish, Old Order Mennonites belong to communities of likeminded members who live nearby and help each other out—this is called a congregation. However, Old Order Mennonites also belong to conferences, which are biannual gatherings of ordained members who together constitute "the highest source of moral authority" (Kraybill 2001: 68).

Old Order Mennonite men do not have beards and communities do not gather at homes every other Sunday for worship service; instead, they gather at meetinghouses, in which the men and the women sit on opposite sides during the service. Bishops are considered to be more spiritually virtuous than regular members and thus have to live up to those standards. They are responsible for many of the same duties as Amish bishops, such as baptisms, weddings, excommunications, confessions, and communions; however, they have the responsibility of interpreting the *Ordnung* and are generally more hands on in their leadership, in contrast to the Amish bishop. The minister preaches in Pennsylvania German at the two-hour Sunday service, and the deacon acts as a spiritual assistant to the bishop and minister. Old Order Mennonites "cast lots" to select deacons, ministers, and bishops.

The process of casting lots begins at the close of a Sunday church service. Members come to the bishop and deacon with nominations. Women are allowed to participate in the nomination process; however, that does not mean that they necessarily do. The next day, the community elders interview the nominees and their wives and assess their suitability for the leadership role. On Tuesday at the community meetinghouse, one candidate is selected for ordination by selecting the songbook with a slip of paper, placed inside by the deacons, which reads, "The lot is cast in the lap, but it falls as the Lord wills" (Prov. 16:33). The candidate who selects the one songbook that contains this slip of paper is ordained right on the spot for either deacon, minister, or bishop.

In contrast to the Amish, not all baptized men can be ministers or other ordained members because not everyone is chosen for this lifelong position by God. Additionally, Old Order Mennonites are more wary of Protestant evangelical influence than Hutterites and Amish. Furthermore, the written *Ordnung* has a much clearer and explicit role in spiritual matters in terms of articulating religious beliefs and guiding community members. In terms of similarities, however, the Amish and the Old Order Mennonites have similar educational systems where local parents and fathers run the school and manage the curriculum, which goes from first grade to eighth grade. They operate with a single teacher who is an unmarried woman in her late teens or early twenties, and the students do not learn about science or sexual education. The focus is on making them good Old Order Mennonites. Old Order Mennonites, like Hutterites and Amish, emphasize separation from the world, humility over pride, faith over arrogance, and the betterment of the group over personal achievement.

Conclusion

There is a phenomenon that occurs when the public and people interested in entrepreneurial endeavors begin to set their gaze on Anabaptists. They have a tendency to either idealize or denigrate the people that belong to this sector of society. There is both an "Othering" and an exoticization that occurs, especially when discussing the Amish, probably the most well known of the Anabaptist groups even though it is not the largest. In his book, *The Amish in the American Imagination*, David L. Weaver-Zercher explores a historical paradox, which has existed since before the twentieth century, about the way in which Anabaptists are considered to be holy saints, representative of good American Christian values, and at the same time backward traditionalists. Americans tend to exoticize the marginalized Anabaptist communities. Weaver-Zercher states: "This study participates in an ongoing conversation about the importance of America's marginal religious groups, not only as sources of intriguing religious activity, but also as conspicuous 'Others' against which mainstream Americans have defined and discovered themselves" (Weaver-Zercher 2001: 7–8). It is important to note that *The Amish in the American Imagination* does not discuss the Hutterites and Mennonites, rather, it focuses on the Amish. The Hutterites are much less visible and conspicuous than the Amish; however, that has not inhibited people from bringing Hutterites into what might be called the Anabaptist imaginaries; that is, the broader tropes and narratives surrounding Anabaptists in America. These tropes tend to perpetuate the paradoxical discourse that Anabaptist are either perfectly righteous saints or somehow uniquely fallen.

One of the most recent incendiary examples of this American tendency to demonize or lionize the Anabaptists was the controversy over the National Geographic television program *American Colony: Meet the Hutterites*, which aired in 2012. Many Hutterites were furious about the way the television show represented their religion and culture. The reality television rendering of Hutterite life attempted to market Hutterites as fallen saints living chaotic lives. However, the opposite perspective, Anabaptists as particularly righteous saints, can be just as misguided and harmful. Thus, it is important that an article this size is only a starting point, a jumping off point, an invitation to acquire more information on Anabaptism. This chapter is comprised of very brief generalizations that cannot compete with actual, everyday Anabaptist life as it is lived on the ground, nor does it cover the vast assortment of other aspects of Anabaptist life. There are many Anabaptist subgroups, not to mention the diverse array of intersectional Anabaptist

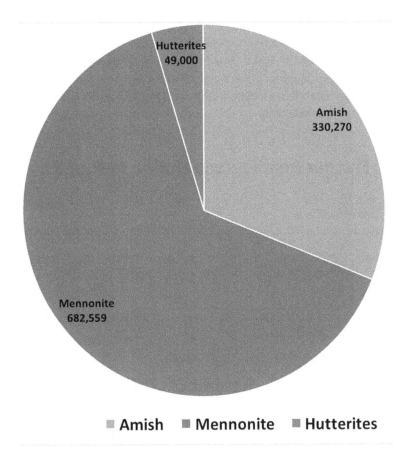

FIGURE 6.5 *Pie chart of the most recent data collected on Mennonite, Hutterite, and Amish populations in North America.* Source: *Graphic by author.*

experiences of race, class, gender, and sexuality that exist across space and time. No account of Anabaptism could ever claim to cover it all.

The Anabaptist story in North America is one of growth and expansion, not of decline and decay. The massive growth and spread of Anabaptism is impressive, considering that Anabaptism is a countercultural movement that has experienced significant persecution, and appears to have values and beliefs that are antithetical to the broader societies in which Anabaptists flourish. The three Anabaptist groups that we have discussed all exist in some way as countercultural movements to the status quo of broader society in the United States and Canada—whether it is their values about selflessness and humility, an aversion to individualistic consumer capitalism, a desire to live separate from the world, or an emphasis on community and communalism. That said, it is important that we avoid overgeneralizing such a diverse religious tradition. Therefore, we must keep in mind that Anabaptists are not some idealized others; rather, they are a complex yet related web of diverse human beings who experience all the benefits and struggles of living a human life. Anabaptists represent an alternative to the broader individualistic consumerism that is prevalent in the United States, Canada, and many other parts of the world. Their countercultural lifestyle has typically been perceived by outsiders as either quite intriguing and a source of transformative insight or considerably antiquated, hypocritical, and problematic, depending on the location and perspective of the observer.

Further Reading and Online Resources

Janzen R.A. and M.E. Stanton (2010), *The Hutterites in North America*, Baltimore: Johns Hopkins University Press.

Kraybill D.B. (2010), *Concise Encyclopedia of Amish, Brethren, Hutterites, and Mennonites*, Baltimore: Johns Hopkins University Press.

Kraybill D.B. and C.F. Bowman (2001), *On the Backroad to Heaven: Old Order Hutterites, Mennonites, Amish, and Brethren*, Baltimore: Johns Hopkins University Press.

Kraybill D.B., K.M. Johnson-Weiner, and S.M. Nolt (2013), *The Amish*, Baltimore: Johns Hopkins University Press.

Scott S.E. (1981), *An Introduction to Older Order and Conservative Mennonite Groups*, Intercourse, PA: Good Books.

References

Global Anabaptists Mennonite Encyclopedia Online (n.d.), "Welcome to GAMEO." Available online: https://gameo.org/index.php?title=Welcome_to_GAMEO (accessed November 6, 2020).

Hostetler J.A. (1997), *Hutterite Society*, 2nd edn., Baltimore: Johns Hopkins University Press.

Hutterian B, ed. (1987), *The Chronicle of the Hutterian Brethren*, trans. Hutterian Brethren, vol. 1, Rifton, NY: Plough Publishing House.

Janzen R.A. and M.E. Stanton (2010), *The Hutterites in North America*, Baltimore: Johns Hopkins University Press.

Kirkby M.-A. (2017), "New Bishop for Schmiedeleut 1 Hutterites." *Polka Dot Press*, September 12. Available online: https://www.polkadotpress.ca/single-post/2017/09/12/New-Bishop-for-Schmiedeleut-1 Hutterites (accessed January 15, 2020).

Kraybill D.B. (2010), *Concise Encyclopedia of Amish, Brethren, Hutterites, and Mennonites*, Baltimore: Johns Hopkins University Press.

Kraybill D.B. and C.F. Bowman (2001), *On the Backroad to Heaven: Old Order Hutterites, Mennonites, Amish, and Brethren*, Baltimore: Johns Hopkins University Press.

Kraybill D.B., K.M. Johnson-Weiner, and S.M. Nolt (2013), *The Amish*, Baltimore: Johns Hopkins University Press.

Riedemann P. (1999), *Peter Riedemann's Hutterite Confession of Faith: Translation of the 1565 German Edition of Confession of Our Religion, Teaching, and Faith, By the Brothers Who Are Known as the Hutterites*, trans. John J. Friesen, Classics of the Radical Reformation, Waterloo, ON: Herald Press.

Weaver-Zercher D.L. (2001), *The Amish in the American Imagination*, Baltimore: Johns Hopkins University Press.

Glossary Terms

Hutterisch Sometimes referred to by Hutterites as low German, this almost exclusively spoken dialect is hundreds of years older than High German and serves as Hutterites first language for everyday communication with fellow Hutterites.

Patriarchy A social system or society in which predominantly men hold positions of power and control.

Pennsylvania German A German dialect spoken by Mennonites and Amish that stems from the Rhineland-Palatinate region in Germany, where a form of the dialect is still spoken today. The dialect is almost exclusively a spoken by Mennonites and Amish rather than written.

Protest Reformation (1517–1648) It is said that it began with Martin Luther nailing his Ninety-Five Theses to the Wittenberg church in Germany in which he criticized the Catholic Church for the selling of indulgences and declared his belief of justification by faith. The extreme displeasure with the corruption in the Catholic Church inspired Protestant reform movements, such as Lutheranism, Calvinism, and others. It was a time period of great religious, social, and technological change.

Radical Reformers A term used to denote Anabaptists as well as other groups that emerged during the protestant reformation, often in opposition to, the dominant authority. These groups were rejected and persecuted by the dominant Roman Catholic, Lutheran, Calvinist, and Anglican traditions.

PART TWO

Race and North American Christianity

7

Race and Christianity

Shuma Iwai

Introduction

Race and Christianity have been—and continue to be—complex issues. Christianity, especially in the North American context, has tended to be a white-dominant religion. Bradley argues that Christianity has "a complex history of both embracing and rejecting cultural norms for demarcating between groups of people according to race" (2016: 132). The Bible says, "God created mankind in his own image, in the image of God he created them" (Gen. 1:26–27), teaching that all humans are equal in the eyes of God. The Bible also claims "There is neither Jew nor Gentile, neither slave nor free, nor is there male and female, for you are all one in Christ Jesus" (Gal. 3:28). Despite these key biblical statements, Christianity has separated racial groups for much of its history.

To discuss how race and Christianity are intertwined with one another, it is important to understand the concepts of race and *racism* in general. This chapter first describes these concepts, then discusses race and racism in the Christian and biblical contexts.

Race and Racism in General

Wijeysinghe, Griffin, and Love describe race as "a social construct that artificially divides people into distinct groups based on certain characteristics such as physical appearance (particularly skin color), ancestral heritage, cultural affiliation, cultural history, [and] ethnic classification" (1997: 88). Little (2016) point out that, through the years, the concept of race has changed. It has lost ancestral and family connections, and has instead focused on physical characteristics to delineate between races. In other words, instead of family and ancestry defining race, race has become a social construct (Little 2016).

Bell defines racism as "a system of oppression that not only stigmatizes and violates the targeted group, but does psychic and ethical violence to the dominator group as well" (2013: 24). David Wellman (1993) argues that racism is a system from which certain people benefit, with privilege based on race. For example, white people, a traditionally dominant group in Western culture, have been accused of taking advantage of their privilege such as in the areas of compensation and education, simply by being white. This theory holds that people of other races do not have as many privileges as white people do. The term "racism" includes one's prejudices and discrimination toward other people based on their race and ethnicity. Beverly Daiel Tatum (2013) writes that individuals in the dominant group often view the subordinate group as inferior or defective in relationship to the norm of the dominant group. Socially constructed norms based on race and racism can cause minority groups to feel marginalized or subordinated.

Race and Racism in a Biblical Context

How does the Bible interpret race and racism? Regarding race, the Bible says "From one man he made all the nations, that they should inhabit the whole earth; and he marked out their appointed times in history and the boundaries of their lands" (Acts 17:26). In this passage, the nations could imply all races and all peoples. God teaches that all humans belong to the same human race, God's people. There are many other passages that address race in the Bible (e.g., Gal. 3:28; Rom. 10:12–13; 2 Tim. 4:7) and all of them seem to describe racism as sin. Human sin began when Adam and Eve fell into disobedience to God (Gen. 3:1–6). With the serpent's temptation, Eve committed her sin and ate fruit from the tree and shared it with Adam. Together they committed the first sin, disregarding God's clear command to not eat the fruit of that tree. In terms of racism in the biblical context, Christian theologian Joseph A. Manickam (2007) argues that racism opposes God's creation of diversity. Manickam explains that socially constructed racism in the modern world has led humans to separate into distinct groups. In other words, while race is considered to be one united human race in the Bible, the separation and inequity of racism in modern society is a sin against God's will and teachings.

Manickam (2007) describes three types of racism: institutional, communal, and personal. Institutional racism is prejudice and discrimination against minority groups on a larger scale, sustained by institutional policies and programs. Communal racism refers to discrimination and prejudice against minority groups because they don't meet certain criteria of the communities (e.g., churches). Personal racism involves attitudes, beliefs, and actions of individuals that are based on ethnic background or appearance. These attitudes, beliefs, and actions can be positive or negative, depending on the situation.

Various Groups of Christians in the United States

There are many Christian minority groups in the modern American context. According to the Pew Research Center (2014), while white is still the dominant Christian group (66 percent of Christians in the United States), 13 percent of Christians are Black, 2 percent are Asian, 16 percent are Latino/a, and 3 percent are other and/or mixed race. Over the course of American history, racism and racial segregation have created the development of churches based on race and ethnicity (Desmond and Emirbayer 2020). The United States is home to numerous ethnic churches—each of which maintains its own history, unique worship style, and distinctive rituals.

Native Americans, also known as Indigenous peoples, were the first minority group in America who experienced racial prejudice. Europeans who sought Christian independence arrived in New England in the early seventeenth century. They took away many privileges including heritage, culture, and beliefs from Native Americans. These Europeans controlled and exploited Native Americans and their land for colonization (Healey and Stepnick 2020). Native Americans combined their Indigenous religions with Christianity and formed the Native American Church during the late nineteenth century.

African Americans experienced racial discrimination most acutely during the period of institutionalized slavery, which began in the early sixteenth century and lasted until the end of the American Civil War in 1865. The Ku Klux Klan, a white supremacist group that began shortly after the Civil War, preached discrimination and racism throughout the twentieth century and influenced many Americans to oppose Jews, Black Americans, and Catholics. In response to these and other discriminative pressures, African Americans developed their own Christian identity and developed their own Black churches, beginning in 1816 with the establishment of the African Methodist Episcopal Church, America's first Black denomination (Lincoln 1984: 63).

The population of Latinos in the United States continues to increase due to Latinos seeking a better life in the face of corruption, violence, and economic collapse in Latin American countries. Latin American countries have the highest percentage of Christians in the world (Daughrity 2014). Pew Research's 2014 survey on Latinos and religion revealed that 55 percent of Latinos are Catholic, while 18 percent are some form of Protestant (Pew Research Center 2014). In 2014, while white was still the largest Catholic population (59 percent) in the United States, 34 percent of Hispanics were Catholic in the United States (Pew Research Center 2018). In some states, such as California and New Mexico, Hispanics now outnumber whites, a trend that will impact other states such as Texas in the near future.

Forty-two percent of Asian Americans are Christians (Desmond and Emirbayer 2020), they too have developed their own churches. Asians are very diverse religiously, for example, 65 percent of Filipino Americans identify as Roman Catholic and 61 percent of Korean Americans are Protestant. Three percent of Asian were Catholic in the United

FIGURE 7.1 *Human hands showing unity.* Source: *Jacob Wackerhausen / Getty Images.*

States (Pew Research Center 2018). Many Chinese and Japanese have also immigrated to the United States, especially during the gold rush in the mid-nineteenth century. For example, Chinese Christians developed the first Asian American Protestant Church in 1852 (Tseng 2012). During the Second World War, many Japanese experienced discrimination and were forced to move to US internment camps, and many of them converted to Christianity during their incarceration (Blankenship 2016).

Conclusion

While the Bible teaches that all humans are made in the image of God, in some spheres, notably in religion, American society has been divided along racial and ethnic lines for generations. Socially constructed racism *influenced*—at times *forced*—separation and division, with each ethnic group developing their own unique Christian churches and ethnic-oriented organizations. However, it is important to note that "Christians are a people who are constituted not by blood [as in the case of Judaism] but by faith" (Berzon 2018: 211). Today many American Christians work hard to challenge racial discrimination, while respecting the unique values and traditions of particular ethnic groups.

Further Reading and Online Resources

Carter J.K. (2008), *Race: A Theological Account*, Oxford: Oxford University Press.
Harvey P. (2016), *Christianity and Race in the American South: A History*, Chicago: University of Chicago Press.

References

Bell L.A. (2013), "Theoretical Foundations," in M. Adams, W.J. Blumenfeld, C. Castaneda, H.W. Hackman, M.L. Peters, and X. Zuniga (eds.), *Readings for Diversity and Social Justice*, 3rd edn., 21–6, New York: Routledge.
Berzon T. (2018), "Ethnicity and Early Christianity," *Currents in Biblical Research*, 16 (2): 191–217.
Blankenship A.M. (2016), *Christianity, Social Justice, and the Japanese American Incarceration during World War II*, Chapel Hill: University of North Carolina Press.
Bradley A.B. (2016), *Something Seems Strange: Critical Essays on Christianity, Public Policy, and Contemporary Culture*, Eugene, OR: Wipf & Stock.
Daughrity D.B. (2014), *Rising: The Amazing Story of Christianity's Resurrection in the Global South*, Minneapolis, MN: Fortress Press.
Desmond M. and M. Emirbayer (2020), *Race in America*, 2nd edn., New York: W.W. Norton & Company.
Healey J.F. and A. Stepnick (2020), *Diversity and Society: Race, Ethnicity, and Gender*, 6th edn., Los Angeles: Sage.
Lincoln C.E. (1984), *Race, Religion, and the Continuing American Dilemma*, New York: Hill and Wang.
Little W. (2016), *Introduction to Sociology*, 2nd edn., Victoria, BC: BCcampus. Available online: https://opentextbc.ca/introductiontosociology2ndedition/ (accessed December 21, 2020).
Manickam J.A. (2007), "Racism," in J. Corrie (ed.), *Dictionary of Mission Theology: Evangelical Foundations*, 326–8, Nottingham: Inter-Varsity Press.
Pew Research Center (2014), "The Shifting Religious Identity of Latinos in the United States," May 7. Available online: https://www.pewforum.org/2014/05/07/the-shifting-religious-identity-of-latinos-in-the-united-states/ (accessed December 15, 2019).
Pew Research Center (2018), "7 Facts about American Catholics," October 10. Available online: https://www.pewresearch.org/fact-tank/2018/10/10/7-facts-about-american-catholics/ (accessed June 8, 2020).
Tatum B.D. (2013), "The Complexity of Identity," in M. Adams, W.J. Blumenfeld, C. Castaneda, H.W. Hackman, M.L. Peters, and X. Zuniga (eds.), *Readings for Diversity and Social Justice*, 3rd edn., 6–9, New York: Routledge.

Tseng T. (2012), "Asian American Religions," in P. Harvey, E.J. Blum, and R. Stephens (eds.), *The Columbia Guide to Religion American History*, 253–64, New York: Columbia University Press.

Wellman D.T. (1993), *Portraits of White Racism*, 2nd edn., Cambridge: Cambridge University Press.

Wijeysinghe C.L., P. Griffin, and B. Love (1997), "Racism Curriculum Design," in M. Adams, L.A. Bell, and P. Griffin (eds.), *Teaching for Diversity and Social Justice: A Sourcebook*, 82–109, New York: Routledge.

Glossary Terms

Race A term used to describe a group of people based on their biological characteristics as well as physical, cultural, and ancestrally inherited characteristics.

Racism Prejudice and discrimination against certain groups of people, often minorities, based on their race, ethnicity, and socially constructed norms.

8

African American Christianities in North America

Darrius D. Hills

Reorienting the Religion of Africans in the New World

The overall trajectory of African American religions, including Christianity, has its roots in the transatlantic slave trade. The role of missionary organizations, such as the *Society for the Propagation of the Gospel (SPG)* throughout the African diaspora, must be linked with not only theological rationales but further with the expansion of Western imperialism. The permeation of Christianity among the enslaved is inseparable, therefore, from the "colonizing creativity" (Long 1999: xvi) practiced by white Europeans, and as reconfigured through present and past expansions of white, American Christianity. The slavery and enslavement system featured the emergence of white racial states, and was built upon notions of white economic, social, and political supremacy. The grand paradox of such systems was exemplified through the conditional, limited deployment of the touted ideals of freedom and liberal democracy, which were assumed solely under the auspices of whiteness and white humanity, while being categorically denied to Blacks (Johnson 2015: 5). Arising from the paradoxes of race demarcated along Black and white lines, were correlating ideological and linguistic subterfuges, which Charles Long referred to as "significations," thereby sustaining and legitimizing hierarchical relationships between European and nonwhite native cultures in other geographic regions (Long 1997: xv).

Long's notion of signification and/or signifying discourses describes the discursive mechanisms that name, characterize, and situate the realities and peoples deemed "novel" and "other" as perceived by cultures of conquest vis-à-vis colonial engagement. At this historical moment, where the imperial interests of whites met the realities of the African, the resulting clash of culture and notions of personhood shook the consciousness and life course of both signifier (European) and the signified (African). This is further compounded through the presumption of centeredness tethered to European self-assessment. From the maiden voyages of Christopher Columbus and his contacts with native populations in the Americas, through the transatlantic slave trade, a significant feature of colonial mobility was the establishment of European hegemony through economic, technological, military, and religious means (Long 1997: 110). One of the privileges conferred through white, European hegemony was/is an unshakeable self-perception of centeredness—a grounding in the insularity of one's capacity for naming place and space—including the place and space of others. This mode of spatial mobility also generated the capacity to shape and envelope those entities and realities considered beyond the pale of established "norms." To be the center, also functions, therefore, like an *ontological* category—an intangible essence that makes one's immediate reality *the* norm—an absolute standard against which other realities and experiences are measured. In the case of the religious apparatus that contoured European reality, as well as European constructs of "civilization," the religious practices of Africans were deemed uncivilized and inhuman, laying beyond the scope of normalcy conferred by the centeredness of Eurocentric norms.

It is critical to recall that prior to their contacts with the United States via slavery, Africans lived their own religious and social practices away from the gazes of whites. The enslaved Africans brought to the New World their own sacred cosmologies, beliefs about the ordering of human life, individual and communal conduct, and a grasp of the harnessing of resources of the physical world to suit their needs (Glaude 2014: 25–31). There have been substantive debates on the extent to which African norms and practices prevailed and held sway in the face of enslavement and the disruption of cultural continuity. Theorists such as E. Franklin Frazier and Melville Herskovits represent two of the noteworthy figures at the center of the debate on African survivals. Frazier argued that "*Africanisms*," or ethnically specific cultural patterns and practices unique to African societies, were essentially obliterated by slavery, while Herskovits found that the cultural vitality of enslaved Africans prevailed in distinctive manners (Baer and Singer 2002: 1). Regardless of the position one supports, what is noteworthy is the centrality of religious life for both enslaved and free African Americans. The character of African religious traditions varied, encompassing folk practices and rites, as well as more established and sophisticated religious worldviews, including Christianity and possibly Islam. The wide array of these traditions, however, did suffer disruption, in form and practice, through the introduction and coercive practice of American Protestant Christianity. This, however, is not the final story. Africans in the New World were not completely untethered from their past. Rather, "slavery in the United States did not wipe away remnants of a former [religious] way of life; instead, it created the conditions for their transformation" (Glaude 2014: 25).

The Christianity imparted to enslaved Africans introduced a paradox. American Christianity was a tool of empire that generated and normalized the subjugation of Black bodies, thereby providing a religious and theological rationale for their enslavement. Frederick Douglass effectively captured the paradox of (white) American "slave holding" Christianity in contrast to the proper and peaceable "Christianity of Christ" (Sernett 1999: 102–11). Douglass's indictment of white Christianity embodied the mood of most African Americans of his time, as many felt deep suspicion and disdain for the Christianity of white America. This was a Christianity that denied the humanity of essentially all communities outside the divine ordinance of the continental United States, sanctioned Black and brown inferiority and servitude, and relegated these communities to *durante vita* second-class (non)citizenship. The practice of American Christianity, as Douglass knew, and as the enslaved knew, was wholly disconnected from the motifs and symbols of a Christianity that spoke spiritual and material liberation, not bondage, to the oppressed. The creativity and genius of the enslaved, and later, free Blacks, involved their pragmatic embrace of their oppressors' religion as a means of realizing their humanity and personhood. Through their own processes of discernment and introspection about the nature of white Christianity, Wilmore notes, African Americans "used Christianity not so much as it was delivered to them by racist White churches, but as its truth was authenticated to them in the experience of suffering and struggle" (1983: 4).

In making Christianity more uniquely their own, African Americans availed themselves of an agency and meaning-making catalyst that preserved their humanity, personhood, and independence as a religious community. As we will see in the section to follow, the journey toward stronger representation as independent African American Christian communities was fraught with its own set of challenges, as well as provided opportunities to establish the modern Black church as a preeminent fixture of Black political and social life.

The Rise of Black Christian Communities

As C. Eric Lincoln and Lawrence Mamiya observed: "Black churches were one of the few stable and coherent institutions to emerge from slavery. Slaves not only worshipped with their masters or under the conditions of their masters' control, they also held their own secret, independent worship services in the backwoods and bayous of plantations, and sometimes in their own slave quarters: a phenomenon [...] called the *'invisible institution'*" (Lincoln and Mamiya 2000: 7–8). In the face of white supremacy and colonial encroachment, enslaved and free Black religious communities embodied the cumulative quest for independence, identity, and refuge under the surveillance of an anti-Black world. Of course, slave religious communities had already become quite practiced in the art of cultivating some mobility and agency in their religious worship spaces under the watchful gaze of whites. Ex-slave Peter Randolph spoke openly of the risk and sense of purpose underscoring the secret religious meetings: "Sometimes the slaves meet in an old log-cabin, when they find it necessary to keep a watch. If discovered, they escape, if possible; but those who are caught often get whipped. Some are willing to be punished thus for Jesus' sake" (Sernett 1999: 67). In thinking about the restrictions cast upon slave religious culture, it is necessary to tie this to the geographies of containment conditioning slave life. Due to the culture of racial surveillance as practiced upon Black bodies during (and after) slavery, it was nearly impossible for African Americans to conduct religious services of their own accord. Concerns over plots of rebellion, for example, prompted additional vigilance from whites, thereby leading to stipulations that these religious services could only be held during daytime hours. Vincent Harding notes that some states, such as South Carolina, even passed laws forbidding Black religious meetings outright, even in the company of whites (Fulop and Raboteau 1997: 111).

For these reasons, it was only under the dark of night, away from the bustle of plantation life, that the enslaved could enjoy clandestine religious worship. In these "hush harbor" meetings, as they were called, Blacks were able to create spaces of meaning in which they could sing, pray, and experience the kind of ecstatic movement of the spirit denied them under the coercive dynamic of white Christianity. Within the spaces of these invisible institutions, African American humanity, voice, and spiritual well-being were privileged—forming a direct assault against the presumed inhumanity, inferiority, and inanity of Black personhood. Away from the watchful gaze of whites, the

FIGURE 8.1 *A prayer meeting.* Source: *Kean Collection / Getty Images.*

enslaved learned, in these secret religious spaces, to draw upon their own cultural and religious resources to instill Black life with a different function and purpose, thereby tethering their quest for freedom and wholeness to a sense of ultimacy beyond the confines of their present reality as slaves.

African Americans' internal yearning for religious independence was generated within the slave quarters, but the desire for a space and place of one's own only intensified with the concomitant pursuit of emancipation. While the invisibility of the early quest for religious identity and freedom of assembly began sporadically, and varied from region to plantation, the abolition of slavery provided African Americans ample opportunity to create substantial Christian organizations and denominations of their own. Before discussing the independent Black church movement, it is necessary to consider a few words about the nature of interracial worship during and after African American emancipation. As Will Gravely has observed, "at many points in the evolution of Black religious independence, White control and Black assertion clashed" (Fulop and Raboteau 1997: 138). There is, however, significant evidence that Black and white Christians were often worshipping in the same congregations during the eighteenth and nineteenth centuries (Boles 1990). In the South, as we have noted, this was particularly noticeable, as Blacks in many states outnumbered whites, so having them worship with whites was typically seen as customary, given fears of rebellion. In this vein, interracial worship was less a praxis of Christian brotherhood and sisterhood, and more aptly a mechanism of white Christian control over potentially dangerous property. Interracial worship services still proved alienating and restrictive. The theologies of white Christian communities in most cases validated the slave system and did nothing to advocate the equality of all human beings, regardless of racial categories. The inclusive humanity suggested in Galatians 3:28: "There is neither Jew nor Greek, there is neither slave nor free man, there is neither male nor female; for you are all one in Christ Jesus" (New American Standard Bible)—was clearly at odds with the theology of race practiced in white Christianity.

Moreover, as a particular source of consternation that bolstered the desire for independence, interracial worship services subjected African Americans to a restrictive form of paternalism—an effort to thwart any effort of Blacks to create their own worship spaces free from the input and specifically, authoritative control, of white ministers and religious leaders. Being subject to the inclinations, wishes, and whims of white religious bodies prompted African American Christians to make parallels to slavery. I make these observations only to underscore the deeply felt drive for independence and the hope for the realization of agency and individual identity that was a critical feature of both slave religious life and the later quest for control that led to the formation of Black churches and denominations. The Independent Black Church movement has a wide assortment of historical characters, organizations, and motivating factors. Rather than attempting a fully exhaustive survey, I will prioritize the histories and polity structures of the early Black Baptists and Methodists, who were and remain arguably the most influential Christian denominations for African Americans.

Black Baptists

The earliest independent Black churches in America were established by Black Baptists. Geographically, most Black Baptist congregations were found throughout the American South, as the restrictiveness of the slave state occasioned the earliest efforts on the part of the enslaved to carve out religious spaces and worship experiences of their own. The larger scope of the Baptist movement began as did most American Christian stories, with the quest for religious freedom undertaken by English Puritans. Roger Williams's arrival in 1631 and the establishment of the colony of Rhode Island led to his forming the first Baptist church in America later in 1639. Gradually, Rhode Island became something of a breeding ground for Baptist churches, eventually leading to the growth of churches further along the East Coast. There are at least two correlating reasons Baptist churches grew during this period and into the eighteenth and nineteenth centuries. First, there was from the beginning, a strong mission-focused praxis that also synced well with the deeply evangelistic character of Baptist preaching and teaching. These attributes were primed to coincide remarkably with the First and Second Great Awakenings in America. The Great Awakenings were periods of great religious revivalism. Beginning sporadically in the 1730s and continuing into the nineteenth century, and taking place in both the north and south, these were periods of renewed interest and enthusiasm in the practice of Christian piety and moral uplift. As was typically the custom during these revival periods, preachers and other associated

FIGURE 8.2 *George Whitefield preaching.* Source: *Culture Club/Getty Images.*

clergy from a variety of Christian denominations would congregate within chosen campgrounds and preach and teach to inspire new converts. Some of the ministers and theologians of renown typically associated with the fervor and excitement of these campground meetings included Jonathan Edwards and George Whitefield.

It was during these revival periods, particularly after the Civil War, that Blacks had ample opportunity to experience an evangelical Christianity beyond the confines of plantation culture. In addition to the interracial fellowship, Black worshippers were also able to wrestle with and experience the growing sense of a democratic ethos undergirding religious experience. Coupled with the missionary zeal of Baptist clergy, many slaves proved to be eager converts. The first Blacks were received into official Baptist church membership in Northeast, but most, to be sure, resided in the south. It is important to again note that the drive for independent Black Christian denominations was in strong measure the result of the desire for agency, free from white denominational control. Slave preachers coming out of the membership of white-controlled churches were often allowed to become licensed as "itinerant" exhorters to slaves at local plantations. The congregation at Silver Bluff, South Carolina, for example, was founded by slaves between 1773 and 1775. As word of the receptivity of white churches to allow Blacks to form their own congregations spread, numerous other independent Black Baptist churches began to spring up in Virginia, Georgia, and North Carolina. It should be noted, however, that the fear of insurrection and rebellion remained a factor underscoring white reluctance to accept independent Black congregations (Baer and Singer 2002: 15).

Slave and ex-slave preachers, over time, not only played significant roles in the building of the first modest independent Black churches but also were key in the formation of organized conventions. These were essentially the governing bodies responsible for validating individual church membership, forming statements of belief and theological tenets, and the allocation of church financial resources. Of these conventional groups, the National Baptist Convention, USA, Inc., and the Progressive National Baptist, Inc. are best known.

Baptist polity structures were particularly attractive to Black Christians, as each individual congregation could maintain its own centralized autonomy, in which local pastors had the freedom to lead their congregations without having to cede authority. As some have observed, separate Black Baptist "churches are a law unto themselves," with the final balance of power residing with the congregation and its board of trustees (Lincoln and Mamiya 1990: 42). In one respect, such polities, or organizational frameworks, would have resonated with both enslaved and freed Black Christians, who were all seeking religious and racial autonomy free from the restraints of white Christian power structures. Unlike other denominations, local Baptist congregations are responsible for the selection of their pastors democratically by way of a vote. This means selected pastors are products of the congregation's express wishes rather than a reflection of bureaucratic process. Looser organizational structures would have also provided Black exhorters and later, licensed ministers, substantially more opportunities to explore and appropriate theologically robust expressions of the faith in their sermons and pastoral activities.

136   CHRISTIANITY IN NORTH AMERICA

While local Baptist congregations did share in the autonomy pertinent to governance and the affairs of local-level church leadership, mission, and worship, they are organized into respective state conventions and/or associations. For Black Baptists, these conventions, or governing bodies, are the National Baptist Convention of America, founded in 1880, and the Progressive National Baptist Convention, Inc., founded in 1961. Like many religious organizations struggling to articulate their identity over time, numerous splits and disagreements have transpired. Eventually, these splits evolved into the formation of larger church conventions and boards, resulting in the broadening of Baptists' reach to members of more diverse and eclectic political and social persuasions.

Black Methodists

The Methodists are distinctive primarily for their denominational commitment to egalitarianism and devotion to spiritual piety, though the church suffered some division when Southern Methodist churches split over the issue of slavery. Early Methodism has its roots in the eighteenth-century Church of England/Anglican Church, when the founder, John Wesley, an English clergyman, distanced himself from the Anglicanism of his upbringing to form a new ministry. Wesley was known for his involvement in "holiness clubs"—study and reflection groups devoted to piety and deepening the knowledge of holiness in everyday life and thought. Given the devotion of these followers and their fastidious approach to scriptural study, fasting, and an ascetic life, they were gradually labeled "methodist" to indicate their methodical approach to Christian faith formation. To be expected, many, if not most, enslaved and free Blacks had their first exposures to Methodist teaching and preaching during the First and Second *Great Awakenings*.

In 1787, local Philadelphia preachers Richard Allen, Absalom Jones, and several of their peers were disrupted during their prayers and pulled from the worship services held at the St. George's Methodist Episcopal Church. When Allen and company refused to return to their segregated seats in the church gallery, the Black worshippers left the service. Allen and Jones went on to pool their resources among their group, and established the *Free African Society (FAS)*, a benevolent society that, among other initiatives, served as a benevolent voluntary association offering economic and social aid to Black Philadelphians. Many of the members remained connected to the Methodist Church, including Allen, but remained steadfast in their desire to have a religious space free from white control, paternalism, and proscription. Notably, what Allen and his peers sought most was to be recognized and accepted as suited to lead and direct their worship experiences and conduct church with the authority reserved for whites. Black church members "insisted that their religious freedom could not be compromised [...] [for] they wanted to elect and be elected to church office, to ordain and be ordained, to discipline, as well as be disciplined, to preach, exhort, pray, and administer sacraments—in sum, to have their gifts and graces acknowledged by the whole community" (Fulop and Raboteau 1997: 138). Seeking this acknowledgment

FIGURE 8.3 *John Wesley.* Source: *National Portrait Gallery / Wikimedia Commons.*

and independence, Allen went on centralize FAS resources to formulate what became the St. Thomas African Episcopal and Bethel African Methodist Episcopal congregations (139). By the nineteenth century, the first Black Methodist denominations, African Methodist Episcopal and African Methodist Episcopal, Zion (AME/AMEZ) were established in Philadelphia and New York, respectively.

The AME and AMEZ denominations comprise the most significant wings of Black Methodism, though the Christian Methodist Episcopal (CME), formerly the "Colored Methodist Episcopal" church, is also included. Methodist polity is characterized by a connectional structure, featuring clergy categories consisting of elders, deacons, local

FIGURE 8.4 *AME congregation holds hands in church.* Source: *Mark Peterson / Getty Images.*

pastors, and lay leaders. Methodist churches typically belong to annual conferences—state governing bodies made up of church delegates—and are led by a bishop. Within separate state conferences, churches are further organized into regional districts. Within the connectional structure, pastors are sent to local churches through the leadership of the office of the bishop and the respective district. On April 30, 2012, the AME and AMEZ, along with three other historically Black denominations, entered into "full communion" with the United Methodist Church, the worldwide representation of Methodism. The pact emerging from this reconciliation called for a recognition of each other's churches, sacraments, and vocational calling of their respective clergy and ministries.

On social issues, Black Baptists and Methodists have been active in the pursuit of platforms for African American flourishing in the public and private spheres, though this is by no means a monolithic trend outright. One example of this is clearly illustrated in the response of the National Baptist Convention (NBC) to the progressive civil rights' campaign of Martin Luther King Jr., who was a Baptist minister. King vented his frustrations with the slow, gradualist, conservative approach to civil rights injustices of Black clergy in his "Letter from a Birmingham Jail" (Sernett 1999: 519–35). The tension between progressive Baptists such as King and the establishment leadership within the denomination on social ills pertaining to racism eventually led to a split, with King and others forming the Progressive National Baptist association. One area where Black Baptists and Methodists have faced additional tension has been on the issue of gender, namely the question of ordaining Black women and issuing them preaching licenses. Black women, for instance Jarena Lee, argued as early as 1836 that the Gospel was not conditionally based upon one sex, and that Jesus died for male and female alike. Lee, like other Black women of her time, was denied ordination within the AME church, and it was not until 1895 that Julia Foote was ordained in the AMEZ church (Baer and Singer 2002: 37–8). Today, both groups have made some small strides in the better treatment of women clergy, as both support the ordination of women as pastors and local preachers, and have devoted more resources toward ministries and programs aimed at addressing women's empowerment. Generally speaking, however, African American Christians and other alternative religious groups within African American communities have long used their religious and theological resources to address pressing social concerns and other issues related to their respective identity formation in American culture (Weisenfeld 2018). Baer and Merrill Singer (2002) document much of this, and highlight the apolitical and/or less socially engaged forms of African American religious expression, within and beyond the mainline Black denominational settings.

FIGURE 8.5 *Richard Allen.* Source: *Hulton Archive / Stringer / Getty Images.*

African American Christians in the Present

According to data from the Pew Research Center on Religion and Public Life, African American Christians overwhelmingly worship in historically Black Protestant denominations and articulate higher measures of religious belief and religious participation than other racial groups (Masci, Mohamed, and Smith 2020). The very brief history of Black Baptists and Methodists should be credited with playing a significant role in galvanizing what appears to be an ongoing resource for African American Christians to create space for religious identity formation. The Independent Black Church movement began as a freedom movement, and the spirit of its influence was also manifest in slave revolts, and later, central to the rationale and motivation(s) driving the civil rights movement. Like any religious community, these denominations have shifted and adapted with the times, places, and people associated with them. In looking at the present landscape, current debates about the place, importance, and function of Black churches are contested terrain.

In an April 2010 *Huffington Post* editorial, Princeton University religion scholar Eddie Glaude noted: "The Black Church, as we've known it or imagined it, is dead [...] the idea of this venerable institution as central to Black life and as a repository for the social and moral conscience of the nation has all but disappeared" (Glaude 2010). What Glaude described in that piece was not necessarily the removal and/or irrelevance of Black churches but rather was an interrogation of the decline of the *centrality* of Black Christian institutions as *"the* institution(s)" of Black social, ethical, and religious life. In my own reflections on this matter, I would only offer some parting thoughts on African American Christianity as but one option in the marketplace of religious (and nonreligious) ideas. African Americans have found a home with varied expressions of the Christian faith, and in the contemporary context the relevance and staying power of the Black church remains intact.

While the Black church still provides a home for many African Americans, there are other factors that further complicate Black religious choices, participation, and commitment. Generally speaking, throughout American culture, there is a rise in secular inquiry and a decline of religious participation, which is not only limited to Christianity. Then, of course, there is the concomitant reality of the *religious "nones"* phenomenon, characterizing those who are nonaffiliated and not tied to any one belief structure or expression of faith. The variety and eclectic mix of African American religious choices, however, is hardly a novel concept. To reduce African American religion to pulpit and pew is to engage in an oppressive essentialism that ignores the human capacity for complex identity formation and the ability to embrace a range of religious choices. As Anthony Pinn observes in *Varieties of African American Religious Experience* (1998), the established canon of what we tend to think and believe about Black religion needs reconstruction and expansion, because not to do so results in the misguided belief that Christianity is normative for Black life and thought.

Mindful of this tension, we are still on the correct side of interpretive approaches by simply reviewing the historical record of the prominent role of Christianity in the drama of African American religious, social, and political experiences in North America. African American commitment to Christianity over time, reflects, it seems, at least one aspect of the cultural and intellectual embrace of religious faith as a mechanism of refuge, identity formation, and social uplift in a racially hostile environment, and within a religiously pluralistic society. The enduring gravitation of African Americans toward the Christian faith, and toward representation within their own denominational enclaves, also reveals the extent to which they have utilized their own cultural resources in formulating a pragmatic religious response to their past and present realities.

Further Reading and Online Resources

Baker J.O. and B.G. Smith (2015), *American Secularism: Cultural Contours of Nonreligious Belief Systems*, New York: New York University Press.
Cone J.H. (2011), *The Cross and the Lynching Tree*, Maryknoll, NY: Orbis Books.
Glaude Jr. E. (2017), *In a Shade of Blue: Pragmatism and the Politics of Black America*, Chicago: University of Chicago Press.
Pinn A. (2012), *Introducing African American Religion*, New York: Routledge.
Smith C. and M.O. Emerson (2000), *Divided by Faith: Evangelical Religion and the Problem of Race in America*, New York: Oxford University Press.

References

Baer H.A. and M. Singer, eds. (2002), *African American Religion in Twentieth Century: Varieties of Protest and Accommodation*, Knoxville: University of Tennessee Press.
Boles J., ed. (1990), *Masters and Slaves in the Household of the Lord: Race and Religion in the American South, 1740–1820*, Lexington: University Press of Kentucky.
Floyd-Thomas S., J. Floyd-Thomas, C.B. Duncan, S.G. Ray, and N.L. Westfield (2007), *Black Church Studies: An Introduction*, Nashville, TN: Abingdon Press.
Fulop T. and A. Raboteau, eds. (1997), *African American Religion: Interpretive Essays in History and Culture*, New York: Routledge.
Glaude Jr. E. (2010), "The Black Church Is Dead." *HuffPost*, August 23. Available online: https://www.huffpost.com/entry/the-black-church-is-dead_b_473815?guccounter=1 (accessed November 16, 2020).
Glaude Jr. E. (2014), *African American Religion: A Very Short Introduction*, New York: Oxford University Press.
Johnston S.A. (2015), *African American Religions, 1500–2000: Colonialism, Democracy, and Freedom*, New York: Cambridge University Press.
Lincoln C.E. and L.H. Mamiya (1990), *The Black Church in the African American Experience*, Durham, NC: Duke University Press.
Long C. (1999), *Significations: Signs, Symbols, and Images in the Interpretation of Religion*, Aurora, CO: The Davies Group.
Masci D., B. Mohamed, and G.A. Smith (2020), "Black Americans More Likely to Be Christian, Protestant than US Adults Overall," Pew Research Center, August 18.

Available online: https://www.pewresearch.org/fact-tank/2018/04/23/black-americans-are-more-likely-than-overall-public-to-be-christian-protestant/ (accessed November 16, 2020).

Pinn A. (1998), *Varieties of African American Religious Experience*, Minneapolis, MN: Fortress Press.

Raboteau A. (2004), *Slave Religion: The "Invisible Institution" in the Antebellum South*, New York: Oxford University Press.

Sernett M.C., ed. (1999), *African American Religious History: A Documentary Witness*, Durham, NC: Duke University Press.

Weisenfeld J. (2018), *New World A-Coming: Black Religion and Racial Identity during the Great Migration*, New York: New York University Press.

Wilmore G. (1983), *Black Religion and Black Radicalism: An Interpretation of the Religious History of African Americans*, Maryknoll, NY: Orbis Books.

Glossary Terms

Africanism A term describing cultural retentions maintained in spite of Africans' acclimation and assimilation to the American slave system.

Clergy The formal description of an established religious leader, namely in the Christian church.

Free African Society (FAS) A benevolent aid society established in Philadelphia by Richard Allen and Absalom Jones in 1787 for free Blacks and their families.

Great Awakening(s) Beginning in the mid-eighteenth century and lasting into the nineteenth, these are periods of heightened religious revivalism, particularly related to the application of Christian piety and morality to American life.

Invisible institution The secret, clandestine religious worship spaces, created by African Americans under the surveillance of the slave state.

Ontology/ontological Relating or pertaining to the nature of being or essence (particularly in human life).

Religious nones Religiously nonaffiliated. This typically refers to a societal demographic that does not ascribe to any particular religious or denominational orientation, and may or may not self-identify as atheist or agnostic.

Society for the Propagation of the Gospel (SPG) in Foreign Parts An eighteenth-century voluntary organization of clergy persons based in England, whose mission was to evangelize and recruit for the Church of England among native, indigenous, and African American populations.

9

Asian Americans and Christianity in North America

Shalon Park

Introduction

During the political turbulence of the 1960s, America faced the post-Second World War challenge of redefining its public religious face. It was an ambivalent era when the golden age of capitalism and radical movements coexisted, such as the movements for civil rights, liberation of women, educational reform, and the end of the Vietnam War. The Third World Liberation Front (TWLF) was one of the most significant social waves of this time, which recognized the post-Second World War American challenge as the larger "problem of the twentieth century," a prognosis made by W.E.B. Du Bois in 1903 (Okihiro 2016). As part of the Third World liberation movement, the Asian American movement emerged as a coalitional response to various social issues, calling for a radical reorientation of social order on a global scale.

The term "Asian American" first appeared in the late 1960s, when the Asian American population was estimated to be around 1.3 million. A significant part of this population was American born, as approximately "80 percent of Japanese Americans and about 50 percent of Chinese Americans and Filipino Americans, respectively, were born in the United States" (Jeung et al. 2019: 10). The social demands of the TWLF and Asian American coalition were beyond the pursuit of the social inclusion of minorities as an extension of the civil rights movement. Instead, as the post-1968 demands for creating ethnic studies were aligned with "the struggles of Third World peoples along the color line" (Okihiro 2016), which challenged modern history shaped by global capitalism. For this reason, understanding Asian American Christianities requires historicizing the Asian American movement and locating the

FIGURE 9.1 *Asian American students' anti-war protest, Berkley, California, 1972.* Source: *Photograph by Ralph Crane / The LIFE Picture Collection via Getty Images.*

study of Christianities and Asian American articulations of faith within the framework of the Third World Liberation movement.

Studying Asian American Christianities, as noted by Helen Jin Kim, also means dealing with the historiographical challenges of studying American religions, which can be limited to "the Atlantic-facing geographic orientation, and black-white binary focus in racial discourse" (Kim 2016: 138–9). While framing the study of Asian American Christianities as a subfield of American religion has limited its discourse to Orientalist and racialized terms, the subject matter can teach us important lessons about world history and religion, especially the formation of American imperialism in relation to Christianity. The task of the study goes beyond a mere addition to the multiculturality of American Christianities but calls for revisiting how Christianity has been integral to constructing imperial relationship with Asia and Asian America. Rather than understanding its task as a form of cultural nationalism, which tends to accentuate difference and cultural diversity within the unified umbrella of America, this essay seeks to historicize Asian relations to America, suggesting that Christianity can be a method for better understanding this relationship, both transnational and domestic. This chapter parses out the threefold relations that connect Asians, America, and Christianity: the Asian making of Asian America, the American making of Asian Christianities, and the Asian American making of Christianities.

The Asian Making of Asian America: The Transnational Formation

The nomenclature of "Asian American"—and as such, the conceptual challenges of representing various forms of racial embodiment—begins with the centuries-long migration histories of Asians to North America. The inception of the term "Asian American" can be traced back to the late 1960s, when the Asian American Political Alliance (AAPA) emerged as a multifarious expression of solidarity with the Black Power movement, the Third World liberation movements, the anti-Vietnam War campaigns.

This coalition was spearheaded by minority students during the San Francisco State strike, which was the earliest campus organizing force in 1968. Asian American students condemned the complacency of San Francisco State College toward poverty among minority residents and scarcity of educational platforms for addressing the structural issues. The student groups that were mobilized for community development, such as Intercollegiate Chinese of Social Action, Philippine Collegiate Endeavor, and Asian American Political Alliance, merged with the Third World Liberation Front to fight for

FIGURE 9.2 *Indian American demonstrating against the Immigration Legislation, 1968.*
Source: *Photograph by Keystone / Hulton Archive / Getty Images.*

promoting admission and curricula for ethnic studies (Liu, Geron, and Lai 2008; Maeda 2011; Wei 1993). Such an ethos was influenced by the 1955 Bandung Conference in Indonesia (Jeung et al. 2019: 13), in which Asian-African solidarity took place against "colonialism in all of its manifestations," condemning the global-scale subjugation of the non-Western regions by two world powers: the United States and the Soviet Union.

Liberationist and anti-imperialist in origin, the movement spread among Asian American students and called for an educational reform according to Third World demands. The statement of "Philippine-American Collegiate Endeavor (PACE) Philosophy and Goals" shows the vast scope and inclusivity of the movement: "We have decided to fuse ourselves with the masses of Third World people, which are the majority of the world's peoples, to create, through struggle, a new humanity, a new humanism, a New World Consciousness, and within the context of collectively control[ling] our own destinies." The Filipino students raised the issues of racism within San Francisco State, in relation to the "the prevailing inadequacies (small number of Filipinos in college, opportunities denied to Filipino professionals in this country, exploitation of Filipino farm workers in Delano working for a few dollars a day)." The educational demands of the coalition were closely linked with the indentured labor condition of Asian immigrants, who together with Mexican American farm workers, led the United Farm Workers movement in the mid-1960s. Sharing the liberationist quest of the New Left movement, this coalitional activism called the legitimacy of imperialist legal, educational, and territorial claims into question (Maeda 2011: 4).

Recent scholarship in migration and Asian American studies has highlighted the transnational continuity between Asian migration history before and after the Chinese Exclusion Act of 1882 (Azuma 2008; Hsu 2015). The history of American making of Asian colonial subjects finds its earliest form in transnational history of Asian migration (Lee 2015). From the history of the Filipino laborers in the Manila galleons to the Chinese migration to Cuba (1874), Asian transnational migration provides the contexts for the coalitional activism of the 1960s surrounding the issues of labor and race.

The indentured labor migration of Asian and Pacific Islanders to North America is traced back as early as 1635, when Chinese barbers arrived in Mexico through the Manila galleon trade, and the transatlantic labor chain spread through the Hawaiian laborers from Peru to Canada (Okihiro 2015). Moreover, a large number of Chinese coolies migrated to Louisiana, as the "labor recruiters hoped that the Chinese could help replace emancipated African Americans, and by 1867 at least 2,000 Chinese had left Cuba for New Orleans" (Lee 2015: 55). The earliest Japanese immigration occurred through private companies that were established in 1891, which sent Japanese farmers to the United States, Canada, Mexico, Peru, and Hawai'i (Lee 2015). Hawai'i was also one of the first locations for Korean immigrants to North America, who worked in the sugar plantations before and after Japan occupied Korea. Many of these laborers were Protestants who carved out their own religious networks, as religion provided them "a bulwark against the effect of white supremacy" (Yoo 2010: 57).

The incarceration of 120,000 Japanese Americans during the Second World War was also a transnational process that has reshaped the cartography of North America.

The wartime policies between North and South America were deeply intertwined in creating the incarceration program, mitigating a mass migration of Japanese Peruvians to the United States from 1942 to 1945. According to Erika Lee, "Peruvian authorities cooperated eagerly, but it was the United States that masterminded, organized, and paid for the forcible deportation of Japanese Peruvians from their homes, their transportation to the United States on American vessels, and their incarceration on U.S. soil" (Lee 2015: 223). The Asian American coalition in the 1960s recognized that this migration history is deeply connected to poverty among Asian American communities, and that such history ought to be taught in higher education alongside the history of slavery and globalization.

The American Making of Asian Christianities

A careful look at multidirectional migration histories (Hsu 2008) explains how the politics of Asian American civic functioning and religiosity were developed in tandem. Christianity in North America has been unquestionably instrumental in constructing the moral basis for the modern nation-state, simultaneously racializing Asians as Oriental subjects. The designation of Asians as undesirable and unfit subjects for a civilized nation is most explicit in a letter entitled "Some Reasons for Chinese Exclusion. Meat vs. Rice. American Manhood Against Asiatic Coolieism. Which Shall Survive?" (1902), by American Federation of Labor, Herman Gutstadt, Samuel Gompers, and Asiatic Exclusion League. He was the leader of the American Federation of Labor, in support of the extension of the Chinese Exclusion Act of 1882. Gompers faults Chinese immigrants for being "unassimilative." He wrote, "They pay little taxes; they support no institutions, neither school, church, nor theater" (26). The letter demonstrates how the exclusion of Asians in America was deemed necessary for the cause of "protection for American labor" (27), as the low wages paid for Asian labor was harmful for "not only men of our own race, but men who have been brought up by our civilization to family life and civic duty" (26). Gompers's rationale, drawing on the essence of Christianity in its alignment with the anti-socialist agenda, illustrates the capitalist basis for excluding and racializing Asians. Asian indentured labor in the United States became an ironic problem, in which migrants were perceived as a "free population" who could ultimately destabilize the American ideal of liberty that was defined by the early settlers (29–30). The Exclusion Act epitomizes the role of religion, and Christianity in particular, in defining the ideal American public life. The category of religion in America was inseparable from Protestantism and its role in the civil sphere (Wenger 2017). Within this, the unregulated religiosity of Asian immigrants—whether mystical, heathen, or even communist—was perceived as non-American, unless Asians became Christian and assimilated to the public life.

In addition to its utilization for exclusionary purposes, Christianity functioned as a rhetorical tool for Asian inclusion based on American sovereignty and internationalism. Christian organizations have been active voices in shaping racial immigration policies. The Federal Council of Churches (FCC), for example, "typified the preference on many

FIGURE 9.3 *Chinese section of hunger parade, Sacramento, CA, 1933.* Source: *Photograph by Bettmann / Getty Images.*

religious groups for broader legislation on the grounds that exclusion was morally problematic, not just in relation to Chinese but all Asian peoples" (Hong 2019: 35). The universality of Christian language has provided a basis for rejecting the codification of racially exclusive immigration policies (Snow 2007). American Protestant missionaries played an important role here too. In particular, American missionaries in China were not only strong advocates for Chinese immigration in America but also were "the most committed and institutionalized constituency working concertedly toward the belief that Chinese could adopt to Western civilization and be converted" (Hsu 2015).

There are two sides to the development of pan-Asian solidarity and the involvement of Christian missionaries in the constituencies and the right of naturalization for Asian immigrants. Solidified by the Open Door policy, a special relationship formed between the US government and China in the early 1900s. This relationship, combined with China's internal struggle for nationalism and US missionary campaigns against Japan's involvement in China, served the interest of US expansion. The Open Door policy, as Gordon Chang points out, symbolized "a unique form of American nonterritorial imperialism" on the one hand, and "elicited the popular expression of moral regard for the welfare of the oppressed Chinese masses," on the other (Chang 2015: 104). Christianity was instrumental for constructing the special bond between China and the

United States, especially through American missionary involvement in foreign affairs. Advocacy for Chinese inclusion within American society and the Christian moral vision for internationalism through Christian missions occurred mostly at the expense of Japanese exclusion (Hong 2019: 36; Wong 2009). While Christian groups such as the Quaker American Friends Service Committee and the Catholic Maryknoll Missionary Society denounced the Japanese incarceration (Blankenship 2016: 8), the notion of pan-Asian American solidarity was hardly a norm, given the intra-Asian violence created by Japanese imperialism (Wong 2009: 81).

The racial representation and the legal category of "Asian" has constantly shifted as immigration policies have evolved. The Yellow Peril, the centuries-old popular depiction of Chinese laborers as an Asiatic economic threat to America, exemplifies how racialization of Asians varied through different modes of European relation to the Orient (Tchen and Yeats 2014).

FIGURE 9.4 *French depiction of Yellow Peril in America, 1908.* Source: *Universal History Archive / Universal Images Group via Getty Images.*

An anonymous report to *The New York Times* on August 2, 1900, titled "How Great Is This 'Yellow Peril'?" exemplifies the ways that Yellow Peril was understood in terms of Christian language and international militarization. The author describes the Battle of Peking (present-day Beijing) in 1900 as the battle between the "Chinese Empire against all foreigners and the combined armies of Christendom," when the Eight-Nation Alliance led by Britain ended the siege of foreign citizens in Peking during the Boxer Rebellion. Arguing that the Yellow Peril is nothing to fear, the article shows how the Chinese persecution of Christians legitimized the diplomatic military force that allowed a coalitional expedition of troops to Peking for protection of Christians, on the battle between "with all of China on the one side and the Christian world on the other." The US coalition with imperial Japan and Russia in forming the eight nations was less relevant than what the Yellow Peril meant for Christianization: "Is it Polyphemus or a pigmy that confronts the Christian powers at Peking? Have we aroused a veritable *monstrum horrendum*, or is it only the familiar and not formidable little Chinese devil with whom the allies are to try conclusions?" ("How Great Is This 'Yellow Peril'?" 1900).

The Immigration Act of 1917 (The Asiatic Barred Zone Act) expanded the categories of "undesirable aliens" by including immigrants from South Asia, Iran, Afghanistan, and the Asia-Pacific islands. Moreover, the ways in which immigration policies are racialized have also taken new forms, particularly during US assertion to reorient its geopolitical place through the Second World War. As the Second World War generated a new flow of immigrants from Southeast Asia, an anti-communist ethos surfaced as the oppositional term for American Christianity.

The 1965 Hart Cellar Act, which removed the national origins quota and prioritized skilled immigrants, family unification, and "refugees from Communist-dominated countries," drew a sizable Christian immigrant flow from Cambodia, Korea, Taiwan, and Vietnam—the territories in which America had formerly established an imperial connection through foreign missions and policies. In a way, the 1965 Act enabled "reworking of the racialization" that gradually transformed the Yellow Peril into the model minority myth (Hsu 2015). The face of Asian immigration changed from the ghettoized laborers to the educated elites and skilled workers, who are fit for obtaining the "successful 'Asian' emphasis on family solidarity, hard work, and education" (Hsu 2015: 237). This was a transformation of the "victims of Communism in the Far East" into the model immigrants who can make "a substantial contribution to the spiritual and material strength of the free word and to the cause of a just and lasting peace" (156). Simultaneously, the institutionalization of Chinese studies in the United States signaled the acknowledgment of Chinese sovereignty, "albeit with the assumption that this would emulate American democracy and Christianity" (57). With an idea that Asian labor can contribute to the free market, Asian Americans became good immigrants—with communism debilitated and Christianity enhanced in the American public.

The dual functions of American Christianity—one that advocates family unification and resettlement programs, and the other that defines the ideological terms for assimilative and acceptable immigrants—have profoundly shaped Asian America, and America more broadly. The transnational formation of Asian migrants through religious

FIGURE 9.5 *Chinese war brides at religious class, Westminster Presbyterian Church in Minneapolis in 1950.* Source: *Photograph © Minnesota Historical Society/CORBIS/Corbis via Getty Images.*

connections under US imperialism cannot be solely explained through immigration policies. For instance, the multidirectional migration of Filipino nurses exemplifies how the exploitation of Asian immigration labor persists through excluding those who do not fall into the category of family cohesion policies (Choy 2003). From the generation of Filipino nurses through American medical missions to their "acceptance" into the country through the US Exchange Visitor Program, by exploiting cheap labor has sustained the Asian impact on America. Today, the same form of labor exploitation persists through the US treatment of the post-1980s Asian and Latina immigrant women as "flexible work force," who can contribute to American transnational industry through cheap labor (Lowe 1996).

Simultaneously, Evangelical Christianity disseminated in East and Southeast Asian territories, spread through a combination of US militarization and humanitarian aid (Yoo 2017). Despite power differentials, the relationship between Asia and America was enmeshed in a religious network. The mutual reinforcement of Christian ideals for Asian Americans—anti-communist, family-oriented, and industrial—thus was a transnational process, in which Asian laborers struggled to identify themselves as national subjects.

This equation of Christian ideals with national identity likewise shaped the spatial boundaries of citizenship for Asian Canadians (Coloma and Pon 2017). Displacement of Japanese Canadians through internment cannot be explained without the colonial cartography of post-Second World War Canada, which was inextricably linked to otherizing the First Nations peoples to subject them to Christian, English-revolving, and British ideals (Miki 2017: 305–7; Oikawa 2017: 103). This process simultaneously involved the disciplining of First Nations children through the Christian residential schools and the federal government's expulsion of Japanese Canadians (Oikawa 2017: 120). Marie Clements's play, "Burning Vision," explores the intricate connection between aboriginal and Asian American, by tracing the history of uranium mining from the First Nations lands of the Sahtu Dene for creating the materials of atomic bombing over Japan during the Second World War. As the play reflects, the myth of Christianization had not only arbitrarily defined First Nations people as unassimilative subjects who fall short of having internal territorial claims as the ideal Canadian citizens but also had resulted in the abominable result of the American international territorial claims, justified by war.

The case of Hmong Christians also exemplifies how indigeneity reflects the larger reality of Asian American Christianities beyond national category. While Hmong Americans constitute a relatively small Asian population in the United States, the resettlement of Hmong people in the 1980s tells us a unique history. An ethnic minority spread in China and South Asia, 45,000 Hmong people migrated to the United States as a result of the Vietnam War through the refugee programs that heavily relied on Christian agencies and church networks. Despite the government effort to create religiously neutral space for refugees, religious practices of Hmong people were seen as incompatible with the Protestant-based norms of religion and not recognized as legitimate religions that needed protection (Borja 2018). Through the dispersal policy that scattered the refugees into California, Wisconsin, and Minnesota, the Hmong community has experienced a rupture from their kin-based religious practices. Consequently, a sizable number of Hmong Americans have converted to Christianity through their entangled settlement connections. Alongside the Hmong American Christians, the cases of Kachin Baptists from Myanmar and Cambodian Christians are the understudied site where the clashes between assimilative and non-assimilative Asian religiously and the national belonging converge.

The Asian American Making of Christianities

Among diverse immigration groups, Christianity becomes a peculiar shared place that connects multiple generations and ethnic groups of Asian Americans. Through Christianity, the ideals of the civic sphere are imbued with defining terms of religion in America, the anxiety for Asian American subjects to assimilate to American public life has been perpetuated.

The two emerging congregation models for Asian American Christians—racially defined Asian American churches and multiethnic churches—reflect what Anne Anlin Cheng terms as the "Asian American hypochondria": "anxieties about the prospect of assimilation for Asian American subjects, caught between the assimilationist model (whereby minority culture are expected to adopt mainstream values or behavioral patterns and the pluralist model (whereby ethnic minority cultures are expected to value and maintain their culture of difference" (Cheng 2000: 69). The incessant demand for Asian Americans to navigate their "assimilating-but-racially-differentiated subjects" (69) has engendered a rupture between the historical formation of Asian America, through the Asian American movements, and the racial identification of Asian Americans today.

The role that Christianity plays in the struggle for Asian American assimilation to American public society has profoundly changed since the 1980s. Glenn Omatsu observes the ideological gap between those who partook in the Asian American activist history of the 1960s and 1970s, and the post-1965 neoconservatives whose religiosity is reshaped by the Reagan platform of struggling to "redefine the language of civil rights by attacking federal government 'entitlement' programs while criticizing the African American 'liberal establishment'" (1994: 84). Noting that the leading figure of the birth of the Asian American movement was Malcolm X, not Martin Luther King Jr., Omatsu explains how Reaganomics' "new mantle of patriotism and economic recovery" shifted the focus of Asian American challenges from liberation to racial identity and representation (57). Within the framework of the latter, which finds the *sine qua non* Asian American experience on racial terms subsequent to the civil rights movement, the questions of labor, religion, and nationhood relative to migration histories become less relevant.

A vast array of Asian American Christian discourse has been done in balance between ethnogenesis and ethnic-racial essentialism. In other words, the task of defining Asian American Christianities necessarily deals with the question of who are Asian Americans, especially in relation to the political identity that was first formed in the 1960s, and what does Christianity have to do with its history. The diverse status of Asian American Christians refuses to "elide significant internal differences within, between, and among different ethnicities or essentialize in other ways what it means to be a person of Asian descent" (Kao and Ilsup 2015: 5).

Moreover, locating the Asian American within the discourse of race inevitably leads to the challenge of substantiating Asian American experience through ambiguities of culture and identity (Choi 2019). The troubling task of designating "Asian American" as the unit of analysis is thus often followed by the problem of homogeneity, as the particularity of "Asian American" persists in ontologizing its identity to the universal: North America. Under this umbrella, various topics of "multi-" Asian American-ness emerge as another form of particularity within, whether divided by subgroups (i.e., "Japanese American," "Cambodian Californians," "Korean American evangelicals") or racialization (i.e., yellow, brown, hapa, blasian, adoptees). American-ness sustains within this multiplicity, preserved through its unchecked relationship with Christianity.

Sociologists tend to pay attention to the ways in which Asian Americans negotiate their religious, ethnic, and national identities. The recent studies on Indian American Christian show how generational differences among Indian American communities reflect the complexity of Christian identity (Kurien 2017). For example, the sense of ethno-religious belonging for the Mar Thoma Syrian Christians, the Indian denomination that traces its history back to the time of Saint Thomas in ancient Kerala, has been drastically changed by the younger generation of Christians. Whereas Christians comprise 3 percent of the population in India, Indian Christians constitute nearly 20 percent of the Indian American population. This brings change to what it means to be Christian, especially for the generation that is becoming more multicultural and multiethnic. Mar Thoma Syrian Christians no longer "use religion as the locus of their ethnic identity," but they tend to search for nondenominational and evangelical church communities that transcend ethnic boundaries. Christianity is no longer a given identity through heritage but a way of forming new identities and national belonging.

A case of Korean American evangelicals is another example that shows how participation of religious communities facilitates the civil incorporation of young Asian Americans. Evangelical, "born-again" identity reshapes Korean American space for civic action and, further, identity as US citizens (Ecklund 2008). Evangelical churches obfuscate the public and private binary, wherein Asian American individuals are encouraged to participate via volunteerism, community service, etc. and as such negotiate between faith and civic engagement. Christianity for Asian Americans becomes a mode of political engagement, mostly congregational and voluntary, creating an alternative space for negotiating their nationhood.

Distinct from the majority scholarship that accentuates the relationship between racial identities and Christian faith, Nami Kim and Wonhee Anne Joh's two edited volumes, *Critical Theology against US Militarism in Asia* (2016) and *Feminist Praxis Against U.S. Militarism* (2019), seek to reformulate the discourse by interrogating the Christian theological underpinnings in constructing the modern nation-state. The volumes pinpoint US militarism as the main problem that links North American transnational histories within which critical Asian American subjectivities are generated. As Joh and Kim argue, "much of US militarist expansionism has been rationalized through specifically Christian language that further buttresses notions like the while man's burden, manifest destiny, and the civilizing mission by the West" (2016: xiv). Joh and Kim call for "critical Christian theology," which "considers the task of Christian theology in relation to critical studies of US imperialism militarism in Asia" (xiv). For such projects, the questions are pointed toward the ways that American borders are made and remade through the amalgamation of Christian language and American exceptionalism: "The expansion of the US military-industrial complex and the global network of US military bases brought changes in racial relations and configurations both inside and outside US borders" (vi).

Translation of ideology (American exceptionalism) to religion (Christian language of sovereignty, martyrdom, triumphalism, suffering, etc.) thus becomes the main site for tracing the mapping of Asian America. For example, the language of martyrdom is deeply ingrained in shaping US militarism today, which is no longer understood as explicitly Christian but can still "signify Americanization and military service eligibility for citizenship for those of Asian ancestry" (Liew 2016: 44). Likewise, one constructive approach to Asian American scholarship is to think of Christianity as a method and analyze the ways that Christian language has been used in constructing the relationship between Asia and America (Chen 2010). When the relationship between Asia and America is treated as the main object of critique, the study of Christianity can be a reflexive method for identifying Christian language that undergirds American imperialism.

Religious trends among Asian Americans keep changing through the translational networks through families, missions, and business. South Asian Canadians and Americans today have formed what Jigna Desai has termed, "Brown Atlantic" identities, which are not reducible to South Asia and North America but expand to Europe and beyond. Many South Asian American Christians are involved in local and global missions, and committed to the idea that church must be a global community that transcends "the barriers of caste, race and language" (Kurien 2017: 74).

Another important component to this topic is its global connection with other religions. For example, Ju Hui Judy Han's "Shifting Geographies of Proximity" interrogates the transnational connections between Asia, Asian America, and Christianity (2018). Han juxtaposes evangelical Christian missions with Islam, arguing how the Korean evangelical pursuit of world evangelization and "Islam missions" was popularized in South Korea, the United States, and Canada, "touted as both a religious necessity and a geopolitical priority" in fortifying the territorial claims of the US empire (Han 2018: 197–8). That Korean-led world evangelism targeted the Muslim majority territory occupied by US troops, which was justified by "conjuring the specter of Islam as geopolitical threat and global competitor" (198), illustrates how globalization of American Christianity creates another expression of Orientalizing Islam (Joshi 2006). This case shows the importance of conceptualizing religion and understanding how its boundaries change through multidirectional and transnational encounters. Evangelical missions today reflect the fluidity of Christianity and the impact of American hegemony on a global scale. Christianity for Asian America(n) not only forms inclusion and exclusion but also creates expressions of difference.

Conclusion

From the Asian exclusion immigration histories to the international enterprise of American expansion, Christianity has been integral to the formation of Asian America. For its indispensable role in constructing North America, Asian American Christianities, while hardly qualifies as an essentialized entity, deserve our attention. This chapter has highlighted the dual function of Christianity as an analytic framework for studying Asian American Christianities. Christianity can function as an instrument for perpetuating

156   **CHRISTIANITY IN NORTH AMERICA**

the American dominance over the marginalized, and Christianity that can function as a method for unravelling its religious history from American history.

As noted by Asian American historians, studying Asian American history requires unearthing the mythical glory of American exceptionalism. This chapter has argued that the study of Christianity has a unique role in such a task. If Asian American subjects "retain precisely the memories of imperialism that the U.S. nation seeks to forget" (Lowe 1996: 117), Christianity is an inescapable reflection of its memory. If the very term Asian America is "an evocative reminder of state-authorized xenophobia and state-sanctioned racism" (Schlund-Vials 2017), the critical study of Christianity demands a reevaluation of the intertwined histories of Asian America and Asian American Christianities. If the "making" of Asian America signals the larger world order of modern history, Christianity entails remaking its historical relationship to world history.

Asian Americans are both the changing faces of American Christianity and the embodiment of American imperial interests and moral dilemma. That Christianity is the largest religious group among Asian Americans today (42 percent), therefore, is not only an index for the changing demographics of American religions but also a medium for questioning where the problem of the color line is drawn for the American public today.

Further Reading and Online Resources

Hsu M.Y. (2015), *The Good Immigrants: How the Yellow Peril Became the Model Minority*, Princeton, NJ: Princeton University Press.
Kao G.Y. and I. Ahn (2016), *Asian American Christian Ethics: Voices, Methods, Issues*, Waco, TX: Baylor University Press.
Lee E. (2015), *The Making of Asian America: A History*, New York: Simon & Schuster.
Lowe L. (2015), *The Intimacies of Four Continents*, Durham, NC: Duke University Press.
Okihiro G.Y. (2015), *American History Unbound: Asians and Pacific Islanders*, Oakland: University of California Press.

References

American Federation of Labor, Herman Gutstadt, Samuel Gompers, and Asiatic Exclusion League (1902), "Meat vs. Rice: American Manhhod Against Asiatic Coolieism, Which Shall Survive?," San Francisco: American Federation of Labor and printed as Senate document 137.
Azuma E. (2008), *Between Two Empires: Race, History, and Transnationalism in Japanese America*, Oxford: Oxford University Press.
Blankenship A.M. (2016), *Christianity, Social Justice, and the Japanese American Incarceration during World War II*, Chapel Hill: University of North Carolina Press.
Borja M. (2018), "'The New Way': How American Refugee Policies Changed Hmong Religious Life," *The American Historian*, November. Available online: https://www.oah. org/tah/issues/2018/november/the-new-way-how-american-refugee-policies-changed-hmong-religious-life/ (accessed November 14, 2020).

ASIAN AMERICANS AND CHRISTIANITY IN NORTH AMERICA

Carnes T. and F. Yang (2004), *Asian American Religions: The Making and Remaking of Borders and Boundaries*, New York: New York University Press.

Chang G.H. (2015), *Fateful Ties*, Cambridge, MA: Harvard University Press.

Chen C. and R. Jeung, eds. (2012), *Sustaining Faith Traditions: Race, Ethnicity, and Religion among the Latino and Asian American Second Generation*, New York: New York University Press.

Chen K.H. (2010), *Asia as Method: Toward Deimperialization*, Durham, NC: Duke University Press.

Cheng A.A. (2000), *The Melancholy of Race: Psychoanalysis, Assimilation, and Hidden Grief*, New York: Oxford University Press.

Chiang M. (2009), *The Cultural Capital of Asian American Studies: Autonomy and Representation in the University*, New York: New York University Press.

Choi K.J. (2019), *Disciplined by Race: Theological Ethics and the Problem of Asian American Identity*, Eugene, OR: Wipf and Stock.

Choy C.C. (2003), *Empire of Care: Nursing and Migration in Filipino American History*, Durham, NC: Duke University Press.

Ecklund E.H. (2008), *Korean American Evangelicals: New Models for Civic Life*, New York: Oxford University Press.

Han J.H.J. (2018), "Shifting Geographies of Proximity: Korean-Led Evangelical Christian Missions and the US Empire," in C. McGranahan and J.F. Collins (eds.), *Ethnographies of U.S. Empire*, 194–213, Durham, NC: Duke University Press.

Hong J.H. (2019), *Opening the Gates to Asia: A Transpacific History of How America Repealed Asian Exclusion*, Chapel Hill: University of North Carolina Press.

"How Great Is This 'Yellow Peril'?" (1900), *The New York Times*, August 2. Available online: https://www.nytimes.com/1900/08/02/archives/how-great-is-this-yellow-peril.html (accessed November 14, 2020).

Hsu M.Y. (2008), "Transnationalism and Asian American Studies as a Migration-Centered Project," *Journal of Asian American Studies*, 11 (2): 185–97.

Hsu M.Y. (2015), *The Good Immigrants: How the Yellow Peril Became the Model Minority*, Princeton, NJ: Princeton University Press.

Hunt M.H. (1983), *The Making of a Special Relationship: The United States and China to 1914*, New York: Columbia University Press.

Jean Yu-Wen Shen W. and T. Chen (2010), *Asian American Studies Now: A Critical Reader*, Piscataway, NJ: Rutgers University Press.

Jeung R., K. Umemoto, H. Dong, E. Mar, L.H. Tsuchitani, and A. Pan (2019), *Mountain Movers: Student Activism & the Emergence of Asian American Studies*, Los Angeles: UCLA Asian American Studies Center.

Joshi K.Y. (2006), *New Roots in America's Sacred Ground: Religion, Race, and Ethnicity in Indian America*, New Brunswick, NJ: Rutgers University Press.

Kao G.Y. and I. Ahn (2015), *Asian American Christian Ethics: Voices, Methods, Issues*, Waco, TX: Baylor University Press.

Kim H.J. (2016), "Asian American Christianity," in G.T. Kurian and M.A. Lamport (eds.), *Encyclopedia of Christianity in the United States*, vol. 5, 137–45, Lanham, MD: Rowman & Littlefield.

Kurien P.A. (2017), *Ethnic Church Meets Megachurch: Indian American Christianity in Motion*, New York: New York University Press.

Lee E. (2003), *At America's Gates: Chinese Immigration during the Exclusion Era, 1882–1943*, Chapel Hill: University of North Carolina Press.

Lee E. (2015), *The Making of Asian America: A History*, New York: Simon & Schuster.

Lee J.H.X., J.N. Iwamura, F. Matsuoka, E. Yee, and R. Nakasone (2015), *Asian American Religious Cultures*, 2 vols., Santa Barbara, CA: ABC-CLIO.

Liew T.-S. (2016), "Militarism, Masculinism, and Martyrdom: Conditional Citizenship for (Asian) Americans," in N. Kim and W.A. Joh (eds.), *Critical Theology Against US Militarism in Asia: Decolonization and Deimperialization,* New York: Palgrave Macmillan.

Liu M., K. Geron, and T.A.M. Lai (2008), *The Snake Dance of Asian American Activism: Community, Vision, and Power,* Lanham, MD: Lexington Books.

Lowe L. (1996), *Immigrant Acts: On Asian American Cultural Politics,* Durham, NC: Duke University Press Books.

Lowe L. (2015), *The Intimacies of Four Continents,* Durham, NC: Duke University Press.

Maeda D. (2011), *Rethinking the Asian American Movement,* American Social and Political Movements of the Twentieth Century series, New York: Routledge.

Miki R. (2017), "Altered States: Global Currents, the Spectral Nation, and the Production of "Asian Canadian," in R. Sintos Coloma and G. Pon (eds.), *Asian Canadian Studies Reader,* Toronto: University of Toronto Press.

Oikawa M. (2017), "Cartographies of Violence: Creating Carceral Spaces and Expelling Japanese Canadians from the Nation," in R. Sintos Coloma and G. Pon (eds.), *Asian Canadian Studies Reader,* Toronto: University of Toronto Press.

Okihiro G.Y. (2015), *American History Unbound: Asians and Pacific Islanders,* Oakland: University of California Press.

Okihiro G.Y. (2016), *Third World Studies: Theorizing Liberation,* Durham, NC: Duke University Press.

Omatsu G. (1994), "The Four Prisons' and the Movements of Liberation: Asian American Activism from the 1960s to the 1990s," in K. Aguilar-San Juan (ed.), *The State of Asian America: Activism and Resistance In the 1990s,* 298–330, Boston: South End Press.

Roland Sintos C. and G. Pon, eds. (2017), *Asian Canadian Studies Reader,* Toronto: University of Toronto Press.

Schlund-Vials C.J., ed. (2017), *Flashpoints for Asian American Studies,* Afterword by V.T. Nguyen, New York: Fordham University Press.

Shanks C. (2001), *Immigration and the Politics of American Sovereignty, 1890–1990,* Ann Arbor: University of Michigan Press.

Snow J.C. (2007), *Protestant Missionaries, Asian Immigrants, and Ideologies of Race in America, 1850–1924.* New York: Routledge.

Tchen J.K.W. and D. Yeats (2014), *Yellow Peril! An Archive of Anti-Asian Fear,* New York: Verso.

Tseng T. and V. Nakka-Cammauf (2009), *Asian American Christianity Reader,* Castro Valley, CA: Pacific Asian American & Canadian Christian Education Project and the Institute for the Study of Asian American Christianity.

Wei W. (1993), *The Asian American Movement: A Social History,* Philadelphia: Temple University Press.

Wenger T. (2017), *Religious Freedom: The Contested History of an American Ideal,* Chapel Hill: University of North Carolina Press.

Wong K.S. (2009), *Americans First: Chinese Americans and the Second World War,* Cambridge, MA: Harvard University Press.

Yoo D. (2010), *Contentious Spirits: Religion in Korean American History, 1903–1945,* Stanford, CA: Stanford University Press.

Yoo W. (2017), *American Missionaries, Korean Protestants, and the Changing Shape of World Christianity, 1884–1965,* New York: Routledge, Taylor & Francis Group.

10

Latinx Christianities in North America

Lloyd Barba

The history of Latinx Christianities in North America is one of global and hemispheric crossings. The encounters in the Americas between European colonizers and Indigenous inhabitants over five hundred years ago should prompt us to consider how such meetings may very well qualify, as one historian noted, "the most astonishing encounter in our history [...] [w]e do have the same sense of radical difference in the 'discovery' of other continents and peoples" (Todorov 1997: 4). Over the next three to four centuries, European (mostly Spanish and Portuguese) colonialization spread rapidly throughout Latin America. From the 1500s to approximately the 1800s, Spanish colonizers imposed new language, institutions, and religion on the Indigenous populations as well as the millions of enslaved Africans brought across the Atlantic, and the mixed-race offspring from all these groups. A complex system of labor, sexuality, race (caste), taxation, law, and religion have since defined social and political relations in Latin America.

A Euro-American gaze at Latin America continues well into this day and has largely been shaped by notions of race and religion. The United States' thinking about Latin Americans has largely informed how Latinxs in the United States are (not) welcomed. Until the 1930s, the vast majority of "experts" of Latin America leveraged arguments that were racially and religiously determined. The former rested on the idea that Latin Americans possessed too much "nonwhite blood" and former on the belief that they were backwards Catholics lacking the virtues of the romanticized Protestant work ethic. From the 1940s to the 1970s historians advanced "modernization theories" and in the 1960s coupled these theories with a "dependency theory" wherein the problems of Latin America and its diasporas owed mostly to forces of colonization and economic globalizations (Chasteen 2006: 21–3). These long-held views about Latin America have largely persisted.

Popular Catholicism thrives across the Latinx Americas both in tension and complementarily to the institutional Roman Catholic Church. Further, as a combination of Iberian Catholicism (especially of a pre-*Tridentine* sensibility), Indigenous spiritualities, and West African religions, Latin American Catholicism looms large in the public (e.g., pilgrimages, feast days) and private spheres (e.g., home altars) (Espín 1997: 117–19). But, while nearly 90 percent of Latin Americans identified as Catholic in the mid-twentieth century, today the numbers are closer to 70 percent, with Pentecostal and Charismatic traditions having made large inroads (Thornton 2018: 858). Nearly a quarter of Latinxs in the United States is a former Catholic, according to a 2014 study (Pew Research Center 2014). An even more recent survey found that Latinx Catholics in the United States, at 47 percent Catholic, have now fallen below the 50 percent majority mark (Pew Research Center 2019). The implications and politics of conversion from Catholicism to Protestantism have only recently begun to be teased out (Mulder, Ramos, and Martí 2017).

The instability of Latin American economies and political regimes have been a major push factor for many to migrate. This brief article will focus on Latinx populations that have arrived in the United States from other points of origin within North America. After discussing the case of Mexicans, who account for the largest of any Latinx population and consequently many of the generalizations about Latinxs, this chapter will turn to populations from the islands of Puerto Rico, Cuba, and the Dominican Republic as well as from El Salvador. The limitation to these five Latinx national populations allows for comparison to the 2014 findings by the Pew Research Center (shown in Figure 10.1). The order of the groups below reflects a chronology of their historical presence and immigration in the United States as well as their numbers from greatest to least. To conclude, this chapter considers how Salvadorans (and Central Americans more generally) are changing the Canadian religious landscape.

Mexicans

The conquest of Mexico at the hands of the Spaniards led by Hernán Cortes was summarily followed by their aggressive religious pacification of the Native peoples through violence and forced conversion. Over the next several centuries biological mixing (much of it through physical violence) resulted in a large class of *mestizos* (mixed blood) in New Spain. The term *mestizaje* would later inform an ideological consciousness of Latin Americans. Such a racial logic of mixing would be encoded into the most ubiquitous religious symbol in the Americas: The Virgin of Guadalupe. The place, symbolism, and language associated with the 1531 apparition of Guadalupe to Juan Diego, is an example of Catholicism mixing (however, unevenly) with Indigenous cosmic spiritualities. Since its fight for independence, Mexico has faced revolutions and political struggles, all of which have generally invoked the power and imagery of Guadalupe. The cultural affinity between nationalism and Catholicism in Mexico is hard to overstate. The fruit of the nation's religio-racial project would in part be borne out

Religious Affiliation, by Hispanic Origin Group

% of Hispanics in each Hispanic origin group who belong to each religious group

	Mexican	Puerto Rican	Cuban	Salvadoran	Dominican
Catholic	61	45	49	42	59
Protestant	18	29	17	37	21
Evangelical	13	22	8	32	16
Mainline	5	8	8	5	6
Unaffiliated	17	20	26	15	16
Other	4	6	8	5	3
Don't know	*	0	*	1	1
	100	100	100	100	100
N	1,843	540	287	228	272

Source: Pew Research Center survey of Hispanic adults, May 24-July 28, 2013. Based on FORM12 and FORMNCO. Figures may not add to 100% due to rounding.

PEW RESEARCH CENTER

FIGURE 10.1 *Religious affiliation, by Hispanic origin group.* Source: *Pew Research Center.*

in the United States where devotion to Guadalupe long preceded the United States' annexation of the southwest.

The racialization and missionization of Mexican Americans stand out as a unique chapter in the United States' religious history. This owes to the fact that Mexicans in the southwest were both an annexed population as well as an immigrant one. As such, Anglo-Americans imputed to them an outsider status after the Treaty de Guadalupe Hidalgo, which ended the US–Mexico War in 1848. Mexicans throughout the southwest would face a "second *mestizaje*" (Elizondo 2000: 13–16).

Some scholars have argued the idea that American expansion was firmly anchored in the notion of Manifest Destiny, which was built on a racist and Protestant logic about the superiority of one race over another. Americans, the argument continues, relegated Mexicans to an inferior "caste-like status" (Gutierrez 1995: 13). Mainline Protestants took charge of missionization efforts, but the undertaking to "make good citizens out of the Mexicans" was by no means one borne out of consensus. While more sympathetic missionaries acted according to a "pious paternalism," others objected to evangelization on the grounds of Mexican inferiority (Espinosa 2014; Machado

2003; Martinez 2006: 28). The pervasiveness of nonwhite European forms of Catholicism among Mexicans heightened the apparent need for missionization. The statistical impact of Presbyterian, Baptist, and Methodist missions in the southwest was only minimal (Banker 1993; Barton 2006; Deutsch 1987; Machado 2003; Martinez 2006; Yohn 1995)

Historically, the overwhelming majority (over 90 percent) of Mexicans have identified as Catholic; the two identities at times have seemed inextricably bound together. Anglo-American Catholics and Protestants alike gave credence to the "Black Legends," myths that advanced the notion that the Spanish-Catholic Empire and its former colonies in Latin America were rapacious and corrupt compared to benevolent Protestant-based British or even French Catholic colonies.

The United States annexed the southwestern states during a period of intense anti-Catholicism throughout the country. These sentiments tainted how Americans viewed the incorporation of the Mexican Catholic population of the southwest. Some missionaries decried the ruinous state of Mexicans as "priest-ridden." Others, seeing the actual paucity of priests serving communities, surmised that in the absence of a robust clergy that many of the southwest's inhabitants had taken Catholicism into their own hands and thus created an even more corrupt version. These sentiments notwithstanding, Anglo missionaries hoped that French and Irish Catholic missionaries could disabuse Mexican Catholics of their folkways (Mora 2011). Later, Protestants in California romanticized the Spanish (Euro) past of the missions at the expense of erasing "Mexican" characteristics (Sagarena 2014). Nevertheless, Mexican Catholicism would expand throughout the twentieth century in numbers as well as in theological and social expressions.

Mexican immigrants in the early twentieth century found work in railroad and agriculture as they fled the long Mexican Revolution (1910–20) and its aftermath. As the century carried on, Mexicans would constitute the overwhelming majority of farmworkers in industrial agricultural, a system rife with exploitation. Labor reform for farmworkers would highlight how Mexicans fused religion and activism, as seen most clearly in the protests of the United Farm Workers led by Cesar Chavez and Dolores Huerta of the Chicano Civil Rights era (Watt 2010). Figure 10.2 captures how their farm labor reforms summoned religious imagery.

For a long time scholars overlooked the crucial importance of religious activism during the Chicano Movement of the 1960s and 1970s. Historians have now shown, for example, how Chavez's mobilization of Catholic Social Doctrine (drawing on the Papal Encyclical Rerum Novarum, 1891) would inspire other grassroots religiopolitical movements such as Católicos Por La Raza, PADRES, Hermanas, and Mexican Catholic participation in the Sanctuary movement as best exemplified in the ministry of Father Luis Olivares (Espinosa, Elizondo, and Miranda 2005; Garcia 2018; Medina 2005). Today, Mexican Catholics represent a vast generational expanse from first generation to over five generations of their piety in practice in the United States (Matovina 2012). The election of the first Latin American pope has caused what many commentators have called the "Francis effect," that is, a measurable difference in the positive view of the Catholic Church. With Latinos comprising 40 percent of United States Catholics

FIGURE 10.2 *Cesar Chavez and Robert F. Kennedy take Communion.* Source: *Michael Rougier / Getty Images.*

and a high-profile papal visit in 2015, many still hope for the Francis effect to improve goodwill for the church domestically.

No single missionary effort would eventually alter the composition of Latinx Protestantism more than the Azusa Street Revival. Many Latinx Pentecostal denominations can lay historical claim to the heyday of the revival and its aftermath in Los Angeles as the genesis of their movement (Espinosa 2014; Ramírez 2015; Sánchez-Walsh 2003). To a smaller extent than has been done in Latinx Catholic history, historians have begun to uncover the often-forgotten role that Protestants have played in social activism. The case of Latino Mennonites represents a fine example of the negotiation of Mexican and Latina/o identity and determination (Hinojosa 2014). Whereas Catholics dominated in previous generations, today 61 percent of Mexican adults in the United States identify as Catholic, 18 percent as Protestant (in which 13 percent evangelical were counted). At 5 percent, Mainline Protestantism is the minority Christian affiliation for Mexican-Americans (Pew Research Center 2014).

Puerto Ricans

A decade before the fall of Tenochtitlan, the Spanish arrived on the shores of Puerto Rico and by royal and religious decree of the *Requerimiento* subjected the native Taínos of the island to the crown and Catholicism. The Spanish relied upon the island colony for agricultural cultivation, and to accomplish this they extracted intensive labor from enslaved Africans and Taínos and their descendants. In such a case of population mixing, it may be more appropriate to speak of a "mulataje," that is, a racial mixture of people (such as Indians and Africans) classified in the colonial *castas* system as "mulattoes." Catholicism in Puerto Rico, unlike that in Mexico, represents a more robust expression of Iberian Catholicism since the Spanish conquest of the island had nearly completely wiped out the entire population. Throughout the centuries of occupation there, the Catholic Church lacked sufficient clerical staffing to minister to the rural and highland populations of the nation, resulting largely in low levels of catechetical instruction and an ambivalent relationship with the official institutions. Many Puerto Rican elites and leaders in the nineteenth century had been educated in European universities and turned to popular religious philosophies of the day including Spiritism, Theosophy, and Masonry. A weakened Catholic Church lost its official state status after the United States' annexation of Puerto Rico (Dolan and Vidal 1994).

More relevant to the diaspora of Puerto Ricans in the mainland, however, is the fact that a majority of Catholics practiced popular Catholicism in which the symbols and imagery supplanted ties to the institutional church. A disconnect between the clergy and laity was palpable. Consider that until the 1960s Catholic Bishops of Puerto Rico were Euro-Americans, phenomena that prefigured their relationship on the mainland (Rivera-Pagan 2006: 150). The Jones Act of 1917 extended citizenship to Puerto Ricans, resulting in an uptick in migration. The earliest waves of Puerto Rican migration to the mainland began just as the United States had passed a series of restrictive national immigration laws in the 1920s. The ease of airplane travel and expansion of jobs after the Second World War facilitated even more migration from the island to New York City as well as in cities along the East Coast and Midwest.

The mixed racial status of Puerto Ricans did not map neatly on to existing notions of race in the United States nor did their language and Catholic culture fit into Euro-American churches. As opposed to waves of Europeans who arrived on Ellis Island in the late nineteenth and early twentieth centuries—and also enjoyed the accommodations of national parishes as a method to foster ethnic solidarity—Puerto Ricans faced years of culturally asphyxiating assimilation policies. One example is the Catholic Church's refusal to implement the ethnic-parish paradigm in Puerto Rican neighborhoods. The case of large-scale Americanization efforts by Cardinal Spellman in New York City for years characterized the attitude of American Catholicism toward Puerto Ricans, especially in the pre-Vatican II era (Dolan and Vidal 1994; Vidal 2004).

Shortly after the Spanish-American War, missionaries hashed out an organized effort (or "comity" agreements) in which they divided the island into regions where certain denomination would evangelize. Presbyterians, American Baptists, Congregationalists, Methodists, and Episcopalians all rushed in to evangelize and offer charitable aid. They also set out to train local religious leader by establishing El Seminario Evangélico de Puerto Rico in 1919. The missionaries only had limited success in reaching out to the rural poor. Later the Christian Church (Disciples), the Christian and Missionary Alliance, the United Brethren in Christ, and the Evangelical Lutheran Church would team up in

FIGURE 10.3 *Sister Teresa at a Pentecostal street service.* Source: *Library of Congress.*

these efforts (Contreras-Flores 2015; Vidal 2004). Puerto Rican migration increased just as Pentecostalism gained steam in the United States and launched missions in Puerto Rico. Juan Lugo is recognized as founding Pentecostalism in Puerto Rico in 1916. Pentecostalism grew rapidly and its presence came to rival Mainline growth on the island to the extent that the terms evangelical Protestant and Pentecostal are almost interchangeable on the island (Contreras-Flores 2015; Espinosa 2014). Pentecostalism gained a major foothold in New York City beginning in the 1980s and the northeast today is a hub of Puerto Rican and Latino Pentecostalism. Current statistics indicate that Puerto Ricans in the United States maintain religious affiliations as follows: 45 percent Catholic, 23 percent evangelical/Protestant, and 8 percent Mainline Protestant (Pew Research Center 2014).

Cubans

Like Puerto Rico, Cuba—immediately following the Spanish-American War—witnessed an influx of Protestant missionaries, intent on implementing Americanization projects via Protestant missions. The Spanish had imposed Catholic beliefs upon all inhabitants for most of the island's history. But by 1898 Catholicism amounted to a severely "weakened" institution, owing largely to an understaffing of clergy beyond Havana, the rise and self-secularization of the sugar plantation in the eighteenth and nineteenth centuries, and the perception of the church as an enemy of independence. The massive plantations further introduced a variation of West African religious traditions (slaves in 1841, for example, accounted for 44 percent of the population) and largely kept them shielded from Catholic missionary enterprises. Although Cuba gained political independence from the United States in 1902, it can be well argued that for most of the early twentieth century the state largely remained financially beholden to corporate US interests in the production of sugar. From 1902 to 1959, Protestant missionaries evangelized throughout the island in hopes of undoing the influence of Catholicism and Santeria, which is a blended religion that draws from West African Yoruba and Catholicism. But different from any Latinx immigrants described in this chapter, Cubans would arrive in the United States largely as exiles (Pérez 1994).

The small population of Cubans in the United States before Castro's ascendance to power would be joined by over half a million Cubans beginning in 1959. Because of the tense relationship between the United States and Cuba since the 1960s, Cubans comprise a unique ethno-religious history of exile, diaspora, and immigration. These exiles (the targets of Castro's regime) largely comprised a wave of wealthier, white, highly educated, and Catholic immigrants into the United States. Because of their status, they quickly established themselves financially in places such as Miami. Given

FIGURE 10.4 *Shrine of Our Lady of Charity in Miami.* Source: *Bohao Zhao / Wikimedia Commons.*

antecedent patterns of Mexicans and Puerto Ricans, it should be of little surprise by now that the US clergy attempted to deal with the influx of Cubans by implementing an Americanization project and refusing to realize an official ethnic parish model. Many Cubans immigrated knowing that they might never return, and because of the relatively strong numbers and socioeconomic status of migrants in the 1960s, Cubans successfully and rather swiftly transplanted educational, civic, and fraternal organizations (Pérez 1994).

The second major exodus in the 1980s fundamentally altered the composition of Cuban Christianity in the United States. When Castro opened the port of Mariel to anyone who could find transportation to leave, no fewer than 120,000 Cubans fled. The media spectacle took special notice of the large number of exiles who fled on portable life rafts. Because they left from the port of Mariel, this wave of exiles came to be known as Marielitos. Generally speaking, Marielitos represented much of what those from the first wave of exiles did not: working class, nonwhite, and many intellectuals, artists, and gays who lived under harsh repression in Castro's regime. During Castro's nearly two decades of power up to that point, many had come to age during his atheistic regime, which made little room for the Catholic Church in society. Many Marielitos practiced Santeria and other Afro-Cuban religions. Their stark social, racial, class, and religious differentiation made for a cold welcome into the United States as well as in Miami where the earlier wave of exiles had established comfortable roots (De la Torre 2004a; Pérez 1994).

The disparities between the more prosperous Cubans in the United States compared to those on the island created a self-understanding among the exiled community in which they thought of themselves as the children of God. The difference lay in those who were "aqui" (here) and proved successful versus those who remained "allá" (there) and continued to struggle. Such a bifurcated identity resulted in a romanticized Cuba "de ayer" (of yesterday), a version that only exists in exilic imagination and an effort to re-create elements of Cuban cultural and religious life in the United States (De la Torre 2004b: 78; Suárez 2006: 155). In the Miami area, where up to 65 percent of the Cuban exile community lives, one can readily detect how religious identities are brought to bear upon national ones. The Cuban national shrine of our Virgin of Charity is a case in point in which nationalism is interwoven into the material and spiritual dimensions of sacred space (Tweed 1997). In nearby Hialeah, we can further detect Cuban-based religion in the practice of Santeria, made public by the series of court cases culminating in 1993, which found the city to be infringing upon the constitutional rights of practitioners. Santeria's saints, beliefs, and rituals (such as animal sacrifice) were quickly sensationalized and exoticized by the American public (De la Torre 2004b). At the time of the revolution, Protestants accounted for only 6 percent of Cubans on the Island. They would not shape the religious contours of the United States in any comparable way to Catholics. Recent surveys indicate that slightly over 49 percent are Catholic, 17 percent evangelical/Mainline Protestant, and 26 percent unaffiliated (Pew Research Center 2014). These numbers certainly are not fixed given the secrecy surrounding the practice of Santeria.

Dominicans

Santo Domingo, the first Spanish settlement in the Americas, long served as the nexus for Spanish colonies. It is also home to Nuestra Señora de la Altagracia Catedral Primada de America, the first Cathedral in the Americas. The city's name itself is a reminder of Spanish religious colonization. Just prior to what would amount to an exodus from the island, the nation's long-time dictator Rafael Leonidas Trujillo had been assassinated in 1961, leaving the country in political and economic turmoil. The field of immigration changed vastly for Dominicans after 1965 when US immigration law would allow for greater numbers to arrive. The vast majority settled in New York City among African Americans and Puerto Ricans. The religious impact of Dominicans in the United States

FIGURE 10.5 *Nuestra Señora de la Altagracia Catedral Primada de America.* Source: *Mario Roberto Durán Ortiz / Wikimedia Commons.*

would mostly go without notice until the last third of the twentieth century. For the sake of comparison, consider that in 1960 fewer than 10,000 Dominicans lived in the United States and by 1980 that number would rise to over 170,000 and top one-million by 2000 after the second wave of migrants.

Catholicism is the official religion of the island nation, per a concordant recognized between the Vatican and the state. Like the abovementioned islands, the Dominican Republic witnessed rounds of Protestant missionary efforts, notably from the African Methodist Episcopal Church (Davidson 2015). But not surprisingly upwards to 90 percent of Dominicans identify as Catholic, and they brought with them national devotions to the Virgin of Altagracia (the patroness of the nation) celebrated annually in the United States on January 21. Devotion to Altagracia can be traced back to the late sixteenth century (Figueroa 2009). San Lazaro, too, carries special importance for the diaspora community. Such devotions are detectable in Miami, Providence, Boston, and Philadelphia. In places such as New York, Catholic ties have stayed intact in large part due to the *transnationalism* of Dominicans living "between two islands." Further, many have faced a similar racialization that Puerto Ricans have due to the islands mulataje legacy and the persistence of Spanish in these transnational communities. At 59 percent, Dominican are only second to Mexicans in the highest percentage of Latino national groups who claim Catholicism. Sixteen percent claim Pentecostalism/evangelicalism while Mainline traditions account for only 6 percent (Pew Research Center 2014).

Salvadorans

Since the Spanish conquest of Cuzcatlan in 1525 of the area that now comprises El Salvador, Catholicism has decidedly shaped Christianity in the Central American nation. Catholics there maintain a special devotion to the country's patron saint El Divino Salvador (the Divine Savior), celebrated since the colonial period and in the United States today acts as a symbol of transnationalism. The devotion to Our Lady of Peace, too, has served as an active symbol of transnationalism.

After independence in 1821, elites of the new nation of El Salvador formed large plantations (*fincas*) relying on the poor populations to carry out the intensive labor. When workers launched large-scale protests in the 1930s, land owners urged the government to react, which resulted in one of the country's most notorious episodes known as *La Matanza* in which the military slaughtered tens of thousands of workers and families over a period of six months. The rest of the century was marked by widespread violence at the hands of the government seeking to suppress revolutionary forces. The Civil War of the 1980s would result in thousands of Salvadorans seeking safety in Mexico and especially the United States, the very country that financed the government's anti-insurgency efforts and trained the military to carry out brutal repression techniques. The conditions that the United States helped to create and maintain pushed migrants out of the country, revealing some of the decade's worst international scandals (García 2006).

Salvadorans in the United States number around 2.3 million, constituting the largest immigrant national group from Central America. While Salvadorans did not begin to arrive in large numbers until the 1980s, by 1950 they outnumbered Mexicans in San Francisco, as the Second World War industries brought in business elites and shipyard workers. The conditions of migration and events in El Salvador, however, would largely shape the perception of Salvadoran immigrants in the United States as entrants that have arrived without documents and from contexts of violence. Because mass Salvadoran immigration into the United States is not only rather recent but also ongoing, they constitute the fifth largest national foreign-born population and one of the fastest growing.

The large-scale arrival of Central Americans (primarily Salvadorans) to the United States created the conditions for the rise of the Sanctuary movement out of Southside Presbyterian Church in Tucson, Arizona. The Sanctuary movement—rooted in Mainline Protestant activism—paved the way for those of other religious traditions to declare their houses of worship to be sacred sites where they could harbor individuals that the state would otherwise deport. Forms of the Sanctuary movement prevail today (Barba and Castillo-Ramos 2019). Church leaders in the 1980s would be among the first and most vocal critics of US involvement in Central America. The crisis quickly became visible on the border. Clergy took notice and began to act, prophetically denouncing the role of the United States abroad and at home.

FIGURE 10.6 *Replica of banners at Southside Presbyterian Church, Tucson, Arizona.*
Source: *Author.*

From Catholicism to Pentecostalism, Salvadoran Christianity appears to be more socially oriented. Compared to other Latinx groups, Salvadorans in the United States view the church more "as a service organization that seeks to remedy material and economic needs" (Menjívar 2003). Catholics are not alone in having a more holistic view of the church in society, as Pentecostals, increasingly so, have begun to view and preach social engagement as part of their mission on Earth to such a degree that the practice of social engagement constitutes a "ritual" (Bueno 2015).

Pentecostalism has arisen in El Salvador almost entirely as a transnational phenomenon. The largest church in El Salvador, Misión Cristiana Elim (MCE), founded in 1977, is a case in point. Under the direction of Mario Vega, the church followed closely the "cell church" model of congregational growth, patterned by Korean megachurch pastor David Yonggi Cho. In 1985 MCE adapted the church model and by 1988 claimed a membership of 20,000. By 2002 it recorded over 150,000 members. Depending on how one enumerates a congregation, MCE can boast the second largest congregation in the world (second only to Yonggi Cho's Yoido Full Gospel Church in Seoul). The growth of Pentecostalism coincided with the nation's civil war, and refugees contributed vastly to the growth of Salvadoran Pentecostalism abroad. MCE keeps a coherent network of cell churches in a hierarchy of pastorates, zones, and districts. Where radio once played a primary role in communication, internet social media and video services have taken over as main media dissemination. MCE's unique cell church model shrinks the normal time for ordination and its highly migratory congregation can plant new "cells" abroad, as the organization has no particular mission plan; it truly follows migrants, equipping the "priesthood" of all believers. In every place where Salvadorans have migrated in substantial numbers (e.g., Los Angeles, San Francisco, Phoenix, New York City, Washington, DC), almost without fail one can locate an MCE church or some type of Pentecostal church (Danielson 2015; Vásquez and Gómez 2003; Wadkins 2017).

In such metropolises we also see robust national expressions of national identity articulated through Catholicism. The feast in honor of the Day of the Salvadoran in Los Angeles, for example, offers a case in point of how nationalism is conveyed through religious symbols. Since 1998, the annual celebration is ushered in by a replica of the national image of El Divino Salvador. Carried in a vehicle from El Salvador to Los Angeles, the statue's journey symbolizes the trek many Salvadorans undergo through Guatemala, Mexico, and into the United States. In the *bajada* (that is, the lowering), the statue descends into a crowd of devotees. While the Virgin Peace occupies a prominent place in Salvadoran devotion, El Divino Salvador engenders a sense of transnational solidarity. The overt Catholic imagery, however, discourages many Pentecostals and Evangelicals from participation in the festivities (Reedy Solano 2004), and in Salvadoran contexts Protestants comprise no small portion. A 2014 study indicated that 42 percent of Salvadorans in the United States identify as Catholic and 37 percent identify as Protestants—among which 32 percent are evangelical/Pentecostal and 5 percent are Mainline (Pew Research Center 2014).

Conclusion: Transnational Latinidad, Multiple Embeddedness, and Canada

The tensions that arise between the devout during the festivities of the Day of the Salvadoran remind us of the stark realities of transnationalism, diasporic communities, and expressions of Latinidad mediated through religious practices. Lest we flatten out differences and the religious contours of communities embedded in new and multiple contexts, we ought to consider the uneven exchanges that often occur. Public devotions and fiestas to local patron saints from home villages do not necessary take place in all diasporic communities. Expressions of religiosity in the homeland often involve *cofradías* and *hermandades* (fraternal orders), which orient one more toward community engagement and well-being (Vásquez 2006: 164). In sites of the public margins in the United States, such replication of hometown religious expressions seems infeasible and heightened visibility can prove dangerous to communities of undocumented immigrants. Migrants' destination may influence how an immigrant Latinx community is welcomed too, Canada serving as a case in point.

Canada's Latinx population pales in comparison to that in the United States. In fact, Latinxs in the United States alone (52 million) outnumber the entire population of Canada (37 million). But as a nation with a much friendlier context for Latinx immigrants, Canada's own "Latino Reformation" (Dias 2013) is worth noting, especially for the growth of Pentecostalism. Rather than Mexicans, Puerto Ricans, Cubans, or Dominicans taking the central role of reverse missions, Central Americans are playing the greatest role in shaping the religious landscape in Canada. Just like the Catholic Church has encouraged Latinxs in the United States to partake in the Charismatic Catholic Renewal, leaders in Canada have taken similar steps to bring Catholicism and Pentecostal-inspired practices into relationship.

To return to the MCE, in Toronto, Rosa Campos in January 2003 gathered with seven members to launch a cell group. Word spread quickly among Salvadorans and after just three months nearly 250 people gathered for services in an auditorium. By mid-2010 the congregation launched other cells that together would account for services with over one thousand people in attendance. While the base is still Salvadoran, the MCE in Toronto draws in a diverse crowd from many Latin American and Caribbean nations (Danielson 2015: 119). In fact, much of the growth of Pentecostalism in Canada owes to immigration, especially from Latin American countries though Canadian policies have not always favored non-European immigrants. Whereas Latinxs in the United States can often claim generational-deep roots in the country, Canada's Latinxs by and large are immigrants themselves. Canada's approximate 750,000 Latinx are concentrated in Toronto, Montreal, and Vancouver. While still mostly Catholic, a religiously diverse group of Central Americans continue to arrive in Canada (Medina 2012: 213).

Much research is still to be conducted on Latinx religiosity. Consider that Latinx Pentecostal and charismatic communities did not significantly register in the United

States' academic publications until the 1990s (Medina and Alfaro 2015). The rise of the Chicano movement in the United States in part elided details about Chicano religious activism and the religious lives of some of its leaders such as Cesar Chavez and Reies Lopez Tijerina (Espinosa, Elizondo, and Miranda 2005). Since the late 1980s and 1990s historians have begun to take notice of the growing field of Latinx religious history (Martínez-Vázquez 2013). The many histories over the past three decades and contemporary accounts of Latinx Christianity today attest to one common feature: Latinx Christianities in North America is a story of past and present crossings whose trajectories will shape the future.

Further Reading and Online Resources

Agosto E. and J.M. Hidalgo (2018), *Latinx, the Bible and Migration*, Cham: Palgrave Macmillan.
Avalos H. (2004), *Introduction to the U.S. Latina and Latino Religious Experience*, Boston: Brill.
Chao Romero R. (2020), *Brown Church: Five Centuries of Latina/o Social Justice, Theology, and Identity*, Downers Grove, IL: IVP Academic.
De la Torre M. and A. Aponte (2020), *Introducing Latinx Theologies*, Maryknoll, NY: Orbis Books.
Martinez J.F. (2018), *The Story of Latino Protestants in the United States*, Grand Rapids, MI: W.B. Eerdmans.
Mulder M., A. Ramos, and G. Martí (2017), *Latino Protestants in America: Growing and Diverse*, Lanham, MD: Rowman and Littlefield.

References

Banker M.T. (1993), *Presbyterian Missions and Cultural Interaction in the Far Southwest, 1890–1950*, Urbana: University of Illinois Press.
Barba L. and T. Castillo-Ramos (2019), "La Migra No Profana El Santuario: The Sanctuary Movement from Reagan to Trump," *Perspectivas* (16): 11–36.
Barton P. (2006), *Hispanic Methodists, Presbyterians, and Baptists in Texas*, Austin: University of Texas Press.
Bueno R.T. (2015), "Translating Pentecost into Transformed Communities in El Salvador: Social Engagement as a New and Contested Ritual," in N. Medina and S. Alfaro (eds.), *Pentecostals and Charismatics in Latin American and Latino Communities*, 67–79, New York: Palgrave Macmillan.
Chasteen J.C. (2006), *Born of Blood and Fire: A Concise History of Latin America*, New York: W.W. Norton and Company.
Contreras-Flores J. (2015), "The Social Impact of the 1916 Pentecostal Revival in Puerto Rico," in N. Medina and S. Alfaro (eds.), *Pentecostals and Charismatics in Latin American and Latino Communities*, 157–65, New York: Palgrave Macmillan.
Danielson R.A. (2015), "Transnationalism and the Pentecostal Salvadoran Church: A Case Study of Misión Cristiana Elim," in N. Medina and S. Alfaro (eds.), *Pentecostals and*

Charismatics in Latin American and Latino Communities, 111–24, New York: Palgrave Macmillan.

Davidson C.C. (2015), "Black Protestants in a Catholic Land: The AME Church in the Dominican Republic 1899–1916," *New West Indian Guide*, 89: 258–88.

De la Torre M. (2004a), "The Cuban American Religious Experience," in Hector Avalos (ed.), *Introduction to the U.S. Latina and Latino Religious Experience*, 66–85, Boston: Brill.

De la Torre M. (2004b), *Santeria: The Beliefs and Rituals of a Religion in America*, Berkeley: University of California Press.

Deutsch S. (1987), *No Separate Refuge: Culture, Class, and Gender on an Anglo-Hispanic Frontier in the American Southwest, 1880–1940*, New York: Oxford University Press.

Dias E. (2013), "Evangélicos!," *Time*, April 15.

Dolan J.P. and J.R. Vidal, eds. (1994), *Puerto Rican and Cuban Catholics in the U.S., 1900–1965*, South Bend, IN: University of Notre Dame Press.

Elizondo V. (2000), *Galilean Journey: The Mexican-American Promise*, Maryknoll, NY: Orbis.

Espín O. (1997), *The Faith of the People: Theological Reflections on Popular Catholicism*, Maryknoll, NY: Orbis.

Espinosa G. (2014), *Latino Pentecostals: Faith and Politics in Action*, Cambridge, MA: Harvard University Press.

Espinosa G., V. Elizondo, and J. Miranda, eds. (2005), *Latino Religions and Civic Activism*, New York: Oxford University Press.

Figueroa A.M. (2009), "Dominicans," in M. de la Torre (ed.), *Hispanic American Religious Cultures*, 205–7, Santa Barbara, CA: ABC-CLIO.

García M.C. (2006), *Seeking Refuge: Central American Migration to Mexico, The United States, and Canada*, Berkeley: University of California Press.

García M.T. (2018), *Father Luis Olivares, A Biography: Faith Politics and the Origins of the Sanctuary Movement in Los Angeles*, Chapel Hill: University of North Carolina Press.

Gutiérrez D.G. (1995), *Walls and Mirrors: Mexican Americans, Mexican Immigrants, and the Politics of Ethnicity*, Berkeley: University of California Press.

Hinojosa F. (2014), *Latino Mennonites: Civil Rights, Faith, and Evangelical Culture*, Baltimore: Johns Hopkins University Press.

Machado D.L. (2003), *Of Borders and Margins: Hispanic Disciples in Texas, 1888–1945*, New York: Oxford University Press.

Martinez J. (2006), *Sea la Luz: The Making of Mexican Protestantism in the American Southwest, 1829–1900*, Denton: University of North Texas Press.

Martínez-Vázquez H. (2013), *Made in the Margins: Latins/o Constructions of US Religious History*, Waco, TX: Baylor University Press.

Matovina T. (2012), *Latino Catholicism: Transformation in America's Largest Church*, Princeton, NJ: Princeton University Press.

Medina L. (2005), *Las Hermanas: Chicana/Latina Religious-Political Activism in the U.S. Catholic Church*, Philadelphia: Temple University Press.

Medina N. (2012), "Hybridity, Migration, and Transnational Relations: Re-thinking Canadian Pentecostalism from a Latina/o Perspective," in M. Wilkinson (ed.), *Global Pentecostal Movements: Migration, Mission, and Public Religion*, 211–26, Leiden: Brill.

Medina N. and S. Alfaro, eds. (2015), *Pentecostals and Charismatics in Latin American and Latino Communities*, New York: Palgrave Macmillan.

Menjívar C. (2003), "Religion and Immigration in Comparative Perspective: Catholic and Evangelical Salvadorans in San Francisco, Washington, DC, and Phoenix," *Sociology of Religion*, 64 (1): 21–45.

Mora A. (2011), *Border Dilemmas: Racial and National Uncertainties in New Mexico, 1848–1912*, Durham, NC: Duke University Press.

Mulder M., A. Ramos, and G. Martí (2017), *Latino Protestants in America: Growing and Diverse*, Lanham, MD: Rowman and Littlefield.

Pérez L. (1994), "Cuban Catholics in the United States," in J.P. Dolan and J.R. Vidal (eds.), *Puerto Rican and Cuban Catholics in the U.S., 1900–1965*, 147–207, South Bend, IN: University of Notre Dame Press.

Pew Research Center (2014), "The Shifting Religious Identities of Latinos in the United States," May 7. Available online: https://www.pewforum.org/2014/05/07/the-shifting-religious-identity-of-latinos-in-the-united-states/ (accessed November 14, 2020).

Pew Research Center (2019), "In U.S., Decline of Christianity Continues at Rapid Pace: An Update on America's Changing Religious Landscape," October 17. Available online: https://www.pewforum.org/2019/10/17/in-u-s-decline-of-christianity-continues-at-rapid-pace/ (accessed November 14, 2020).

Ramírez D. (2015), *Migrating Faith: Pentecostalism in the United States and Mexico in the Twentieth Century*, Chapel Hill: University of North Carolina Press.

Reedy Solano J. (2004), "The Central American Religious Experience in the U.S.: Salvadorans and Guatemalans as Case Studies," in Hector Avalos (ed.), *Introduction to the U.S. Latina and Latino Religious Experience*, 116–39, Boston: Brill.

Rivera-Pagán L. (2006), "Puertorriqueõs/as," in E. Aponte and M. de la Torre (eds.), *Handbook of Latina/o Theologies*, 144–51, St. Louis, MO: Chalice Press.

Sagarena R.L. (2014), *Aztlán and Arcadia: Religion, Ethnicity, and the Creation of Place*, New York: New York University Press.

Sánchez-Walsh A. (2003), *Latino Pentecostal Identity: Evangelical Faith, Self, and Society*, New York: Columbia University Press.

Suárez M.M.W. (2006), "Cubana/os," in E. Aponte and M. de la Torre (eds.), *Handbook of Latina/o Theologies*, 152–9, St. Louis, MO: Chalice Press.

Thornton B.J. (2018), "Changing Landscapes of Faith: Latin American Religion in the Twenty-First Century," *Latin American Research Review*, 53 (4): 857–62.

Todorov T. (1997), *The Conquest of America*, San Francisco: Harper Perennial.

Tweed T. (1997), *Our Lad of Exile: Diasporic Religion at a Cuban Shrine in Miami*, New York: Oxford University Press.

Vásquez M.A. (2006), "Central and South Americans, and 'Other Latinos/as'," in E. Aponte and M. de la Torre (eds.), *Handbook of Latina/o Theologies*, 160–8, St. Louis, MO: Chalice Press.

Vásquez M.A. and I. Gómez (2003), "Saving Souls Transnationally: Pentecostalism and Youth Gangs in El Salvador and the United States," in M.A. Vásquez and M. Friedman Marquardt (eds.), *Globalizing the Sacred: Religion across the Americas*, 119–44, New Brunswick, NJ: Ruthers University Press.

Vidal J.R. (2004), "The Puerto Rican Religious Experience," in Hector Avalos (ed.), *Introduction to the U.S. Latina and Latino Religious Experience*, 42–65, Boston: Brill.

Wadkins T.H. (2017), *The Rise of Pentecostalism in Modern El Salvador: From the Blood of the Martyrs to the Baptism of the Spirit*, Waco, TX: Baylor University Press.

Watt A.J. (2010), *Farmworkers and the Churches: The Movement in California and Texas*, College Station: Texas A&M Press.

Yohn S.M. (1995), *A Contest of Faiths: Missionary Women and Pluralism in the American Southwest*, Ithaca, NY: Cornell University Press.

Glossary Terms

Mestizaje The racial and cultural mixing of people groups, which in the Americas generally includes persons of African, Native American, and European extraction origins.

Popular Catholicism The everyday or ordinary practices of Catholics that fall beyond institutionalized approval. The approach of popular religion, more generally, seeks to understand religion as it is practiced in everyday settings rather than how it is practiced are mandated by any one institution.

Transnationalism The sustained operation of people and groups across borders in a way that forms a mutually reinforcing benefit between country of origin and destination.

Tridentine The Council of Trent (1545–1663) in which the Roman Catholic Church made reforms in response to the burgeoning Protestant Reformation.

11

Native Americans and Christianity in North America

Joseph J. Saggio

Roman Catholic Missionary Efforts

The opportunity to explore the New World held untold opportunities to achieve wealth and status, and financial gain was an important motivation for many. However, this was also a time of deep religious sentiment, a sense pervading all social strata of society and motivating missionary enterprises throughout the Americas. Both explorers and missionaries were part of early explorations to the New World. While some individuals pursued great opportunities for wealth, others sought a chance to further Christianity (Shea 1855: 20). Thus, the motives for exploring the New World was a study in diverse motivations. These disparities gave rise to cynicism, as motivations are subject to historical analysis and review. Were the early explorers interested in "saving souls," gaining material wealth, or perhaps a mixture of both?

Early Roman Catholic missions among Native Americans in North America were conducted primarily by four religious orders: the Order of Preachers (Dominicans), the Order of Friars Minor (Franciscans), the Society of Jesus (Jesuits), and the Order of Friars Minor Capuchin (Capuchins). In addition to these four orders, work was also conducted by two distinct groups of clergy: (1) the seminary priests of Quebec, and (2) the Society of Saint-Sulpice. These two groups were not part of a canonically established order but were more loosely organized communities of diocesan priests.

The Spanish Catholic missionaries were the first to begin missions work among Indigenous inhabitants, evangelizing the Southeast (including Florida, Georgia, and the Carolinas) beginning circa 1530. This was followed by work in the southwestern United States (Texas, New Mexico, and Arizona). By then, the British and French were

CHRISTIANITY IN NORTH AMERICA

establishing missions in the St. Lawrence and Great Lakes regions (from Maine to New York and on to Wisconsin) and also to the Middle Atlantic region (where efforts were almost exclusively focused on Maryland). Because of the intercolonial wars beginning about 1680, missionary efforts then spread to the Mississippi Valley region (from Illinois to Louisiana). Finally, with the threat of Russia, England, and the newly established United States, efforts were concentrated on the Pacific Coast (Kiemen 1946: 7–8).

Seminal efforts by Roman Catholic missionaries in the sixteenth century were often marked by extraordinary sacrifice, courageous energy, and singularity of purpose in promoting Christianity. The level of personal sacrifices was enormous, and only the hardiest of missionaries could handle the rigor of these enterprises. A multitude of tribes existed throughout North America, each with their own language, tribal culture, and religion, often living in isolation from other tribal entities making it necessary for early missionaries to be exposed to a multitude of languages and cultures as they sought to proselytize. Moreover, many tribes did not welcome the missionaries' attempt at evangelism, thus adding to the danger.

The Jesuits and others encountered numerous obstacles including floods, wild animals, hostile audiences, and inclement weather. Missionaries Jean de Brebeuf and Juan Baptista de Segura were martyred. René Menard died in the wilderness, others froze to death or died of heat exposure. Historically it is said that the Jesuits never receded one foot in their efforts to propagate the Gospel. Many of these early missionaries took literally the Christian injunction to reach all the nations with the Gospel of Jesus Christ (see Mt. 28:18–19; Shea 1855: 20-2, 26).

Historically, the legacy of early Spanish Roman Catholic mission's efforts is viewed either positively or pejoratively, depending on the historical vantage point. The major criticism of early missionaries was that they had only a veneer of Gospel outreach and were primarily agents to enslave the Indigenous population. Even staunch defenders of these efforts concede that cruelties existed but deny that they were as widespread as reported (Shea 1855: 39). Historical records are difficult to interpret because the vantage point of the historians must be taken into account to get to the truest, most accurate accounts. The fact that there is a great deal of written history both lauding and criticizing early missionary work strongly suggests that there is a great deal of truth in both camps, thus differing accounts must be reconciled to attain to the greatest level of historical accuracy.

Perhaps the most well-known critic of Native missionary efforts was Bartolomé de las Casas (1484–1566), named a saint by the Roman Catholic Church, and designated as "Protector of the Indians" during the time he served as the bishop of Chiapas, Mexico. Bishop de las Casas's criticisms of the treatment of the Native peoples brought him into sharp dispute with many colonial Spanish leaders. The bishop had great affection for the Native people and spent a great deal of his life as an advocate for their humane treatment. Spending more than fifty years among the Indians, he had a tremendous grasp of the issues. He died before completing his magnum opus *History of the Indies*, which would not be published until the middle of the nineteenth century. In the prologue of that work he indicated his purpose was:

> To call the attention of the readers to the terrifying disparity between the missionary purpose of the encounter between Christian Europeans and Native Americans and the brutal exploitation of the second by the first.
>
> (Rivera-Pagán 2003: 117)

Bartolomé de las Casas notes that the exploitation of the Indians began immediately after the arrival of the Spaniards in the New World. He mentions slaughter, harsh working conditions, not even sparing women and children from these atrocities (de Las Casas 1689: 3–4). The bishop also notes that the Indigenous inhabitants were subjected to working conditions that caused their premature deaths, thus decimating the population. Bishop de Las Casas details: "They snatcht young Babes from the Mothers Breasts, and then dasht out the brains of those innocents against the Rocks; others they cast into Rivers scoffing and heering them and call'd upon their Bodies when failing with derision, [*sic*]" (5).

FIGURE 11.1 *Bartolomé de Las Casas, "Protector of the Indians."* Source: DEA / ICAS94 / Getty Images.

While Spanish colonial efforts at establishing Roman Catholic Christianity were taking place among their colonies, the French were also expanding their missions outreach. Whereas many of the Spanish missionaries worked independently, the French efforts were more unified. Jacques Cartier held a commission authorizing him to explore "in order the better to do what is pleasing to God, our Creator and Redeemer, and what may be for the increase of his holy and sacred name, and of our holy mother, the Church" (Shea 1855: 123). French missions' work began as early as 1608, a bit later than the start of Spanish efforts. The first French Roman Catholic settlement among the Natives on Boon Island in what is present-day Maine, and eventually moved to the opposite shore at Port Royal (today known as Annapolis). Pierre Dugua De Monts, who established Acadia, a colony of New France in northeastern North America, was required to have the Indians in that region instructed and indoctrinated in Christianity. He was succeeded by Jean de Biencourt de Potrincourt, who sought the pope's blessings on his work among the Micmacs (or Souriquois of Nova Scotia) and the Abnakis, but unfortunately his efforts were destroyed by English violence. Eventually, much of the work in the region was carried out by the Jesuits and in fact their efforts to spread Christianity among the Native population helped them to gain young Jesuits throughout Europe. French-speaking Roman Catholics who decried atrocities against Indians included Pierre-Jean de Smet (1801–73), a Belgian priest who (like Bartolomé de las Casas before him) denounced the ill-treatment of Native people. European missionary work among Indians in North America remained largely unchanged from the sixteenth through the nineteenth century, perpetuating a paternalistic model that kept Indigenous inhabitants in a subordinate status.

Only in recent years has Indigenous recognition developed to any extent. Today, according to the Roman Catholic Church's figures, of the 2.9 million self-identified Native Americans in the United States, an estimated 580,000 are Catholic (approximately 20 percent). Moreover, many Native Catholics also strongly identify with their Native religion's tradition despite embracing Catholicism. Especially noteworthy among the American Indian Roman Catholic community was the canonization of Saint Kateri Tekakwitha (1656–80) in 2012 as the first Native American Catholic saint in the Roman Catholic Church. Also, in 1986, Donald E. Pelotte of the Abenaki tribe became the country's first Native American bishop of the Diocese in Gallup, New Mexico (Cavanaugh 2017). Sadly, Native Americans have been slow to ascend to positions of leadership in many denominations, not just the Roman Catholic Church. Native activist Vine DeLoria Jr. (1988: 122–3) frequently decried the lack of Native Indigenous leadership frequently marginalized at the expense of developing Anglo clerics. This problem is pervasive throughout many denominations and is slowly being rectified.

FIGURE 11.2 *Statue of St. Kateri Tekakwitha, first Native American Catholic saint in North America.* Source: *Stan Honda / Getty Images.*

Protestant Missionary Efforts

Roughly contemporaneous with early Roman Catholic efforts at reaching Native Americans with the Christian Gospel were labors by various Protestant groups beginning in 1620 with the arrival of Pilgrims at Plymouth Rock. Not only seeing great opportunities to settle in new territory that would give them religious freedom from the oppression of the Church of England, the early Puritans also saw themselves as the ones who could bring "light" to the "spiritual darkness" experienced by the North American Indians. One of the ways Puritans chose to do this was through the founding of Harvard College in 1636. In its original inception, Harvard College was created to perpetuate an educated class of Puritan ministers in the New World. The

New England First Fruits Plaque located at the entrance to Harvard Yard bears witness to this with: "And Perpetuate It to Posterity Dreading to Leave An Illiterate Ministry to The Churches When Our Present Ministers Shall Lie in the Dust [sic]" (quote taken directly from the plaque). By 1650, Harvard expanded its original charter to include the education of Native ministers for the ministry and to serve as religious leaders among their own. However, early results were mixed. Caleb Cheeshateaumuck was an Algonquian Indian from Martha's Vineyard admitted to Harvard. In addition to his Native language, Caleb learned to read and write English, Greek, and Latin. Unfortunately, he died several months after graduation, falling victim to one of the many "white man's diseases" to which he had no natural immunity. Sadly, at that time very few other Native men enrolled at Harvard and the dedicated dormitory for them was converted into housing for white male students (Wright and Tierney 1991: 11–18). This type of setback made it difficult to establish a class of Indigenous Native ministers in the New World.

Additionally, missionaries such as Thomas Mayhew, John Eliot, and David Brainerd were other pivotal Protestant leaders who gave active service toward reaching Indians with Christianity. Both Eliot and Mayhew established a number of "praying villages," which were Christian enclaves where Native Christians lived in a small Christian society where they were taught doctrine, baptized, and adopted the Christian faith. Eliot (1604–90) was particularly diligent, having spent fifty-eight years of his life in this enterprise while concurrently pastoring a church in Roxbury, just three kilometers outside Boston. Because of his legendary accomplishments and zeal, he was affectionately known as "Apostle to the Indians" (Calhoun 1989: 36). Critics contend that Eliot was promoting British cultural hegemony as much as Christianity since he required the learning of the English language before potential converts would be taught the catechism. Nevertheless, critics still credit Eliot with reaching more than 20 percent of the Indian population in New England with Christianity and despite the slaughter during King Philip's War (also known as Metacom, King Philip's tribal name) in which Christian Indians were pitted against non-Christian Indians in an internecine conflict. During that period, more than half of the Native converts remained faithful to Christianity (Lomawaima 1999: 10–11). Eliot must also be credited with incredible resiliency since copies of his translation of the Bible into Algonquin were destroyed along with many of the praying villages—essentially thirty years of his life's labors. Eliot spent the last fifteen years of his life diligently rebuilding his work despite advancing age and heartbreaking disappointment (Eden 2014: 42–3; Calhoun 1989: 37–8).

Brief mention must also be made of David Brainerd, known more for his piety and prayerfulness than for actual achievement since his life was tragically cut short at age twenty-nine. Melancholic by nature, his journal entries show a man of stoic disposition and character: "May 18.- 'My circumstances are such that I have no comfort of any kind, but what I have in God. I live in the most lonesome wilderness; have but one single person to converse with that can speak English'" (Edwards 1978: 5). Brainerd traveled throughout New England, preaching the Gospel to Indians. Despite tuberculosis, which eventually took his life, Brainerd worked tirelessly in his vocation, giving unflinching

FIGURE 11.3 *John Eliot of Roxbury, Massachusetts, "Apostle to the Indians."* Source: *Kean Collection / Getty Images.*

devotion to the Native people he so desperately wanted to reach. Brainerd Hall at Yale was named in his honor.

Despite some of these early attempts at spreading Protestant Christianity among Indians, evangelistic efforts were largely tainted by such events as the *Indian Removal Act of 1830* in which President Andrew Jackson authorized the forced removal of Indians on the eastern seaboard to lands west of the Mississippi River, an event also known as the "Trail of Tears." Those ordered to flee included the Cherokee, Choctaw, Chickasaw, Creek, and Seminole Indian nations known as the Five Civilized Tribes. Although some went peaceably, many (both Indians and non-Indians) loudly protested this inhumane action. Moreover, the Indian Removal Act forced thousands to leave their sacred lands, banished to remote regions in the western United States. This did not help in the spread of Christianity since this was seen by some as the "policy of Christians." However, in some cases the white Christian missionaries joined the march with their Indian congregants to the lands west of the Mississippi, refusing to abandon their congregants.

Also tainting the efforts of Christian missionaries was the *Sand Creek Massacre* of the Southern Cheyenne Indians in Colorado Territory, perpetrated in 1864 by Col. John Chivington, a former Methodist minister turned US Army colonel. The massacre was ostensibly to stem what Chivington believed was the beginning of an Indian uprising. One hundred and fifty people were killed by his soldiers including women and children (Fowler 2015: 378–9). As a result of this brutal massacre, Col. Chivington was widely

FIGURE 11.4 *The 1864 Sand Creek Massacre.* Source: *DEA PICTURE LIBRARY / Getty Images.*

criticized by many, yet lionized by others. Nevertheless, he ended his military career in disgrace, yet defending his actions for the rest of his life.

Another resurgence of efforts to reach Native Americans occurred in the mid-nineteenth century. Missionaries such as Dr. Marcus Whitman and his wife Narcissa, along with Jason Lee, Henry H. Spaulding, and many others, answered the "Macedonian call" reminiscent of when the Apostle Paul sensed a divine call to help the Macedonians receive the Gospel of Jesus Christ (see Acts 16:9). The results were often mixed. Although Jason Lee's efforts were largely successful, Dr. Whitman and his wife were massacred by Cayuse Indians who mistook his efforts at medical treatment as an effort to harm them. Today, Whitman and his wife are regarded by many as martyrs for the Christian faith.

Boarding School Movement

The Boarding School Movement (1879–1978) was a mixture of federal policy and religious indoctrination attempts (both Roman Catholic and Protestant) existing in both the United States and Canada. Although ostensibly an attempt to inculcate cultural indoctrination and assimilation, strong exposure to religious teaching took place either at or alongside the boarding schools. Examples of these schools include the infamous *Carlisle Boarding School* in Carlisle, Pennsylvania; the *Chilocco Indian Agricultural*

School in Chilocco, Oklahoma; and *St. Mary's Indian Residential School* (actually two different schools with the same name) in British Columbia at Frasier River Park.

The most well known of these schools was the Carlisle Boarding School run by General Richard Pratt, whose motto was "kill the Indian in him, and save the man" (Lomawaima and Ostler 2018: 81). This referenced Pratt's idea of "killing" the Indian culture in his students, yet redeeming the "person" whom he considered valuable and worth saving, but in need of redeeming from his "savage nature." The boarding schools also served to "Christianize" Indian students, effectively outlawing Native expressions of traditional religion, language, and culture. Students were frequently required to attend Christian churches while enrolled at boarding schools operated by the Federal Government, and were often taken by force from their homes and forcibly moved hundreds of kilometers. According to Lomawaima "Civilization and Christian conversion were assumed for centuries to be the same thing [...]. The separation of church and state, a foundation of our public school system, was not initiated in federal Indian boarding schools until the 1930s" (1999: 6). Since 1978 with the passing of the Indian Child Welfare Act, Native students are no longer compelled to attend the off-reservation schools although they may choose to attend one voluntarily such as the Sherman Indian High School (operated by the Bureau of Indian Affairs) in Riverside, California.

Women's Contributions

Although not always at an egalitarian level, women have held a pivotal role in the spreading of Christianity among American Indians although their contributions are not often as well publicized. During the time of the French Jesuit missionary ventures beginning in the 1600s, convents of Ursuline and Hospital nuns came to carry out practical efforts through care for the sick and instruction of the young in catechism and other subjects (Shea 1855: 124–5). The aforementioned Narcissa Whitman, martyred in 1847, worked alongside her missionary physician husband, Dr. Marcus Whitman as a co-laborer. In 1880, Annie Armstrong, one of the founders of the Southern Baptist's Women's Missionary Society established a school for Native Americans in Maryland (Roach 2017).

On a bit more of an "egalitarian" level, Ethel Marshall along with her husband founded the first Assemblies of God Church among the Indians of Arizona at the San Carlos Apache Reservation in 1936. Alta W. Washburn, a missionary pastor, established a church, All Tribes Indian Assembly of God, in Phoenix in 1948. In 1957 Washburn established a Bible school at the church to train Native pastors that is still in existence, known today as Southwestern Assemblies of God University, American Indian Campus. Tarango (2014: 108–9) regards Washburn's work as iconoclastic since she advocated using Native pastors as full-fledged ministry colleagues, flying in the face of the paternalism of that time.

Native Leaders' Concerns with Christianity

Iconoclastic Native activist and scholar Vine Deloria Jr. was very critical of Christian attempts to spread their teachings among Native Americans, believing them to be harmful to traditional Native American culture. Ironically, Deloria himself was a seminary graduate, coming from a long line of Lakota Christian leaders. Despite his personal rejection of Christianity, Deloria conceded that if Christianity is to succeed among Native Americans, it should take on a more indigenous expression:

> The best thing that the national denominations could do to ensure the revitalization of Christian missions among Indian people would be to assist in the creation of a national Indian Christian Church. Such a church would incorporate all existing missions and programs into one national church to be wholly in the hands of Indian people.
>
> (Deloria 1988: 122–3)

Likewise, Richard Twiss was also very critical of Christianity's work with Native Americans and accused many of practicing cultural hegemony by imposing an Anglo-centric approach. Like Deloria, Twiss felt that Native Christian leaders were denied opportunities to be full-fledged colleagues in ministry. However, unlike Deloria, Twiss remained within the scope of mainstream Christianity throughout his lifetime, choosing to promote more indigenous expressions of Christianity while also working alongside sympathetic non-Indians. Twiss reported "I would love to see some of our Anglo church leaders, when asked to help a Native church, say, 'yes, but on one condition: only if you will in turn send your pastors and leaders to come and equip us with the grace and gifting God has given as Native people'" (2000: 58).

Despite criticisms, there are still many Native Americans who proudly embrace Christianity. Interdenominational organizations such as CHIEF Ministries (Christian Hope for Indian Eskimo Fellowship) promote Indigenous Christian ministry among Native Americans (including Alaska Natives, see CHIEF n.d.). Parallel organizations such as the Native American Fellowship of the Assemblies of God (AG NAF) promote Indigenous Native ministry within the context of denominational structures (Native American Fellowship Assemblies of God 2019). Craig Smith (1997), a Chippewa Christian leader, argues that Christianity is very relevant to Native Americans and when properly contextualized it is possible to have great success reaching Indians despite past failures. According to Smith in reference to the Christian God, "He makes us fully complete, no matter who we are or what part of Indian culture we belong to" (1997: 130).

The Church of Jesus Christ of Latter-Day Saints (Mormon) Missionary Efforts

Outside the more mainstream of Christianity, including the aforementioned Roman Catholicism and Protestantism, the Church of Jesus Christ of Latter-day Saints (LDS) instead traces its origins to its founder, Joseph Smith (1805–44) of Palmyra, New York.

NATIVE AMERICANS AND CHRISTIANITY IN NORTH AMERICA

He claimed to have had visions of the need to reform Christianity. Smith believed that Jesus Christ came to North America to evangelize, leaving additional writings such as *The Book of Mormon* as a record of those visits, and as an additional testament of his teachings beyond *The Holy Bible*. Much like its Catholic and Protestant counterparts, Mormonism's relationship with Indians has been problematic. Especially troublesome to some was the belief that North American Indians were part of the *Lamanites*, a cursed race of dark-skinned people described as "a filthy people, full of idleness and all manner of abominations" (*Book of Mormon*, 1 Nephi 12:23). Mormons believed that the Lamanites rejected the teachings of Christ when he came to the New World; however, Christ's teachings were embraced by the Nephites, who were marked by their light-colored skin, "white and delightsome." The Lamanites were then said to have killed many of the Nephites bringing upon themselves a curse of dark skin to show their "fallen" nature.

Mormon evangelistic efforts have centered on bringing Lamanites (including Indians and other "dark-skinned" people) into the Mormon faith so that they can be restored to proper relationship. Early Mormon leader Oliver Cowdery expressed a strong desire to reach the Lamanites. In a letter dated May 7, 1831, he states:

> I am informed of another Tribe of Lamanites lately who have abundance of flocks of the best kind of sheep & cattle and manufacture blankets of superior quality. The tribe is very numerous. They live three hundred miles west of Santa Fe and are called Navahos. Why I mention this tribe is because I feel under obligation to communicate to my brethren every information respecting the Lamanites [...] to you all my Labours and travels, believing as I do that much is expected from me in the cause of our Lord [*sic*].
>
> (Cowdery 1831)

Indeed, Mormon outreach to the Navajo and other tribes has been fairly extensive and has included efforts at evangelizing them with the Mormon Gospel through evangelist efforts with children. For a number of years there was a program in place to do so (1947–2000). According to Landry (2017) the Mormon Church had a Indian Student Placement Program, which placed Indian children in Mormon homes where they received doctrinal teaching, as well as moral and cultural practices of the LDS church. These homes served as foster homes and many children became committed Mormons while others felt culturally marginalized from their tribal background and families. At the program's height, over three thousand students were enrolled. The program was controversial in part because of the stigma of being "Lamanite," which was seen as a designation of a "cursed" race. Since Mormon doctrine teaches that the righteous Mormons are "white and exceedingly fair and delightsome" Indian students were, at times, expected to undergo physical changes in their appearance, becoming lighter in skin pigmentation.

On June 1, 1978, a pivotal change in Mormon theology took place when then President Spencer W. Kimball announced that he had received a divine revelation announcing the lifting of the Lamanite curse, which said that men of dark skin could not hold the Mormon priesthood because of the curse of Cain marking their previous rebellion. This ban on the priesthood existed since 1852 with few exceptions. In Official Declaration 2, the President of the Latter-day Saints announced the "lifting" of the curse, clearing the way for African Americans, Indians, and other dark-skinned ethnic men to hold the priesthood. This has been the official policy of the Mormon Church ever since, and has cleared the status of Native American men to hold the full status of priesthood within the LDS Church.

The Native American Church

The Native American Church (or Peyote Road) is a widespread, loose confederation religious movement rather than a monolithic group. They seek to integrate Christian life with Indigenous Native traditions into a spiritual belief system that is both Christian and uniquely Indigenous (The Pluralism Project: Harvard University 1997–2019). According to Feeney (2016) the practices of the Native American Church have historical antecedents in traditional Indigenous religious expressions dating back several millennia. In its most modern permutation, the usage of Peyote as a religious expression of the Native American Church began in the late nineteenth century and takes place in the United States, Mexico, and Canada. The use of peyote is a pan-Indian religious expression connecting multiple tribal groups in its usage. Contemporary usage is traced to 1891 among the Kiowa who sat in a circle inside a sacred tipi around a fire during which time the participants ingested the peyote while singing and drumming. These all-night ceremonies are held for purposes of prayer, healing, and meditation.

Although claiming ties to Christianity, the Native American Church is highly controversial because of their use of peyote cactus buttons as a sacrament believed to have spiritually medicinal properties. Peyote is classified as a hallucinogenic drug and is known for its mind-altering qualities. Courts have generally held since 1965 that peyote usage should be allowable when used in conjunction with the religious practices of the Native American Church by Native American practitioners. The laws typically interpret "Native Americans" as people with at least 25 percent Indian blood quantum. Critics have argued that some are using these exemptions as a "shield" for the illicit usage of drugs for purely recreational purposes. Moreover, allowing the use of Peyote to a religious group primarily limited by ethnicity, also provides a racially based sectarian exemption that the constitutional framers might have never intended. The Native American Church has also been offered additional legal coverage through the *American Indian Religious Freedom Act (Public Law 95–341)* signed into law by President Carter in 1978. This statute allows Indigenous people in the United States the freedom to practice their traditional beliefs without governmental interference.

Outside the more mainstream expression of Christianity, the Native American Church argues that it provides a uniquely Native American expression of Christianity blending Christian and traditional Native beliefs into a theological framework more inclusive of Native peoples. Nevertheless, Christian leaders have frequently opposed

FIGURE 11.5 *The Peyote plant used in Native American religious practices.* Source: *DEA / A. MORESCHI / Getty Images.*

the practices of the Native American Church, citing the danger of peyote usage and its other *syncretistic* practices as antithetical to the teachings of biblical Christianity.

The Native American Church currently exists today as the Native American Church of North America (NACNA) to broadly represent practitioners in the United States (with chapters in twenty-four different states), as well as in Canada and Mexico. Its core values include brotherly and sisterly love, care of family, self-reliance, and the avoidance of alcohol in any form. Despite its controversial nature it shows no current signs of abatement.

Conclusion

Christianity in its various expressions has become a part of the religious landscape of Indigenous peoples in North America since the arrival of the first Roman Catholic missionaries in the sixteenth century. Often existing alongside traditional Native beliefs, and sometimes in opposition to them, Christianity continues to grow and even thrive, often taking on a DNA uniquely Indian or tribal in its influence. Yet, the number of Native people identifying as Christian is still relatively small. Estimates vary as to their exact numbers. The aforementioned Catholic numbers estimate 20 percent of Indians are

Roman Catholic, with some of those same Native people also adhering to traditional tribal beliefs (Cavenaugh 2017). Other estimates are that only about 10 percent identify with any form of Christianity, thus making it a minority religion among Indians ("Christianity Grows Among Native Americans" 2016). Still, the sacrifices and efforts of the early missionaries along with current Indigenous ministry have guaranteed these expressions of Christianity a *bona fide* place in the cultural and religious mosaic of Native peoples in North America. Despite relatively low numbers, many Native Americans have yet come to embrace Christianity as part of their own tribal and Indigenous heritage.

Further Reading and Online Resources

Brown D. (1970), *Bury My Heart at Wounded Knee*, New York: Owl Books, Henry Holt and Company.
Deloria V. (1988), *Custer Died for Your Sins*, Norman: University of Oklahoma Press.
Smith C.S. (1997), *Whiteman's Gospel*, Winnipeg: Indian Life Books.
Twiss R. (2000), *One Church Many Tribes,* Ventura, CA: *Gospel Light*.
Yong A. and B. Brown Zikmund, eds. (2010), *Remembering Jamestown: Hard Questions About Christian Missions*, Eugene, OR: Wipf and Stock Publishers.

References

Calhoun D.B. (1989), "John Eliot: Apostle to the Indians," *Presbyterion*, 15 (4): 358.
Cavenaugh R. (2017), "The Resilience of Native American Catholicism," *The Catholic World Report*, November 23. Available online: https://www.catholicworldreport.com/2017/11/23/the-resilience-of-native-american-catholicism/ (accessed August 6, 2019).
Christian Hope Indian Eskimo Fellowship (CHIEF) (n.d.), "CHIEF." Available online: https://chief.org/ (accessed November 29, 2020).
"Christianity Grows among Native Americans" (1986), *Evangelical Focus*, July 12. Available online: http://evangelicalfocus.com/world/1777/Christianity_grows_among_Native_Americans (accessed May 2, 2020).
The Church of Jesus Christ of Latter-Day Saints (1978), Official Declaration 2, September 30. Available online: https://www.churchofjesuschrist.org/study/scriptures/dc-testament/od/2?lang=eng (accessed August 1, 2019).
Cowdery O. (1831), "Letter, Kaw Township, MO," May 7, in *Joseph Smith Letter Book 1*, 12–13. Available online: https://www.josephsmithpapers.org/paper-summary/letter-from-oliver-cowdery-7-may-1831/1#ft-source-note (accessed July 31, 2019).
de Las Casas B. ([1689] 2007), *A Brief Account of the Destruction*, The Project Gutenberg Ebook. Available online: http://www-personal.umich.edu/~twod/latam-s2010/read/las_casasb2032120321-8.pdf (accessed June 24, 2019).
Deloria V. (1988), *Custer Died for Your Sins: An Indian Manifesto*, Norman: University of Oklahoma Press.
Eden J. (2014), "Therefore Ye Are No More Strangers and Foreigners," *American Indian Quarterly*, 38 (1): 36–59.

NATIVE AMERICANS AND CHRISTIANITY IN NORTH AMERICA

Edwards J. (1978), *The Life of Rev. David Brainerd, Chiefly Extracted from His Diary*, Grand Rapids, MI: Baker Book House.

Feeney K.M. (2016), "Peyote & The Native American Church: An Ethnobotanical Study at the Intersection of Religion, Medicine, Market Exchange, and Law," PhD diss., Washington State University. Available online: http://neip.info/novo/wp-content/uploads/2018/06/Feeney_Dissertation_Peyote_NAC_2016_NEIP.pdf (accessed August 3, 2019).

Fowler L. (2015), "Arapaho and Cheyenne Perspectives from the 1851 Treaty to the Sand Creek Massacre," *American Indian Quarterly*, 39 (4): 365–90.

Kiemen M.C. (1946), *Colonial Indian Missions: The Record of Catholic Missioners to the American Indians, 1521–1848*, New York: The America Press. Available online: https://archive.org/details/colonialindianmi00kiem (accessed June 8, 2019).

Landry A. (2017), "How Mormons Assimilated Native Children," *Indian Country Today*, October 7. Available online: https://newsmaven.io/indiancountrytoday/archive/how-mormons-assimilated-native-children-Cc6f97ZsA0mL7eCMcnQG6g/ (accessed July 31, 2019).

Lomawaima K.T. (1999), "The Unnatural History of American Indian Education," in K.G. Swisher and J.W. Tippeconnic III (eds.), *Next Steps: Research and Practice to Advance Indian Education*, 1–32, Charleston, WV: ERIC Clearinghouse on Rural Education and Small Schools.

Lomawaima K.T. and J. Ostler (2018), "Reconsidering Richard Henry Pratt: Cultural Genocide and Native Liberation in an Era of Racial Oppression," *Journal of American Indian Education*, 57 (1): 79–100.

Native American Fellowship Assemblies of God (2019), "Home." Available online: https://agnaf.org/ (accessed November 29, 2020).

The Pluralism Project: Harvard University (1997–2019), "Native American Church." Available online: http://pluralism.org/religions/native-american-traditions/native-peoples-experience/native-american-church/ (accessed August 1, 2019).

Rivera-Pagán L.N. (2003), "A Prophetic Challenge to the Church: The Last Word of Bartolomé de las Casas." *Princeton Seminary Bulletin*, 24 (2): 216–40. Available online: https://ia801209.us.archive.org/19/items/princetonseminar2422prin/princetonseminar2422prin.pdf (accessed June 19, 2019).

Roach D. (2017), "Native American Evangelism: Past and Present Examined," *Baptist Press*. Available online: http://www.bpnews.net/49293/native-american-evangelism-past-and-present-examined (accessed April 1, 2020).

Shea J.G. (1855), *Catholic Missions among The Indian Tribes of the United States, 1529–1854*, New York: T.W. Strong, Late Edward Dunigan & Brother, Catholic Publishing House. Available online: https://books.google.com/books?id=3ZsMFapSs9EC&printsec=frontcover&dq=inauthor:%22John±Dawson±Gilmary±Shea%22&hl=en&sa=X&ved=0ahUKEwi0ubLtn-ziAhUCrZ4KHRjUA5wQ6AEIKjAA#v=onepage&q&f=false (accessed June 15, 2019).

Smith C.S. (1997), *Whiteman's Gospel*, Winnipeg: Indian Life Books.

Tarango A. (2014), *Choosing the Jesus Way: American Indian Pentecostals and the Fight for the Indigenous Principle*, Chapel Hill: University of North Carolina Press.

Twiss R. (2000), *One Church Many Tribes: Following Jesus Way God Made You*, Ventura, CA: Regal Books.

Wright B. and W.G. Tierney (1991), "American Indians in Higher Education: A History of Cultural Conflict," *Change*, 23 (Spring 1991): 11–18.

Glossary Terms

American Indian Religious Freedom Act (Public Law 95-341) A law passed during President Carter's administration in 1978 that allowed for the protection of traditional Indian religious practices including the use of Peyote, a hallucinogenic drug used in the Native American Church (aka as Peyotism).

Carlisle Boarding School An Indian boarding school that existed in Carlisle Pennsylvania (1879–1918) that was founded and established by General Richard Pratt. Its specific purpose was to indoctrinate Native American children in mainstream educational knowledge, trade skills, and cultural practices but also to suppress traditional tribal religious, cultural, and linguistic practices. It was the first of five off-reservation schools established by an executive order of President James Garfield.

Chilocco Indian Agricultural School Located in Chilocco, Oklahoma, this was an Indian boarding school that operated from 1884 to 1980. The name "Chilocco" is believed to be derived from a Muscogee word meaning "big deer" or horse. Like the Carlisle Boarding School, the Chilocco school also depended on military-like drilling and training of the students and was also one of the five residential off-reservation schools established by President Garfield's executive order. It was very controversial due to allegations of ill-treatment, poor nutrition for the students, and forced religious indoctrination of Christianity.

Indian Removal Act of 1830 A highly controversial act signed into law in 1830 by President Andrew Jackson wherein Native peoples on the eastern seaboard were forcibly resettled west of the Mississippi River. Some tribes peacefully complied but many resisted this forced relocation policy. Approximately 100,000 Indians were forced into this march with estimates that 25 percent of them perished in route.

Indigenous Of or relating to the original inhabitants of an area or region. In North, South, and Central America this would refer to the hundreds of Indian tribal groups residing in the western hemisphere in pre-Columbian times up to the present.

Lamanites According to the *Book of Mormon*, a religious text of the Church of Jesus Christ of Latter-day Saints (LDS), who along with the Nephites, was a group of Indigenous people in North America at the time of Jesus Christ's alleged appearance in the New World. Unlike the Nephites, the Lamanites rejected and resisted the early message and were marked for this rebellion through "dark skin" and were considered cursed by Mormon doctrine, thus barring dark-skinned men from the priesthood. In 1978, this ban was lifted after LDS President Spencer C. Kimball had a revelation that this ban was to be rescinded paving the way for dark-skinned people (including Native Americans, Pacific Islanders, and men of African descent) to be able to join the Mormon priesthood and enjoy full status within the Mormon Church.

Native American Church A loose confederation of Native American religious believers who combine the use and ingestion of Peyote (a hallucinogenic drug) along with Christian teachings. Their use of Peyote has been ruled to be protected through the American Indian Religious Freedom Act (Public Law 95-341), which allows for its usage when utilized in conjunction with Peyote religious ceremonies. Largely criticized by mainstream Christians, especially missionaries to Native Americans because of its combination of both traditional Native religious practices

NATIVE AMERICANS AND CHRISTIANITY IN NORTH AMERICA

and Christianity, which are believed by many orthodox Christians as being incompatible.

Saint Mary's Indian Residential School There were actually two schools by this name: a Roman Catholic boarding school and later a federal school operated by the Canadian government. Both schools were located in Mission, British Columbia, Canada. The Roman Catholic school operated from 1863 to 1961. It was closed in 1961 due to its deteriorating infrastructure and replaced by the federal school of the same name until its closure in 1985. Like boarding schools in the United States, these schools were very controversial for their alleged mistreatment of Indian students, which to date has never been officially acknowledged.

Sand Creek Massacre A brutal massacre of Southern Cheyenne Indians in the Colorado Territory in 1864 perpetrated by Col. John Chivington, a former Methodist minister, who ordered the slaughter that resulted in the killing of one hundred and fifty Indians—including women and children—in retaliation for an alleged uprising. Chivington's actions brought loud protests by some, yet he was lionized by others. The Sand Creek Massacre ultimately caused him to end his military career in disgrace although he defended his actions for the rest of his life.

Syncretistic Combining elements of two or more different religious systems or practices not normally found together. For example, the Native American Church combines the consumption and use of peyote, a hallucinogenic drug tied to indigenous religious beliefs with the teachings of Jesus Christ and Christianity into a single, unified religious system.

PART THREE

Critical Issues

12

Missionization and Christianity

Thomas E.I. Whittaker

Colonial Missions

Starting in the 1520s, Franciscan missionaries were recruited to begin the process of evangelizing New Spain, and they were soon joined by Dominicans, including Bartolomé de las Casas, an advocate for the rights of Native peoples. The friars' attempt to Christianize the Indians continued beyond the colonial period. Its geographical reach stretched from the missions of Alta California, New Mexico, and Texas, into South America. In New France, the dynamic of evangelization was led by the Jesuits.

In both contexts, a process of indigenization marked the synthesis between Catholic and Indigenous practices. In Mexico, Indian converts translated their pre-Hispanic divinities into appropriately Catholic forms as saints, including the Virgin of Guadalupe, who may have been considered a continuation of the Aztec goddess Tonantzin (González and González 2008). Catholics also incorporated Indigenous saints into their pantheon. After the death of the Mohawk convert Kateri Tekakwitha in 1680, she quickly became venerated by Indigenous Catholics in Canada (Greer 2004).

Among Protestants, the dynamics of syncretism are much more difficult to discern. Scholars have worked hard to differentiate the conversion narratives of the Natick, Massachusetts converts of the Congregational minister John Eliot, from their white contemporaries.

Eliot's mission, sponsored by the English missionary society known as the New England Company, began in the 1640s. Eliot translated the Bible into the Massachusetts language and gathered native converts into "praying towns." But the mission largely ended in disaster during King Philip's War from 1675 to 1678, when Christian Indians found themselves perilously poised in a deadly no-man's-land between non-Christian Natives and a hostile white population (Cogley 1999).

The parallel work of the Mayhew family in Martha's Vineyard, protected by its insular position, lasted over a century and a half.

On the mainland, with New England Indian populations decimated, these missions continued fitfully, even as they gained the additional support of the Society in Scotland for Promoting Christian Knowledge. A movement of support for Indian missions in the 1760s, led by the evangelical ministers Eleazar Wheelock and Samson Occom, the latter a Mohegan convert, managed to gain influential British sponsors. But to Occom's dismay, the proceeds were redirected by Wheelock from Moor's Indian Charity School in Connecticut to the creation of Dartmouth College (Silverman 2010).

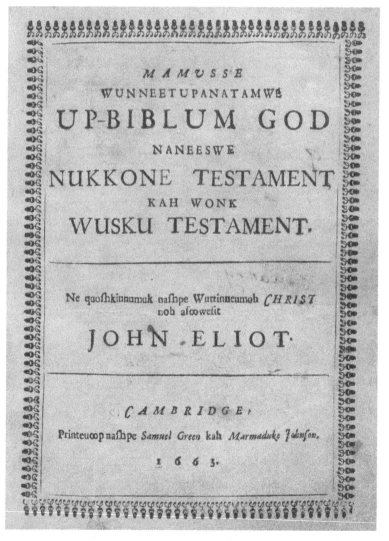

FIGURE 12.1 *The Eliot Bible, in Massachusetts, an Algonquian language, was printed in Cambridge, Massachusetts, in 1663.* Source: Wikimedia Commons.

The other major Protestant missionary enterprise in the period was organized by the Moravians in middle colonies, who established settlements of Christian Indians drawn from the Delaware and Mohican tribes. Just as in King Philip's War, the liminal nature of these Christian Indians could be their undoing. During the American Revolution, the settlement of Gnadenhutten in Ohio became the site of a massacre of ninety-six Moravian Indian men, women, and children by frontier militiamen (Wheeler 2008).

During the colonial period, churches in the British metropole were also concerned with ensuring that white settlers had access to the Word and sacraments. The Society for the Propagation of the Gospel (1701), an Anglican institution, conducted missions to slaves in the British West Indies and to some extent in North America, but the majority of its efforts on the American mainland went toward importing and supporting English ministers (Glasson 2011).

Despite being the established church in most of its American colonies, the Church of England was impeded by the absence of an American bishop. While prospective Anglican clergy needed to return to England for ordination, the Congregational clergy of New England were trained at the local colleges of Harvard and Yale and ordained within their local churches. Especially after the evangelical awakenings of the mid-eighteenth century, the momentum in churching the British colonies shifted to evangelical Presbyterians and Baptists (Isaac 1982).

Missions in the Benevolent Empire

By the nineteenth century, the religious future of the North American continent had become an open question. The continual increase of immigration brought new ethnic groups who arrived in the New World with distinctive religious backgrounds. The United States attracted large numbers of Irish, Germans, and Scandinavians, joined at the turn of the twentieth century by Italians, Czechs, and Poles. The tides of immigration led to increasing numbers of Catholics in a nation once dominated by Protestants.

In Canada, the central Francophone–Anglophone split between the Québécois and the descendants of American Loyalists was complicated first by large numbers of British and Irish migrants in the nineteenth century, and then a similar trend of continental European immigration. This dynamic was never as strong in Mexico, where Spanish immigrants remained the most common arrivals, joined by smaller numbers of French, Germans, Irish, and English.

The upsurge in migration to the United States in the early nineteenth century corresponded to the revivals and missionary activism of the Second Great Awakening. The Methodists and Baptists exploded across the country, especially in the south and the west, aided by networks of tireless itinerants. They embraced populist versions of evangelical theology that encouraged lay leadership and rejected the necessity of an educated ministry (Hatch 1989). Large numbers of African Americans were converted

FIGURE 12.2 *Presbyterian Sabbath school scholars in Caledonia, Columbia County, Wisconsin, in 1900.* Source: *Presbyterian Board of Publication, Philadelphia / Flickr.*

by means of these movements, in turn founding their own institutions, such as the African Methodist Episcopal Church (1816) (Frey and Wood 1998). Meanwhile, a new "benevolent empire" of evangelical voluntary societies, wary of the danger of frontier "infidelity" and immigrant "popery," sought to ensure that the American republic rested on a Protestant foundation. Organizations such as the American Bible Society (1816), the American Tract Society (1825), and the American Sunday School Union (1817) joined with missionary societies like the American Home Missionary Society (1826) to form a phalanx of evangelical missionary endeavor.

Foreign missions from the United States also coalesced out of this movement, most importantly the American Board of Commissioners for Foreign Missions (1810), which by the 1820s had missionaries stationed in the Pacific, the Middle East, and South Asia, as well as among Native American tribes in the United States (Conroy-Krutz 2015). Sharing a desire with the missionaries to instill "civilization" among the Indians, starting in 1819, the Federal Government began to fund educational missions organized by the missionary societies.

The Twentieth Century

By the turn of the twentieth century, Catholic and Jewish immigration began to dramatically reshape the North American ethnic and religious landscape. In an effort to stall the ethnic transformation, the US government imposed a quota system to restrict immigration in 1924. American home missionaries responded by protesting racial quotas and promoting assimilation (Pruitt 2017). Immigrant assimilation was aided by the two world wars, in which Catholics and Jews proved their patriotic attachment to the nation.

In the wake of the Second World War, the Christian understanding of nationhood began to be challenged, when Will Herberg's *Protestant—Catholic—Jew* (1955) posited a new understanding of "Americanism" that incorporated not only Catholics but Jews as well (Schultz 2011). Meanwhile, mainline Protestants began to draw back from conversionistic missions work in the wake of decolonization and a newfound respect for non-Christian religions (Hollinger 2013).

At the same time, another wave of immigration that began in the United States with the Immigration and Nationality Act of 1965 and in Canada with the Immigration

FIGURE 12.3 *An image from* The Home Missionary, *the periodical of the American Home Missionary Society, encouraging American Protestants to welcome Italian immigrants in 1905.* Source: *Wikimedia Commons.*

Act of 1976 brought a new influx of immigrants from East and South Asia, Africa, the Caribbean, and Latin America. This was a continuation of much older trends: Puerto Ricans had become American citizens in 1917 and the American Southwest retained important Mexican–American populations that increased exponentially by immigration starting in the 1970s. Large numbers of Chinese migrants had arrived on the West Coast starting in 1849, only to be confronted with restrictive laws in the United States (1882) and Canada (1885), and expulsion from Mexico in the 1930s. But from the 1960s, Asian immigrants carried with them religious traditions such as Buddhism, Hinduism, and Islam that further loosened Christian hegemony and attracted converts from Christianity (Mann, Numrich, and Williams 2008).

In recent decades this new pattern of immigration has also given rise to a new form of missionization, the work of the so-called "reverse missionary." Christians from Africa, Asia, and Latin America, viewing North America as a mission field in its own right, have established churches seeking to stem the secularization of the Western world (Kim 2015). Although most churches established by reverse missionaries cater to migrants from the same region of the world as their pastor, they are consciously entering into the discourse of an enterprise that has been ongoing for almost five centuries across the North American continent.

Further Reading and Online Resources

Butler J. (1990), *Awash in a Sea of Faith: Christianizing the American People*, Cambridge, MA: Harvard University Press.

Chang D. (2010), *Citizens of a Christian Nation: Evangelical Missions and the Problem of Race in the Nineteenth Century*, Philadelphia: University of Pennsylvania Press.

Finke R. and R. Stark (2005), *The Churching of America, 1775–2005: Winners and Losers in Our Religious Economy*, rev. edn., New Brunswick, NJ: Rutgers University Press.

References

Cogley R.W. (1999), *John Eliot's Mission to the Indians before King Philip's War*, Cambridge, MA: Harvard University Press.

Conroy-Krutz E. (2015), *Christian Imperialism: Converting the World in the Early American Republic*, Ithaca, NY: Cornell University Press.

Frey S.R. and B. Wood (1998), *Come Shouting to Zion: African American Protestantism in the American South and British Caribbean to 1830*, Chapel Hill: University of North Carolina Press.

Glasson T. (2011), *Mastering Christianity: Missionary Anglicanism and Slavery in the Atlantic World*, New York: Oxford University Press.

González O.E. and J.L. González (2008), *Christianity in Latin America: A History*, New York: Cambridge University Press.

Greer A. (2004), *Mohawk Saint: Catherine Tekakwitha and the Jesuits*, New York: Oxford University Press.

MISSIONIZATION AND CHRISTIANITY

Hatch N.O. (1989), *The Democratization of American Christianity*, New Haven, CT: Yale University Press.

Herberg W. ([1955] 1983), *Protestant–Catholic–Jew: An Essay in American Religious Sociology*, Chicago: University of Chicago Press.

Hollinger D.A. (2013), *After Cloven Tongues of Fire: Protestant Liberalism in Modern American History*, Princeton, NJ: Princeton University Press.

Isaac R. (1982), *The Transformation of Virginia, 1740–1790*, Chapel Hill: University of North Carolina Press.

Kim R.Y. (2015), *The Spirit Moves West: Korean Missionaries in America*, New York: Oxford University Press.

Mann G.S., P.D. Numrich, and R.B. Williams (2008), *Buddhists, Hindus, and Sikhs in America: A Short History*, New York: Oxford University Press.

Pruitt N.T. (2017), "Open Hearts, Closed Doors: Native Protestants, Pluralism, and the 'Foreigner' in America, 1924–1965," PhD diss., Baylor University.

Schultz K.M. (2011), *Tri-Faith America: How Catholics and Jews Held Postwar America to Its Protestant Promise*, New York: Oxford University Press.

Silverman D.J. (2010), *Red Brethren: The Brothertown and Stockbridge Indians and the Problem of Race in Early America*, Ithaca, NY: Cornell University Press.

Wheeler R. (2008), *To Live upon Hope: Mohicans and Missionaries in the Eighteenth-Century Northeast*, Ithaca, NY: Cornell University Press.

13

Masculinity and Christianity

Seth Dowland

American Christians have always held particular ideas about how men should appear and act, but fear of an increasingly feminized culture in the late nineteenth century encouraged some to take a more assertive approach in defining *masculinity*. Beginning in the 1870s, a group of white Protestant men began advocating "*muscular Christianity*." The movement had its origins in Great Britain but took root in American churches and parachurch organizations, such as the Young Men's Christian Association (YMCA). These "muscular Christians" worried that the faith had become feminized, thanks to the preponderance of women in the pews, and what they saw as a misguided focus on the meekness of Jesus. They called for depictions of a masculine savior, accompanied by a reinvigoration of church life. The YMCA insisted that physical activity went hand in hand with spirituality. Muscular Christianity's most famous proponent, President Teddy Roosevelt, insisted that if one "reads the Bible aright," he would find it advocated work "that can be done only by the man who is neither a weakling nor a coward" (Putney 2003: 78).

When President Roosevelt and other muscular Christians advocated for American boys and men to toughen up, they almost always had white Protestants in mind. The industrializing of the American economy had placed numbers of these white men into management positions, where their work no longer involved strenuous physical activity. To combat physical flabbiness, muscular Christians extolled adventurous, ambitious projects. These included the YMCA's expansion around the globe, where it spread the Gospel of Christianity and sports alongside a growing American empire. The Edinburgh Missionary Conference of 1910—chaired by YMCA stalwart John R. Mott—epitomized the grand ambitions of muscular Christianity.

Back home in the United States, muscular Christians worried that their churches had become overly feminine. The expansion of Protestant Sunday schools and missionary societies in the nineteenth century had created massive opportunities for women. But

FIGURE 13.1 *The YMCA helped spread muscular Christianity around the globe, often working in tandem with the US Military. This image shows the YMCA providing rations to American soldiers in Liverpool during the First World War.* Source: *A. R. Coster / Stringer / Getty Images.*

muscular Christians feared that female majorities in the church had driven men away. In 1911 to 1912, the short-lived "Men and Religion Forward" placed advertisements in newspapers across the country calling on "3 million missing men" to find their way back to America's pews (Bederman 1989).

Fundamentalists were convinced that these "missing" men in liberal congregations had led those churches down the path of doctrinal error. Conservative Protestants (who had taken the name "fundamentalist" as a way of signaling their commitment to the "fundamentals" of Christian faith) associated masculinity with certitude. They not only resisted female leadership in the church; they charged liberal men with effeminacy. Fundamentalist preacher Arno Gabelein described liberal theologians as "little infidel preacherettes," while his colleague William Bell Riley preached a sermon entitled, "She-Men, or How Some Become Sissies" (Bendroth 1996: 66).

In the first decades of the twentieth century, a looming fear of "race suicide" caused white Protestant Christians to worry about the virility of their men—and about the growing threat of immigrants, Catholics, and African Americans. The rise of muscular Christianity took place at the same time as legislators drafted hundreds of segregation laws. Concern for racial purity seeped into the muscular Christian movement, which

MASCULINITY AND CHRISTIANITY

ensured that depictions of ideal Christian men were white. Artistic representations of Jesus produced during this era portrayed him as a tall, Nordic deity—the epitome of "pure" manhood, at least in the minds of muscular Christians (Blum and Harvey 2012).

The racial overtones of Christian masculinity buttressed nativist politics. During the 1920s, groups such as the American Legion and the Ku Klux Klan grew rapidly by preaching a message of white Christian nationalism. They depicted native-born white Protestants as the only true Americans and enacted violence against immigrants, Catholics, socialists, and African Americans. Muscular Christianity developed as a way to bring the Gospel to men around the world, but the nativist politics of the 1920s revealed racist tendencies within the "manly Christianity" movement (Baker 2011).

At the same time, groups outside the white Protestant mainstream worked to establish their own versions of muscular Christianity. Roman Catholics used boxing as a way to prove their masculinity. Their devotional culture, in which suffering was seen as redemptive, made boxing's brutality into a manifestation of male spirituality. Catholic immigrants could find in their boxers physical signs of the suffering savior. On occasion, they could also exult in a boxing triumph over nativist Protestants (Koehlinger 2019).

African American Christians also placed an emphasis on masculine faith in the early twentieth century. They linked respectable manhood to their quest for civil rights and made defending their women's honor a marker of Black masculinity. Black ministers urged their male congregants to practice sobriety, industry, and protectiveness as a way of demonstrating their manhood. White Protestants perpetuated stereotypes of Black men, for example, as being overly sexual animals, underscoring an ubiquitous anti-Black racism of the early twentieth century.

The rise of big-time sports helped to challenge the racism of muscular Christianity. During the 1950s and 1960s, new evangelical organizations devoted to ministry among athletes emerged. The Fellowship of Christian Athletes grew rapidly among college football teams—particularly in the South—at the same time as that region was experiencing the convulsions of the civil rights movement. Racial desegregation of schools (and, by extension, football teams) in the late 1960s presented a challenge and opportunity for proponents of muscular Christianity. Interracial groups of young men slugging it out on the gridiron became models of a new kind of "colorblind" Christian masculinity.

This type of muscular Christianity reached its apex in the 1990s, when the evangelical men's group Promise Keepers (PK) burst onto the stage. Founded by University of Colorado football coach Bill McCartney, PK called on men to dedicate themselves to God, their church, and their families. McCartney demonstrated a commitment to racial reconciliation, arguing that white men needed to seek forgiveness from people of color. PK's message combined colorblind conservatism with an emphasis on masculine leadership, and it resonated widely. Nearly one million men gathered on the National Mall in Washington for PK's most successful event, the 1997 "Stand in the Gap" rally (Dowland 2015: 207–27).

PK's commitment to racial reconciliation and men's emotionalism proved difficult to sustain. The group fell off the national radar after its budget shrunk dramatically in the

FIGURE 13.2 *In October 1997, men from around the country descended on the National Mall in Washington, DC, for the Promise Keepers "Stand in the Gap" rally.* Source: *Brooks Kraft / Getty Images.*

late 1990s, giving way to more hard-edged masculine ministers. The most prominent, including Al Mohler, Mark Driscoll, and John MacArthur, hailed from the Reformed wing of evangelical Christianity. Reformed evangelicals follow the teachings of sixteenth-century theologian John Calvin. They see Calvin's doctrine of predestination as an unflinching confrontation with the harsh truth of the Gospel. For Mohler, Driscoll, and MacArthur, only Calvinism offers a belief structure sufficient to combat the scourge of postmodern relativism.

These Calvinists' certitude contributed to a combative style that brooked no compromise with liberals. Driscoll was the most notable in his transgressive preaching; he boasted about firing elders, cataloged explicit sexual instructions for married couples, and referred to Promise Keepers as "pussified [...] homoerotic worship loving mama's boys" (Johnson 2018). Such rhetoric was atypical (and Driscoll apologized for this particular quote), but it signaled the increasingly confrontational style emerging among conservative evangelicals in the early twenty-first century.

Aggressive, confrontational masculinity had emerged as a hallmark of conservative American Christianity by the 2016 election, when 81 percent of white evangelical voters supported Donald Trump (Martínez and Smith 2016). Journalists and scholars scrambled to explain how a thrice-married casino mogul and reality television star captured the votes of white evangelicals, who had previously defended "family values" and social conservatism. Trump's combative approach partly explains this unlikely alliance. White evangelicals prized his aggressive, politically incorrect masculinity.

The aggressive masculinity exhibited by Trump and celebrated by his white evangelical supporters showed both continuities and breaks with earlier versions of muscular Christianity. Like the fundamentalists of the 1920s, twenty-first-century evangelicals see their opponents as effeminate ("snowflakes" instead of "sissies"). But the nationalism of twenty-first-century Christian manhood contrasts with the social Gospel-influenced muscular Christianity of the early twentieth century. Those men wanted to bring the world together under the banner of Christ—an internationalist vision. Today's muscular Christians emphasize borders and walls, reflecting the nativism and nationalism central to Trumpism.

As liberal Christians have become comfortable with feminist-inspired calls for gender-neutral language and women clergy, conservative evangelicals have increasingly monopolized the language of Christian manhood. Online searches for Christian masculinity result in a preponderance of evangelical sites. This has marked a shift from the early days of muscular Christianity and has resulted in a narrower understanding of what it means to be a godly Christian man.

Further Reading and Online Resources

CBMW (2017), "The Nashville Statement." Available online: https://cbmw.org/nashville-statement (accessed November 5, 2020).
Kobes Du Mez K. (2020), *Jesus and John Wayne: How White Evangelicals Corrupted a Faith and Fractured a Nation*, New York: Liveright.
University of Minnesota (2020), "Kautz Family YMCA Archives." Available online: https://www.lib.umn.edu/ymca (accessed November 5, 2020).

References

Baker K. (2011), *Gospel According to the Klan: The KKK's Appeal to Protestant America, 1915–1930*, Lawrence: University Press of Kansas.
Bederman G. (1989), "'The Women Have Had Charge of the Church Work Long Enough': The Men and Religion Forward Movement of 1911–1912 and the Masculinization of Middle-Class Protestantism," *American Quarterly*, 41 (3): 432–65.
Bendroth M.L. (1996), *Fundamentalism and Gender, 1875 to the Present*, New Haven, CT: Yale University Press.
Blum E. and P. Harvey (2012), *The Color of Christ: The Son of God & the Saga of Race in America*, Chapel Hill: University of North Carolina Press.
Dowland S. (2015), *Family Values and the Rise of the Christian Right*, Philadelphia: University of Pennsylvania Press.
Johnson J. (2018), *Biblical Porn: Affect, Labor, and Pastor Mark Driscoll's Evangelical Empire*, Durham, NC: Duke University Press.

Koehlinger A. (2019), "Why Boxing Was the Most Catholic Sport for Almost 100 Years," *American Magazine*, March 8. Available online: https://www.americamagazine.org/faith/2019/03/08/why-boxing-was-most-catholic-sport-almost-100-years (accessed November 5, 2020).

Martínez J. and G. Smith (2016), "How the Faithful Voted: A Preliminary 2016 Analysis," Pew Research Center, November 9. Available online: https://www.pewresearch.org/fact-tank/2016/11/09/how-the-faithful-voted-a-preliminary-2016-analysis/ (accessed November 5, 2020).

Putney C. (2003), *Muscular Christianity: Manhood and Sports in Protestant America, 1880–1920*, Cambridge, MA: Harvard University Press.

Glossary Terms

Masculinity The attributes, behaviors, and traits cultures associate with men. Some Christians have viewed masculinity as created by God rather than constructed by culture. These Christians view effeminate men (or masculine women) as disordered.

Muscular Christianity A movement of Protestant Christians in the late nineteenth century and early twentieth century that connected physical fitness to spiritual vitality. Muscular Christians in organizations such as the Young Men's Christian Association (YMCA) promoted sports, personal hygiene, and spiritual discipline as essential to the Christian life.

14

Women and Christianity

Emma Rifai

According to the Pew Research Center, women in the United States are more likely than men to believe in God, consider religion to be an important part of life, attend religious services, pray, participate in religious education, meditate, read scripture, and believe in heaven and hell. Furthermore, a greater percentage of women identify as Catholic, Evangelical Protestant, Historically Black Protestant, Jehovah's Witness, Mainline Protestant, and Mormon than do men. It turns out that, in terms of Christian traditions, it is only in Orthodox Christianity that men outnumber women. Further, the pervasive presence of women in Christianity is not new. For example, even in early seventeenth-century New England, women had an easier time attaining full membership in Puritan churches than did men. While women may have historically been less likely to serve in leadership positions in Christian institutions—though there are notable exceptions including Mary Baker Eddy, Ann Lee, and Aimee Semple McPherson—women have overwhelmingly filled the pews and the coffers of Christian churches in North America.

Why, then, is the topic of "Women and Christianity" merely a sidebar "hot topic" issue in a collection on North American religions? On the surface, this framework suggests that men's experiences with Christianity stand in for the universal, neutral, and even natural North American Christian experience. This privileging of the male perspective in our historical narratives exaggerates the degree to which declension, feminization, and secularization have impacted Christianity in North America today. Rather than focusing on the absence of men, we should, instead, focus on the presence of women. One scholar writes: "Women are present in every class, race, and ethnicity: they are immigrants and natives, old and young, educated and illiterate, northern and southern, Mexican and Canadian. They reside in every geographical area, they are urban and rural, single and married, theologians and devotees" (Braude 1997: 90).

FIGURE 14.1 *Mary Baker Eddy.* Source: *Hulton Archive / Stringer / Getty Images.*

There are two common ways scholars attempt to correct the canonical histories of Christianity in North America to better account for the experiences of women. First, we might look for examples of women assuming the types of leadership roles in Christianity often associated with men. We have a wealth of examples of women as itinerant preachers (e.g., Jarena Lee [1783–1864], the first woman of color preacher in New England), religious reformers (e.g., Anne Hutchinson [1591–1643], who was banished from the Massachusetts Bay Colony because her religious convictions defied established Puritan doctrine), and denominational founders (e.g., Mary Baker Eddy [1821–1910], who established the Church of Christ, Scientist in New England, a faith popularly known as Christian Science today). This approach is valuable insofar as it recovers alternate histories of women who have, in fact, been influential figures in the history of Christianity in North America. On the other hand, this approach employs the same logic as canonical histories: privileging a "great figure" as the primary force of historical change.

The second approach we can use to recover the history of women in North American Christianity is to analyze the various institutional and structural barriers women have historically faced when attempting to access public religious experiences in North

America. For example, various Christian communities refuse to ordain women into clerical positions (e.g., Roman Catholicism, Orthodoxy, the Lutheran Church–Missouri Synod, and the Southern Baptist Convention). In many congregations, women also face more mundane, daily inequalities that diminish their ability to participate fully in their religious communities. For example, the types of auxiliary work women often do in their religious communities (e.g., cooking, teaching Sunday School, and maintaining religious spaces) is often overlooked and underappreciated. Again, attending to these structural barriers provides an important corrective to histories that ignore the experiences of women altogether. However, this approach is still essentially reactive to systems, organizations, and institutions that actively marginalize the breadth of experiences available to women in religious public life.

While making important contributions to the recovery of women's experiences within Christianity in North America, these two approaches often overlook some of the creative and innovative ways women participate in religious public life *alongside* various structural and institutional barriers. For example, Sarah McFarland Taylor explores the fascinating work and lives of American nuns at the forefront of the environmental movement practicing what they call "spiritual ecology." Marie Griffith has written about the experiences of women in Protestant parachurch organizations—such as Aglow International—with complex leadership hierarchies that seemingly empower women while simultaneously affirming *gender complementarianism*. That word, "complementarianism," is a crucial one in the literature on women and religion today. It is the belief that men and women should perform different but complementary roles; women are typically assigned more supportive tasks while men assume leadership positions. While not always recognized for their contributions, women have always been active participants in the history of Christianity in North America, and we can recover these stories when we actively attend to women's experiences as leaders, followers, reformers, founders, and believers.

Finally, it is important to note that a number of Christian communities today practice some form of *radical inclusivity*—the attempt to embrace and welcome diversity in terms of sexual orientation, race, age, citizenship, ethnicity, ability, and socioeconomic status. For example, in 2008, Pastor Nadia Bolz-Weber founded an Evangelical Lutheran Church of America (ELCA) denomination called House for All Sinners and Saints in Denver, Colorado. Her church defines itself as "a group of folks figuring out how to be a liturgical, Christo-centric, social justice-oriented, queer-inclusive, incarnational, contemplative irreverent, ancient/future church with a progressive but deeply rooted theological imagination." It is also important to note that even when institutionalized Christian communities perpetuate certain exclusions, there are people, *within those very groups*, who think differently. For example, Catholics for Choice is a reproductive rights advocacy group in Washington, DC, that believes abortions should be safe, legal, and accessible for everyone. Similarly, a Methodist organization called Reconciling Ministries Network advocates for the inclusion of all sexual orientations and gender identities in the United Methodist Church.

The goal should be to treat women as full participants and citizens in religious public life. We should recognize and embrace their contributions in canonical histories of

Christianity in North America. Moving beyond gendered categories will allow us to consider the experiences and contributions of queer, transgender, non-binary, and non-gender-conforming individuals. If we include these other categories to those of cisgender categories, then our histories of Christianity in North America will be more authentic, complexified, and nuanced.

Diverse, seemingly sidebar, histories of Christianity *are* the histories of Christianity in North America. If women were included fully in North American histories of Christianity, then we would not need "hot topic" sections like this one. Ultimately, therefore, we should hope to reach a point where these sections become redundant as our canonical histories better reflect the experiences of everyone who has contributed to religious public life and to academic scholarship on Christianity in North America.

Further Reading and Online Resources

Braude A. (2001), *Radical Spirits: Spiritualism and Women's Rights in Nineteenth-Century America*, Bloomington: Indiana University Press.

Braude A. (2008), *Sisters and Saints: Women and American Religion*, Oxford: Oxford University Press.

Brekus C.A. (1998), *Strangers and Pilgrims: Female Preaching in America, 1740–1846*, Chapel Hill: University of North Carolina Press.

Brekus C.A. (2007), *The Religious History of American Women: Reimagining the Past*, Chapel Hill: University of North Carolina Press.

Griffith R.M. (2000), *God's Daughters: Evangelical Women and the Power of Submission*, Berkeley: University of California Press.

Nabhan-Warren K. (2005), *The Virgin of El Barrio: Marian Apparitions, Catholic Evangelizing, and Mexican American Activism*, New York: New York University Press.

Reference

Braude A. (1997), "Women's History Is American Religious History," in T.A. Tweed (ed.), *Retelling U.S. Religious History*, 87–107, Berkeley: University of California Press.

Glossary Terms

Gender complementarianism The belief that men and women should perform different but complimentary roles.

Radical inclusivity The attempt made by religious communities to embrace and welcome diversity in its many forms.

15

Sex, Sexuality, and Christianity

Kristy L. Slominski

Sex and sexuality, along with closely related issues of *gender*, have been consistently hot topics among American Christian communities. These topics have included—but are not limited to—women's ordination; lesbian, gay, bisexual, transexual (LGBT) inclusion; sex education; abortion; evangelical marital sexuality and purity culture; and sexual scandals.

In the nineteenth century, one disagreement between and within Christian communities was whether women should be ordained. Some Protestant denominations, for instance Quakers, allowed women to preach from their beginning. In the twentieth century, the number of mainline denominations allowing female ordinations grew, although some restricted ordained women from holding leadership roles beyond the congregational level. Other Protestant groups, along with Catholics and Eastern Orthodox Christians, rejected female ordination, holding to church tradition or biblical passages that they interpreted as preventing female clergy. While the problem has shifted within communities that ordain women to the related challenge of implementation, Catholics and some Protestant denominations continue to face agitation from members to break their patriarchal traditions of male-only clergy (Knoll and Bolin 2018). The Roman Catholic Women Priest movement has gone beyond protest and asserted their authority to ordain women against the doctrines of the Vatican.

Many mainline Protestant denominations that came to accept female ordination would later debate the degree to which homosexuals should be included in church life and doctrine, a topic that caused and continues to cause internal divisions. Reflecting the expansion of lesbian, gay, bisexual, transgender, intersex, and queer/questioning (LGBTIQ) activism, later discussions addressed the inclusion of people who identified as LGBTIQ, along with debates over LGBTIQ ordination and same-sex marriage. The Metropolitan Community Church, the first denomination for gay and lesbian Christians, was created in Los Angeles 1968, offering a religious refuge from the homophobia that plagued denominations and the anti-religious sentiment prominent in LGBT circles (Wilcox 2003: 170). At the time, same-sex intercourse remained a crime in most US states, with Illinois being the first to repeal its sodomy laws in the early 1960s. Some liberal clergy actively engaged in the early gay rights movement, although the National Council of Churches, the largest organization of mainline Protestant denominations in the United States, refused the Metropolitan Community Church's repeated requests for membership (Gerber 2018: 256). In 1972, the United Church of Christ became the first mainline Protestant denomination in America to ordain an openly gay person. Scholars Heather R. White and Rebecca L. Davis have shown that early liberal Protestant efforts to challenge religious prohibitions against homosexuality had ambivalent consequences. By defining the "homosexual" according to therapeutic-psychological trends, liberal Protestants provided fuel for later anti-homosexual views among conservative evangelicals, who continued to perpetuate the view of homosexuality as a disease long after it was renounced by the American Psychological Association and progressive activists (Davis 2011: 361; White 2015: 1–14). Although stances on LGBTIQ inclusion often follow liberal and conservative theological divides, these debates remain unsettled in many religious communities. In 2019, the United Methodist Church reinforced its ban on LGBTIQ ordination and same-sex marriage, reflecting a deep chasm within their denomination between supporters and protesters of the decision.

Beyond internal debates, American Christians have engaged debates about sexuality in the public sphere as well. Intense controversies emerged in the late 1960s over whether comprehensive sexuality education belonged in public schools. This form of sex education had been the brainchild of progressive Quaker Mary Steichen Calderone, who promoted sexuality as a health topic. With clergy from the National Council of Churches, she created the Sex Information and Education Council of the United States in 1964. Liberal Protestants and some progressive Catholics had long been a part of national organizations promoting public education about sexuality, beginning with their involvement in the creation of the American Social Health Association in 1914. Earlier campaigns focused on educating communities about the dangers of syphilis, gonorrhea, and having sex with prostitutes. In the 1920s, Christian sex educators began to push the sex education movement toward teaching sexuality as part of family life education, a framework that came to dominate the movement by mid-century (Slominski 2021).

In the 1960s, comprehensive sexuality education faced greater opposition from conservative Protestants, including those of the Christian Crusade, who opposed teaching about sexuality outside of Christian contexts and divorced from their biblical interpretation that sexual behavior belonged only within marriage. Their protests related to broader concerns about the removal of public prayer and sponsored Bible readings from public schools. The 1968 to 1969 sex education controversies served as an early example of alliances between conservative Christians over sexual politics, providing a model for the development of the so-called Christian right and its pro-family political agenda (Irvine 2002: 2–3; Slominski 2021). In the 1980s, some evangelical leaders of the Christian right proposed an alternative form of public sex education now

FIGURE 15.1 *Mary Steichen Calderone, known as the founder of comprehensive sexuality education.* Source: *Smithsonian Institution Archives.*

known as abstinence-only education. The AIDS crisis posed challenges to abstinence-only education because alarming infection rates led to a greater emphasis on condoms and same-sex sexual behavior, both of which abstinence-only excluded. Evangelicals felt additional defeat when Surgeon General C. Everett Koop, a prominent evangelical, endorsed AIDS education in 1986 and soon after launched one of the largest sex education campaigns in national history (Petro 2015). In 1996, however, abstinence-only advocates won a significant and long-lasting victory when the federal government began to fund abstinence-only education with fifty million dollars a year.

FIGURE 15.2 *Norma McCorvey ("Jane Roe," left) and her lawyer on the steps of the Supreme Court in 1989.* Source: *Lorie Shaull.*

Abortion debates in many ways came to mirror sex education debates, with vocal liberal and conservative Christian leaders defining opposite sides and many lay Christians maintaining more moderate views in between the public extremes. However, at the time of *Roe v. Wade*, a 1973 Supreme Court decision that lifted state bans on abortions before the point of fetal viability, these familiar contours of later debates had not yet developed. Up until the 1970s, Catholic physicians and clergy led the right to life movement, later called pro-life. As historian Daniel K. Williams argues, the pro-life movement originated the language of human rights in the abortion debates because they argued for the right to life of the unborn long before proponents of legalizing abortion adopted arguments for women's rights (2016: 4–5; 114–15). In the early 1970s, some Protestants joined pro-life Catholics, including social liberals who linked pro-life activism to anti-war efforts. Most conservative Protestants, however, remained either indifferent or supportive of the *Roe v. Wade* decision. It was not until the late 1970s that evangelicals became leaders within the pro-life movement around the same time that they became closely associated with the Republican Party. The pro-choice movement, which organized around 1970 with the influences of feminism and, to some degree, liberal Protestantism, became aligned by the end of the decade with the Democratic Party (Williams 2016). Despite religious and political pro-life efforts, including an increasing number of state laws in the twenty-first century adding additional restrictions on abortion, the Supreme Court has yet to fully overturn the *Roe v. Wade* decision.

Both the abstinence-only and pro-life movements have been profoundly shaped by evangelical sexuality, which upholds heterosexual Christian marriage as the only context for sexual behavior. Evangelicals created a vibrant publishing industry of evangelical manuals that celebrate marital sexuality, arguing that married Christians have the best sex with the Bible as their ultimate guidebook (DeRogatis 2015). They have extended this message to create marital sexual ministries online (Burke 2016) and to develop a popular Christian purity culture, which praises premarital abstinence and depicts premarital sexuality as dangerous. Purity culture includes, among other things, purity literature, purity pledges, and father-daughter dances known as purity balls in which fathers promise to protect their daughters' chastity (Gardner 2011; Moslener 2015). Purity culture has been critiqued for creating a culture of guilt around sexuality, for shaming people who engage in premarital sexual behavior, including those subjected to sexual violence, and for promoting patriarchy, heterosexism, and homophobia. These critiques have been strengthened by the loss of one of the purity movement's most outspoken champions—Joshua Harris—author of *I Kissed Dating Goodbye*. In 2018 Harris expressed strong regret for spreading the purity message, and even claimed to have broken with Christianity altogether. Evangelicalism's stance against homosexual behavior also received media attention when Exodus International, an evangelical ex-gay ministry that sought to convert people from homosexual lifestyles, declared its conversion therapy methods to be harmful; they closed their doors in 2013 (Erzen 2006).

While many Black churches uphold evangelical beliefs and sexual ethics, they focus on aspects important to the history and lives of Black people. Evangelical sexual ministries for Black women, including televangelism, conferences, and other forms of media, "adjust the white-dominant message to reflect a history wherein a woman's purity is not automatically considered the property of her father, a woman's purity can be denied because of stereotypes of her being sexually available, sexual pleasure can be discussed, and a woman's path to a God-given marriage is not guaranteed" (Moultrie 2017: 4). These adaptations respond to common stereotypes of the oversexualized "Jezebel" and the asexual "Mammy," which have been negotiated in terms of the "politics of respectability" within Black churches to restrict the articulations of women's sexuality (7–8).

Sex scandals have punctuated conversations about Christianity and sexuality in the twenty-first century. The topic, of course, is not new; among other cases, scholars have documented clergy sexual misconduct in nineteenth-century America and as part of the televangelist "telescandals" of the late twentieth century (Gedge 2003: 23–74; Harding 2001: 247–69; Krivulskaya 2018: 1–27). Cases of child sexual abuse by Catholic priests were also known, but new investigations uncovered the extent of involvement by Catholic hierarchs who helped in transferring accused priests to new congregations. Attention has also been directed toward cases of sexual abuse committed by Protestant clergy and the related involvement of denominational leaders who knew about them. While there is never a good time for a scandal, these have hit the churches at a time when many Christian denominations are losing members.

Further Reading and Online Resources

DeRogatis A. (2015), *Saving Sex: Sexuality and Salvation in American Evangelicalism*, New York: Oxford University Press.

Griffith R.M. (2017), *Moral Combat: How Sex Divided American Christians and Fractured American Politics*, New York: Basic Books.

References

Burke K. (2016), *Christians under Covers: Evangelicals and Sexual Pleasure on the Internet*, Berkeley: University of California Press.

Davis R.L. (2011), "'My Homosexuality Is Getting Worse Every Day': Norman Vincent Peale, Psychiatry, and the Liberal Protestant Response to Same-Sex Desires in Mid-Twentieth-Century America," in C.A. Brekus and W.C. Gilpin (eds.), *American Christianities: A History of Dominance and Diversity*, 347–65, Chapel Hill: University of North Carolina Press.

DeRogatis A. (2015), *Saving Sex: Sexuality and Salvation in American Evangelicalism*, New York: Oxford University Press.

Erzen T. (2006), *Straight to Jesus: Sexual and Christian Conversion in the Ex-gay Movement*, Berkeley: University of California Press.

Gardner C.J. (2011), *Making Chastity Sexy: The Rhetoric of Evangelical Abstinence Campaigns*, Berkeley: University of California Press.

Gedge K.E. (2003), *Without Benefit of Clergy: Women and the Pastoral Relationship in Nineteenth-Century American Culture*, New York: Oxford University Press.

Gerber L. (2018), "We Who Must Die Demand a Miracle: Christmas 1989 at the Metropolitan Community Church in San Francisco," in G. Frank, B. Moreton, and H.R. White (eds.), *Devotions and Desires: Histories of Sexuality and Religion in the Twentieth-Century United States*, 253–76, Chapel Hill: University of North Carolina Press.

Harding S.F. (2001), *The Book of Jerry Falwell Fundamentalist Language and Politics*, Princeton, NJ: Princeton University Press.

Irvine J.M. (2002), *Talk about Sex: The Battles over Sex Education in the United States*, Berkeley: University of California Press.

Knoll B.R. and C.J. Bolin (2018), *She Preached the Word: Women's Ordination in Modern America*, New York: Oxford University Press.

Krivulskaya S. (2018), "Paths of Duty: Religion, Marriage, and the Press in a Transatlantic Scandal, 1835–1858," *Journal of American Studies*: 1–27. https://doi.org/10.1017/S0021875818000981.

Moslener S. (2015), *Virgin Nation: Sexual Purity and American Adolescence*, New York: Oxford University Press.

Moultrie M.N. (2017), *Passionate and Pious: Religious Media and Black Women's Sexuality*, Durham, NC: Duke University Press.

Petro A.M. (2015), *After the Wrath of God: AIDS, Sexuality, & American Religion*, New York: Oxford University Press.

Slominski K.L. (2021), *Teaching Moral Sex: A History of Religion and Sex Education in America*, New York: Oxford University Press.

White H.R. (2015), *Reforming Sodom: Protestants and the Rise of Gay Rights*, Chapel Hill: University of North Carolina Press.

Wilcox M.M. (2003), *Coming Out in Christianity: Religion, Identity, and Community*, Bloomington: Indiana University Press.

Williams D.K. (2016), *Defenders of the Unborn: The Pro-Life Movement before Roe v. Wade*, New York: Oxford University Press.

Glossary Terms

Gender Feminine, masculine, or androgynous qualities or actions, which are shaped by culture-specific assumptions about what it means to be a man or a woman.

Sex A term with multiple meanings, from the act of intercourse to the category that includes male, female, and intersex. Intersex refers to individuals whose sexual biology does not conform to typical medical distinctions between males and females and is associated with a variety of causes and conditions. Although it may be convenient to distinguish sex and gender by saying that the former is about biology and the latter is about culturally assigned characteristics, also cultural assumptions about what it means to be a man or a woman profoundly influence the categories of male and female and are therefore not "scientifically objective" categories.

16

On Christians and the Abortion Divide/Debate in North America

Kristy L. Slominski

United States

Abortion debates have become associated with the pro-life and pro-choice movements in the United States, a reflection of the perceived conservative verses liberal "culture wars" dividing Americans. *Roe v. Wade*—a 1973 Supreme Court decision that overturned many state and federal abortion restrictions on first and second trimester abortions—is another household phrase linked to these debates. Religious people, especially Christians, have been involved in conversations and stances about abortion within their own communities and in the public sphere. Reflecting the diversity of Christianity in the United States, Christians span the spectrum of opinions on abortion and its regulation by the government.

The idea promoted by pro-life movements that life begins at conception is a fairly recent one. Before the nineteenth century, the time at which a woman could feel the fetus moving inside of her, or the moment of "quickening," was seen as the first signs of life in the womb, and this often occurred around twenty weeks of pregnancy (McLaren and McLaren 1997: 39). This corresponds to the belief of numerous religious groups that "ensoulment" occurred not at conception but at a later stage of fetal development. Abortion before this point of pregnancy was more generally accepted. Even the medieval Catholic Church, which condemned any means of limiting fertility and reproduction, had leaders who considered early abortion to be a less grievous sin than murder. By the nineteenth century, views on abortion began to change. Physicians pushed to institute state laws that banned abortion except when a pregnancy was deemed life-threatening. As sociologist Gene Burns argues, these laws championed doctors' control over abortion procedures rather than abortion as a moral issue (2005: 162). At the same time, illegal abortions and advertisements for abortifacients (abortion drugs) continued, putting many women at risk for medical complications. Although the laws were not intended to support Catholics, they aligned with Catholic views, and the Catholic Church issued a pronouncement in 1869 called *Apostolicae Sedis* reminding its constituency that abortions at any point in pregnancy would result in excommunication.

The beginning of the abortion debate in the United States can be traced to the 1930s. The growing support for contraception at this time, along with the strain on resources created by the Great Depression, led some doctors to begin campaigning for the decriminalization of abortion in limited cases such as rape (Williams 2016: 20). The campaign to expand pregnancies that qualified for legal abortion before the 1960s represented "a medical or population control movement, not a women's rights cause" (xii). The most vocal promoters of abortion reform were progressive Jewish doctors committed to saving women's lives, helping the poor, and improving society. The antiabortion movement that opposed these campaigns was led by Catholic doctors organized within the National Federation of Catholic Physicians' Guilds, while most Protestant doctors stood somewhere in the middle and remained relatively silent on the issue (26–7).

Even as the divide between supporters and opponents of the liberalization of abortion laws continued to widen during the following decades, relatively few people were involved and the issue received little public attention. After the Second World War, Catholic doctors and theologians increasingly drew comparisons between abortions and the eugenic campaigns to murder Jews during the Holocaust, a comparison that was rejected as offensive by supporters of abortion reform. Sex researchers, inspired by the reports about American sexual practices published by Alfred Kinsey and his associates in 1948 and 1953, produced further documentation about the high rates of illegal abortions, providing data to support arguments for the liberalization of abortion laws to make abortions safer (Williams 2016: 38–40). In 1961, the National Council of Churches, which represented many mainline Protestant denominations, announced support for limited forms of abortions, specifically when the woman's health was at risk. The 1962 case of Sherri Chessen Finkbine, who was denied an abortion in Arizona for her pregnancy with a high risk of birth defects, received national media attention and highlighted a divide between Catholics and non-Catholics on their support for her decision (Burns 2005: 166–7; Williams 2016: 41–3). The following year, several states proposed legislation to liberalize abortion laws, all of which were struck down before reaching public votes. These victories for the antiabortion movement "probably made Catholics overconfident," leaving them unprepared for the next round of abortion reforms (Williams 2016: 50).

The medical framing of abortion continued to dominate legislative discussions through the 1960s. Between 1966 and 1970, numerous states passed bills to expand legal abortion beyond those that could save a woman's life to those that a physician deemed necessary to improve her physical and mental health or in cases of rape, incest, or fetal impairment. These reforms passed in many southern states, where moral controversy was minimal in part because they had smaller Catholic populations, and most evangelical Protestants supported abortion in limited cases such as rape

(Burns 2005: 182). In the meantime, a growing movement influenced by second-wave feminism began to replace conversations about physicians' rights with women's rights, advocating for repeal instead of reform of abortion laws (Luker 1985: 92–125). They, however, were not the first to introduce the language of individual rights into the abortion debates; antiabortion advocates had long based their arguments on the rights of the fetus (Williams 2016: 4–5, 114–15). Planned Parenthood, the National Organization for Women, and the National Association for the Repeal of Abortion Laws (NARAL) joined pro-choice alliances, along with liberal Protestant clergy, forming a grassroots pro-choice movement. Abortion repeal laws introduced in the early 1970s, however, provoked heated controversy and were largely unsuccessful.

Despite the lack of success at the state level for abortion repeal laws, January 22, 1973, marked a landmark victory for the pro-choice movement. The Supreme Court decision in *Roe v. Wade* overturned a Texas antiabortion law, ruling that a woman's right to an abortion was protected under her "right to privacy" by the Constitution's Fourteenth Amendment. This right, however, was to be balanced with concern for the fetus. In the eyes of the court, the fetus' rights became more pressing as the pregnancy developed, especially after the point at which the fetus could live outside of the womb, which the courts identified at twenty-eight weeks. *Doe v. Bolton*, a decision issued concurrently with *Roe v. Wade*, overturned abortion restrictions in Georgia and confirmed that even after the point of fetal viability an abortion may not be restricted if it protects the woman's health.

FIGURE 16.1 *Norma McCorvey ("Jane Roe," left) and her lawyer on the steps of the Supreme Court in 1989.* Source: *Lorie Shaull.*

The antiabortion movement up until the end of the 1960s had been led by male Catholic physicians and clergy, with few Protestants or Jews participating (Williams 2016: 66). By then, Catholics increasingly recognized the need to diversify the movement so that it was no longer seen as just a Catholic issue. The Catholic Church had faced a long history of anti-Catholicism from American Protestants, and its authority among its own members on reproductive issues had been challenged after the Second Vatican Council of the 1960s. Vatican II had initiated widespread change within the church but ultimately did not change the church's stance against artificial birth control as many lay Catholics had hoped. Subsequently, lay Catholics embraced the idea that Catholic doctrine could change and felt more comfortable explicitly rejecting church teachings on birth control (Tentler 2004). To progress the antiabortion cause after *Roe v. Wade*, Catholics made it into a single-issue movement, separating it from their previous ties to rejecting contraception because most Protestants and Jews saw no moral issue with birth control. The National Right to Life Committee was created as an independent national organization that would coordinate local groups beyond the leadership of Catholic bishops (Williams 2016: 58–9).

This "right to life" movement, which was later shortened to pro-life, succeeded in recruiting non-Catholic leaders and women. In the first half of the 1970s, pro-life activists spanned the social and political spectrum, including social progressives who linked their pro-life stance to anti-war activism. Even though most Catholics were Democrats, neither the Democratic nor the Republican Party rallied behind them. It was not until the late-1970s that Republican strategists saw the political advantage of supporting the pro-life movement, a move that was linked to their new constituency: conservative evangelicals—along with their pro-life family platform (Ginsburg 1998: 43–4; Luker 1985: 126–57). After this point, the public face of the pro-life movement also became associated with the so-called Christian right, led largely by white evangelicals. In the 1980s and 1990s the movement became publically associated with the actions of its more militant members, including violence against abortion clinics (Burns 2005: 234–5).

Evangelicals have embraced the pro-life stance as part of the movement's identity and agenda, although scholars have challenged the common myth that the Christian Right emerged from protests of *Roe v. Wade*. At the time of the landmark decision, conservative Protestants tended to be either ambivalent or supportive of *Roe v. Wade*. Antiabortion activism did not become a central part of the Christian right's platform until the late-1970s, before which time they saw it as predominantly a Catholic issue (Balmer 2014; Dowland 2015: 114). Several scholars, most notably Randall Balmer, have pointed to the desegregation of American schools—and especially the denial of tax-exempt status to private schools that refused to racially integrate in the 1970s—as the "real origins" of the Christian right (Balmer 2014). In other words, Balmer argues that conservative Protestants came together politically not out of a shared opposition to abortion but based on the impulse to defend their Christian schools against forced integration and the government interference that it represented. Many scholars now acknowledge racial politics as at least one of the factors in the rise of the Christian right.

FIGURE 16.2 *A clinic escort outside of a Planned Parenthood clinic.* Source: *Robin Marty.*

Later Supreme Court decisions challenged aspects of the *Roe v. Wade* ruling, although attempts to completely overturn it have been unsuccessful. In 1989, *Webster v. Reproductive Health Services* ruled that states could prohibit abortions in public hospitals and could restrict access to abortion earlier than twenty-eight weeks if the fetus proved viable. In 1992, *Planned Parenthood of Southeast Pennsylvania v. Casey* proclaimed that states could do the following: introduce waiting periods, mandate education and counseling that promoted negative portrayals of abortion, and require facilities to report the number of abortion procedures performed (Burns 2005: 232–3). The core rulings from the 1989 and 1992 cases remain in place.

In the twenty-first century, abortion has faced increasing restrictions at the state level. Numerous states proposed so-called "heartbeat bills," which banned abortion after the fetal heartbeat could be detected instead of the later point of fetal viability. Courts have struck down some of these laws. In 2019, Alabama passed HB 314, which criminalized doctors who perform abortion procedures, with exceptions only for cases that seriously threaten the pregnant woman's health, ectopic pregnancies, and those in which the fetus could not survive birth. Along with efforts to restrict education about abortion through abstinence-only education and to defund abortion providers, state-level legislative attempts have been made to require the burial of aborted fetuses, to increase required delays and permission processes, and to forbid abortions in cases of genetic abnormalities. Pro-life advocates hope that these state bills, which have faced legal action from the American Civil Liberties Union and Planned Parenthood, will lead to the eventual overturning of *Roe v. Wade* if they make it to the Supreme Court.

Canada

In Canada, the 1988 Supreme Court case *R v. Morgentaler* is the case that comes to the fore in abortion discussions because it overturned the law outlawing most abortions in Canada. Strongly influenced by British law, Canada had banned both contraceptives and abortion—except to save the woman's life—starting in the nineteenth century. In 1969, contraception was legalized and abortion allowed if performed in a hospital and approved by an official therapeutic abortion committee, which considered cases that threatened the woman's health and not just her life. Mainline Protestant communities gave the 1969 reform conditional support, including the United Church, Unitarians, Presbyterians, Anglicans, as well as Reform Jews. Although they supported expanding legal abortions beyond just life-threatening cases to include other threats to a woman's health, most "stressed they were against abortion for social and economic reasons" (Morton 1992: 21). Opponents to the reform included the Canadian Catholic Conference. Catholic politician Joseph "Joe" Borowski became the main spokesperson for the Canadian pro-life movement of the late 1970s and 1980s, sacrificing his political career for his activism for the unborn (22, 14–16). Lay Catholics, however, were divided on the

FIGURE 16.3 *Henry Morgentaler, pro-choice abortion activist in Canada.* Source: *John Mahler / Toronto Star via Getty Images.*

issue, as "Catholics were just as likely as Protestants to avail themselves of abortion services, and Quebec was the province that manifested the nation's most liberal views on the subject" despite their overwhelming affiliation with Catholicism (McLaren and McLaren 1997: 146). Part of this can be attributed to the fact that the Canadian Conference of Catholic Bishops had already challenged the Vatican's pronouncements against contraception in their 1968 Winnipeg Statement, opening the door for Canadian Catholics to disagree with official pronouncements on many reproductive issues.

Henry Morgentaler, a Jewish Holocaust survivor who became a doctor and reproductive rights advocate, drew the attention of the law and eventually the nation through his civil disobedience of performing abortions in clinical settings outside of hospitals and without the required committee approval. After facing numerous legal charges, including imprisonment in 1975, his 1988 case made its way to the Supreme Court, which declared the 1969 abortion restrictions to be unconstitutional under the 1982 Canadian Charter of Rights and Freedoms. After the 1988 ruling in favor of Morgentaler, no specific law governed abortion, which was thereafter to be treated like other medical procedures without being singled out with additional limitations. Therapeutic abortion committees were disbanded and abortion clinics outside of hospital settings increased, leading to greater access to safe abortion services, although access continues to be a struggle for Canadian women in remote areas. The 1989 Supreme Court case *Tremblay v. Daigle* denied the fetus legal standing as a person, further supporting abortion rights (McLaren and McLaren 1997: 144). Legislative attempts have been made to reintroduce abortion bans but have been unsuccessful (Norman and Downie 2017). However, some news media report that the increase in antiabortion bills in the United States in 2019 has inspired the Canadian pro-life movement and may lead to a reopening of abortion debates in Canada.

Mexico

In Mexico, the strong presence of the Catholic Church and its antiabortion stance has often stifled public debate on the issue. Abortion procedures have been illegal in Mexico through state-level legislation, most of which was based on a 1931 penal code and allowed abortions only in limited cases such as rape, incest, or situations lethal to the woman. Legislative changes in 2000 expanded exemptions in some states to include cases of significant fetal defects, involuntary artificial insemination, and situations that seriously threatened aspects of the woman's health, even if non-life-threatening (Kulczycki 2007: 51–2). However, even for those who met these conditions, many states denied petitions for abortions, and medical procedures remained difficult to access, especially for poor women and those living in rural locations. Illegal abortions were prevalent and caused high rates of female death and serious health complications.

Increased federal resources for family planning programs since the 1970s, including government approval of emergency contraception in 2004, have helped some women

230 CHRISTIANITY IN NORTH AMERICA

to prevent unplanned pregnancies. These programs, however, have not reached many women and consciously excluded abortion services. In 2007, Mexico City became the only place in Mexico to legalize elective abortions within the first twelve weeks of pregnancy and provided free services to uninsured residents. Although this has increased access to safe abortion procedures for those in and surrounding the city, many other states doubled down on their abortion restrictions, defining human personhood at the point of egg fertilization or conception and enforcing their abortion laws to a greater extent (Kulczycki 2011: 208).

When abortion debates have surfaced in Mexican politics, feminists have led the charge for decriminalizing abortion while Catholic lay organizations such as Pro-Vida, Legionnaires of Christ, and Opus Dei have rallied against such reform. Because Mexico has one of the largest Catholic populations in the world, the Catholic hierarchy has taken a special interest in the country and maintaining its laws against abortion. Pope John Paul II, for example, visited five times during his papacy and spoke out against abortion. Pope Benedict XVI spoke out in 2007 against Mexico City's abortion reform. However, some Mexican Catholics have disagreed with the Catholic hierarchy on this issue, represented by the organization Catholics for a Free Choice (Kulczycki 2007: 58).

Further Reading and Online Resources

Burns G. (2005), *The Moral Veto: Framing Contraception, Abortion, and Cultural Pluralism in the United States*, New York: Cambridge University Press.
Guttmacher Institute (n.d.), "United States: Abortion." Available online: https://www. guttmacher.org/united-states/abortion (accessed September 15, 2019).
Kulczycki A. (2007), "The Abortion Debate in Mexico: Realities and Stalled Policy Reform," *Bulletin of Latin American Research*, 26 (1): 50–68.
Morton F.L. (1992), *Pro-Choice v. Pro-Life: Abortion and the Courts in Canada*, Norman: University of Oklahoma Press.
Williams D.K. (2016), *Defenders of the Unborn: The Pro-Life Movement before Roe v. Wade*, New York: Oxford University Press.

References

Balmer R. (2014), "The Real Origins of the Religious Right," *Politico Magazine*. Available online: https://www.politico.com/magazine/story/2014/05/religious-right-real-origins-107133 (accessed September 15, 2019).
Burns G. (2005), *The Moral Veto: Framing Contraception, Abortion, and Cultural Pluralism in the United States*, New York: Cambridge University Press.
Dowland S. (2015), *Family Values and the Rise of the Christian Right*, Philadelphia: University of Pennsylvania Press.
Ginsburg F.D. (1998), *Contested Lives: The Abortion Debate in an American Community*, Berkeley: University of California Press.
Kulczycki A. (2007), "The Abortion Debate in Mexico: Realities and Stalled Policy Reform," *Bulletin of Latin American Research*, 26 (1): 50–68.

Kulczycki A. (2011), "Abortion in Latin America: Changes in Practice, Growing Conflict, and Recent Policy Developments," *Studies in Family Planning*, 42 (3): 199–220.

Luker K. (1985), *Abortion and the Politics of Motherhood*, Berkeley: University of California Press.

McLaren A. and A.T. McLaren (1997), *The Bedroom and the State: The Changing Practices and Politics of Contraception and Abortion in Canada, 1880–1997*, 2nd edn., New York: Oxford University Press.

Morton F.L. (1992), *Pro-Choice v. Pro-Life: Abortion and the Courts in Canada*, Norman: University of Oklahoma Press.

Norman W.V. and J. Downie (2017), "Abortion Care in Canada Is Decided between a Woman and Her Doctor, Without Recourse to Criminal Law," *British Medical Journal*, 356: 1–2.

Tentler L.W. (2004), *Catholic and Contraception: An American History*, Ithaca, NY: Cornell University Press.

Williams D.K. (2016), *Defenders of the Unborn: The Pro-Life Movement before Roe v. Wade*, New York: Oxford University Press.

17

Christianity and Politics in North America

Anthony J. Miller

Introduction

In November of 2019, US Energy Secretary Rick Perry, an ardent Protestant evangelical, declared to the American press his belief that President Donald Trump was "chosen by God." Perry's conviction reflected an evangelical's conception of God selecting "imperfect" leaders—even those such as the president who were prone to frequent ethical lapses such as adultery—as "chosen" to lead the nation. Conversely, it also seemed clear that like many other prominent Christian conservatives, Perry was invoking Christianity as a political defense for a president embroiled in scandal. That fall in the lead up to the congressional inquiry into Trump's relations with Ukraine, evangelist Franklin Graham had labeled the mounting criticism of Trump from the Democratic Party the work of "demonic forces" (Cummings 2019). With Congress lingering on the question of moving forward with impeachment, Trump's supporters were drawing spiritual "lines in the sand," pinning their hopes for the president's political salvation on the mobilization of the conservative Christian base. To supporters, those that stood with Trump even despite his "imperfections," whether immoral or illegal, were standing with God's anointed leader in a turbulent moment in the nation's history.

Graham's and Perry's statements are two examples that could be used to illustrate the influence of Christianity on politics in the twenty-first century. More can be found in Mexico and Canada, where like the United States, Christianity has long been a decisive political force. According to the Pew Research Center on Religion & Public Life, North America in 2010 was home to over 266,000 million Christians, nearly 77 percent of the total population. Not surprisingly then contemporary media across North America regularly features pundits, journalists, and academics forecasting how Christians will mobilize voters and push political candidates to embody Christian values.

FIGURE 17.1 *President Donald Trump with Governor Greg Abbot and Secretary Rick Perry.*
Source: *United States Department of Energy / Wikimedia Commons.*

Scholars have long researched Christianity's impact on political life in Mexico, Canada, and the United States. With a history in the "New World" that dates back to the collision between European explorers and Native Americans in the fifteenth century, Christianity has been a potent political force shaping the development of nations. Since that time, scholars from a range of disciplines—history, political science, sociology—have pursued a number of critical research questions: What role did Christianity play in the quest for revolution and later civil rights? Or, alternatively, how have Christian clergy, churches, and grassroots campaigns promoted conservatism and fought to preserve "traditional" values?

Scholars also benefit by asking questions that compare Christianity's role in the political sphere in Canada, the United States, and Mexico. For example, how does the Christian religion infuse political discourse, values, and the ideas of various political parties, leaders, and government in the United States, Canada, and Mexico? These questions are especially useful in examining how Christianity has influenced modernization in North America, as a friend or foe of capitalism and the development of secular and pluralistic societies. Especially in the past few decades, researchers have investigated how Christianity colors the attitudes of Canadians, Mexicans, and Americans toward globalization. This chapter introduces the reader to the subject of Christianity and politics in North America via a number of important themes such as colonialism, civil rights and progressivism, conservatism, and the culture wars.

Christianity, Colonialism, and World Missions

Since its arrival in the "New World" more than four hundred years ago, Christianity has been deeply embedded within the politics of North America. The journal of Christopher Columbus (1451–1506) in 1492 predicted a rapid expansion of Christianity across the New World, "I believe that they would easily be made Christians, as it appeared to me that they had no religion" (Columbus 1893: 37). His comment reflected an age of colonization in which Europeans anticipated wealth and prestige to flow from the New World to their empires back home. In exchange, Native Americans would "benefit" from the transformative experience of Europeans exposing them to Christianity, an ideology justifying conquest and exploitation that historians typically refer to as the "civilizing mission."

In reality, the exploration and conquest of North America turned the Spanish monarchy into the world's leading power by siphoning off the wealth of the Aztecs and Incas, while diseases brought by Europeans decimated Native Americans. Christianity remained integral to the collision between Native American cultures and Europeans for centuries thereafter as new European powers such as the Dutch, French, and English followed in Spain's wake.

Christianity did not always stand steadfastly behind European imperialism. Christian leaders were sometimes very critical of the colonial project. Ironically, one such figure was a biographer of Columbus, Dominican Priest Bartolomé de Las Casas (1484–1566). Writing to the King of Spain in 1542, De Las Casas rebuked the Spanish Conquistadores for their brutal exploitation of Native American groups and for disguising their lust for wealth in the veneer of serving Christendom. He wrote: "The Spaniards first assaulted the Innocent Sheep, so qualified by the Almighty, like most cruel tigers, wolves, lions, hunger-starved, studying nothing, for the space of Forty Years, after their first landing, but the Massacre of these Wretches, whom they have so inhumanely and barbarously butchered and harassed with several kinds of Torments" (de Las Casas 2007: 9–16). His writings marked an early, important step in employing Christianity as the voice of conscience.

More frequently though from the sixteenth to nineteenth centuries, Christianity's role in the "civilizing mission" justified the continued expansion of European settlement and displacement of Native Americans across North America. The creation of new nation-states in the form of the United States, Mexico, and Canada marked the culmination of the mission to extend Christianity to the far reaches of the New World. The religious identity of these North American states as "Christian nations" was firmly established in these centuries and shaped their diplomatic relations for generations to come. For example, in the 1630s and 1640s, amidst persecution from King Charles I (1625–49), thousands of English Puritans were led to settlements in New England under leaders such as John Winthrop (1587/8–1649). Unlike their counterparts in Virginia, the New England settlers declared their mission to erect a "City on a Hill," or, a model Protestant

FIGURE 17.2 *Bartolomé de Las Casas.* Source: *Wikimedia Commons.*

utopia whose church and political leadership would be an example to the Church of England back home.

In the centuries after the American Revolution, Winthrop and the Puritan's mission infused the mythos of American exceptionalism as citizens of the United States imagined their nation and society as a source of inspiration and model to be emulated by the world. Canadians similarly saw themselves as a "Christian" nation with a "special mission" to extend their values abroad. Centuries after European missionaries brought Christianity to Canada and the United States, Protestant missions from the

CHRISTIANITY AND POLITICS IN NORTH AMERICA

United States and Canada in the late nineteenth and early twentieth centuries now joined Europeans in the grand "civilizing mission" in Africa, Asia, and the Middle East.

American and Canadian missionaries urged their governments to adopt a mixture of benevolent and paternalistic relations with Asians and Africans that was intended to modernize them, yet subject them. After decades of building churches, hospitals, schools, and YMCAs, rapid decolonization after the Second World War saw millions across the globe liberated from foreign, Western rule. It also alarmed Christians in North America, as nations such as the People's Republic of China moved to expel Christian missions (Tyrell 2010).

After 1945, American Christians entered the Cold War—a religious war in which the United States and its allies such as Canada stood as the defenders of freedom and human rights endowed by God, from the atheistic communism represented by the Soviet Union. Intellectuals, American clergy, and policymaking elites such as John Foster Dulles saw Christianity as an instrument to contain communism and expand Western influence in Asia and Africa. Both Catholics and Protestants trained missionaries to compete with communist revolutionaries overseas and joined with politicians such as Walter Judd at home to form organizations like the "Committee of One Million Against the Admission of Red China to the United Nations" to isolate communist countries (Inboden 2008).

Much like with the ideology of the "civilizing mission," Christianity informed a foreign policy that was meant to expand US power on the world stage. Since the end of the Cold War, American and Canadian churches and international organizations continue to engage in missions worldwide, building churches, medical clinics, and schools around the globe. But the impact of these missionaries on the foreign relations of the United States and Canada has far less weight than that of their predecessors in the Cold War or early twentieth century. Today, Canadian and American missionaries are still often seen as humanitarians and agents of global Christianity, but their connection to American foreign policy is not as obvious now as it was then.

It is also true that alongside Christianity's service to imperialism ran strong undercurrents of progressive causes within the world of Christian missions emanating out from Canada and the United States. Groups such as the American Board of Commissioners for Foreign Missions, and Women's Christian Temperance Union were often critics of American and European imperialism (Tyrell 2010). Along with likeminded missionaries working in the Middle East, Africa, and Asia, these organizations exported campaigns against slavery, opium, alcohol, and promoted the expansion of women's rights across the globe. Similarly, from the early 1900s to the end of the twentieth century, a large number of missionaries and children of missionaries such as novelist Pearl Buck influenced foreign policy, higher education, and literature to reflect the values of anti-colonialism and pluralism in North America (Hollinger 2019). Moreover, the increasing visibility of churches formed by North Americans of Asian and African descent after 1945 has contributed greatly to political views that support diversity and racial equality.

Reform and Progressivism

Another important area of study for scholars is how Christianity has fueled revolutionary movements, campaigns for women's and civil rights, and progressive politics in North America. For example, historians of the First *Great Awakening* (1730–50) have connected the spread of revivalist preachers and their teachings to the growing impatience of colonial society toward British rule before the American Revolution. In the eighteenth century, new congregations formed by Baptist and Methodist preachers reflected a restless, fluid society where artisans, printers, merchants, and lawyers chafed at the social and political hierarchy of the Anglican Church. Eventually, the egalitarianism and individual conscience within these new churches spilled over into a quest for liberty from the British Crown that spawned American independence (Kidd 2010).

In Canada, however, Christianity helped delay the move toward independence until the mid-nineteenth century. In many areas of British North America, congregations of Presbyterian and even Methodists sought a strong church–state relationship rather than a revolt against provincial governors and the British Crown. Within the Maritimes and Upper Canada in the years after the American Revolution, the Anglicans came to function as an established church, similar to the position it held in England. The strength of the Anglican and Congregationalist churches encouraged the loyalty of colonists to the Crown even as their American brethren tried to push them into rebellion by invading Quebec in 1775 (Murphy and Perrin 1996).

By the early nineteenth century, Christianity in both the United States and Canada was riven by the political controversy surrounding slavery. Inside the United States, antislavery campaigns formed first among Quakers and later spread rapidly as many northern states emancipated slaves after the American Revolution. Meanwhile, evangelical churches spanning the Atlantic from Britain to Canada combined to call for the end of the slave trade and supported Black Canadians in winning manumission (release from slavery) via the courts. And yet, across the ideological and geographic divide, southern US Christians grounded their defense of slavery in scripture. Even after the Civil War, southern Christians opposed Reconstruction and by drawing upon the Bible to justify Jim Crow, the legal codes that enforced segregation and a racial caste system denying African Americans equality (Noll 2002).

More important to the struggle against slavery in the modern world was the spread of Christianity among free Blacks and enslaved African Americans. Finding in their faith a basis for a politics of liberation, Christianity proved a potent force for resistance to slavery and the pains of discrimination faced by free Blacks. By 1831, Black Christianity had become a fountain for revolt as Nat Turner (1800–1831) led an uprising of free and enslaved Black men against slaveholders in Southampton County, Virginia, after reading the biblical passage "Seek ye the kingdom of Heaven and all things shall be added unto you" (Turner 1831). Although the uprising failed, African American Christians such as Frederick Douglass (1818–95) formed the backbone of the abolitionist movement. Meanwhile, the abolishment of slavery in Canada after 1834 led a minority of free

CHRISTIANITY AND POLITICS IN NORTH AMERICA

Blacks to travel along the Underground Railroad from the southern United States to safe havens and new lives in Ontario.

Similarly, Christian women from within the antislavery movement formed the vanguard of the campaigns for women's rights. The Grimke Sisters—Angelina (1805–79) and Sarah (1792–1873)—gained notoriety as advocates for abolition and later women's rights based on their Christian virtues. Generations of Christian women from Abigail Adams (1744–1818) to Elizabeth Cady Stanton (1815–1902) demanded female suffrage on gendered interpretations of Christian teachings that hallowed women's superior morality and virtue. Across the northern border, Canadian Christian women founded the Women's Christian Temperance Union to fight for rights to property, education, and suffrage in campaigns that forged allies in the United States, the United Kingdom, and all over the world (Noll 2002).

After the Civil War, Christian reformers in both the United States and Canada turned to issues related to industrialization, urbanization, and the flow of millions of immigrants to North America. Applying Christian ethics to social problems ranging from inequality, class conflict, labor conditions, and the hazards of urbanization, what came to be known as the "*Social Gospel*" saturated the progressive politics of new parties and politicians promising to make government an engine for social change. Inspired activists in the United States and Canada, including social worker Jane Adams (1860–1935) and farmer W.C. Good (1867–1967), employed Christian solutions to modern society (Noll 2002).

Black Christian churches continued to be the bedrock of resistance to racial discrimination and inequality. Ida Wells (1862–1931) stridently denounced the lynching of African Americans, while her tours abroad to England forged ties of solidarity between African American churches and Europe. It is also possible to trace the critical role of Black liberation theology from the revolts of slaves to the modern civil rights movement. Several scholars argue that the civil rights movement of the mid-twentieth century was in fact a religious revolution led by a number of Black Christian activists such as Martin Luther King Jr. (1929–68) and the Southern Christian Leadership Conference (Selby 2008).

For much of the nineteenth and twentieth centuries, Christianity was integral to the core of numerous rights movements in North America. However, controversies surrounding the US involvement in the Vietnam War, the sexual revolution, and the eruption of second-wave feminism produced a sharp counterreaction from conservative Protestants and Catholics. At the same time, the Christian Left fell from the vanguard of progressive political movements to the rearguard, at least in terms of ideology and leadership, as new, secular influences took the mantle for leftist politics in Canada and the United States. Christian women, for example, in the United States and Canada experienced great success as part of a broader feminist movement that won suffrage in both countries by the 1920s. Thereafter the mainstream of women's rights movements distanced itself from Christianity, which increasingly was associated in media after 1945 with forces opposed to the causes of second-wave feminism's campaigns for reproductive rights and sexual liberation (Manning 1999).

FIGURE 17.3 *Cornel West.* Source: *Gage Skidmore / Wikimedia Commons.*

Still, many liberal Protestant churches have fought to make theology and the social praxis of Christianity relevant to rights movements and minority groups. The most successful came in inner city churches where new pastors and lay leaders at Philadelphia's Deliverance Temple and New York's Iglesia Cristiana Juan led campaigns against drugs, gun violence, and most recently police brutality. Intellectuals such as Cornel West (1953–) inherited the mantle of King and Fannie Lou Hamer (1917–77) in generating Christian critiques of Black oppression and white racism (West 1999).

Separation of Church and State: Catholicism in Quebec and Mexico

US citizens have long prided themselves on achieving a government that separates church and state, equating that with a more tolerant society and greater religious freedom for citizens. Conversely, in other areas of North America such as Mexico and Quebec the line drawn between church and state—the government and Catholic Church—has often been blurred. While Catholics are a salient political force as a religious minority in the United States, they have long been the dominant majority in Mexico and Quebec. In French-speaking Quebec, the Roman Catholic Church dominated politics from the seventeenth century well into the late twentieth century. Following the founding of Quebec City by French explorer Samuel de Champlain in 1608, the French Catholic Church was granted immense tracts of land in the new colony building churches, schools, and convents from the wealth derived from a thriving fur trade.

Quebec was nearly 80 percent French and Catholic, with a state—church system in which the provincial governor and legislature worked closely with the clergy. Protective of the status quo, the province was slow to enact many societal reforms even after it was absorbed by Canada because of the Catholic Church's influence. For example, it was not until 1940 that Quebec granted women the right to vote, the last such area in North America to do so. From the 1930s onward new elements in Quebec challenged traditional theology and the politics of the Catholic Church. Inspired by reformers and intellectuals in France, a younger generation of Quebec's Catholics such as Pierre Eliot Trudeau (1919–2000) transformed Christianity into a vehicle for social justice, and mobilized women and the working class on the political front. Still, the Catholic Church there largely works politically to retain its influence over education, morality, and the cultural identity of the province (Murphy and Perrin 1996).

To a greater degree than in Quebec, the Roman Catholic Church has been an integral part of the political landscape in Mexico. Today, the country stands as the second largest Catholic nation in the world (after Brazil). Yet, Mexico for over 125 years had no relations with the Vatican due to conflict between church and state. The Catholic Church was transported to "New Spain" in the wake of conquistador Hernan Cortes' (1485–1547) destruction of the Aztec Empire in the sixteenth century. The Spanish Crown's policy tasked missionaries with Christianizing Indigenous men and women. Ideologically, the goal of winning souls was equal to that of profiting from the resources drawn from the New World as Spanish missionaries built schools, convents, and churches to help build a new society. The campaigning of de Las Casas managed to convince the Spanish Council of the Indies to abolish the system of slavery that had enslaved Native populations (Hamnet 2019).

Catholicism proved vital in the movement toward Mexican independence in 1810, sparked by the martyred parish priest Miguel Hidalgo's (1753–1811) cry of "Viva Mexico." After independence though the Catholic Church became a divisive institution. Mexican liberals denounced the church's large landholdings and privileges and worried about the loyalty it commanded from the populace as a rival to the government. The rise of President Benito Juarez (1806–72) introduced reform laws designed to curtail the power of the church and its clergy. Church courts for the first time were placed under civilian authorities, properties were confiscated, and clergy were forbidden from appearing in public fully garbed as bishops and priests (Hamnet 2019).

Meanwhile, conservative Mexican voices defended the Catholic Church as a source of unity and nationalism. As a result, in the 1860s, the Mexican Catholic Church threw its support behind conservatives to install a foreign ruler in power, the Austrian aristocrat Maximilian I. This experiment was short-lived (1864–7) as Juarez came back to power and Maximilian was executed. For the rest of the nineteenth century, Mexico's political system was wracked with instability and violence as caudillos, or dictators, held power. The Catholic Church largely functioned as an apologist for dictatorial rule (Butler 2007).

In the early twentieth century, the Mexican Catholic Church again became the target of revolutionary currents. Urban poor, farmers, and reformers joined with the Mexican Liberal Party to assail the Catholic Church as the enemy of equality. Following the Mexican Revolution and Civil War (1910–20), a new constitution was adopted that introduced a number of anti-clerical measures. The Constitution of 1917 nationalized Mexican Catholicism, demanding all priests hail from Mexico, forgo owning property, voting, and even discussing politics. At times, the enforcement of such laws was lax, but under President Plutarco Elias Calles in the 1920s and 1930s these laws served as the grounds for relentless persecution of the Catholic Church. Mexican clergy led loyal Catholics in violent clashes against authority, leading to reprisals by government forces that hunted down renegade priests (Butler 2007).

In the 1940s, the Mexican government swung back to the Right, allowing the Catholic Church to establish more cordial relations with the state. In the early Cold War, Mexican clergy were welcomed as partners in the fight to contain communism. With Fidel Castro's regime in Cuba looming as an inspiration for Mexico's students, workers, and radicals, the church angrily denounced communism as a plague on humanity and Latin America. The highest levels of the Catholic hierarchy bestowed spiritual legitimacy on the elites and industrialists that dominated Mexico (Hamnet 2019).

In the 1960s and 1970s, the spread of Liberation Theology—a movement of Latin American Catholics incorporating Marxist politics into Christian theology—inspired a minority of Catholics to join with progressive forces to fight against oppression. For example, in Oaxaca, Catholic nuns, scholars, and Indigenous women allied to promote feminism and challenge inequality in mainstream society. On the matter of reproductive rights for women, though, the vast majority of Mexican Catholics remained solidly in the conservative camp as opponents to abortion. This is true of the Catholic Church in Canada, too, after the Second World War. There, like in Mexico, Catholics tended to be more conservative on issues such as birth control or divorce, but far more liberal in supporting welfare and state intervention for the poor.

The restoration of ties between the Mexican Catholic Church with the Vatican in 1992 introduced new political tensions. Since then Mexican Catholicism has had an estranged relationship with the government. For the most part, Mexican Catholicism

FIGURE 17.4 *Pope Francis visits Mexico.* Source: *Marko Vombergar / Aleteia Image Department / Wikimedia Commons.*

eschews social issues in favor of popular piety comfortably practiced in the privacy of the church and family home. But the position of Rome has been a source of constant tension between church and state. In 2016, Pope Francis visited after calling attention to Mexico's problems with security, violence, and inequality (Agren 2016). Later in 2019, the Pope addressed the immigration crisis along the US–Mexican border with a donation of $500,000 for migrants, while leveling criticism at the policies of Washington and Mexico City (La Croix International Staff 2019). The effect has been to reignite the long-standing questions about the political loyalty of Mexican Catholic clergy and churches even as the faith remains integral to the nation's modern identity.

Conservatism and Culture Wars in the Twentieth Century

More commonly from the late twentieth century to the present, Christianity has been associated with the cause of conservative politics. Since the 1980s, Christianity has shaped politics in the United States, Mexico, and Canada via religious media and the capacity to mobilize large voting blocs behind rightist politicians. Scholars have devoted their attention to exploring how Fundamentalist Christians—Catholics, Protestants, and Mormons—have entered the fray on myriad political and social issues such as abortion;

capital punishment; lesbian, gay, bisexual, transgender, and queer/questioning (LGBTQ) rights; and the teaching of scientific theories (evolution and climate change). Ironically, this has all come long after Fundamentalist Christianity was seemingly vanquished after the *Scopes Monkey Trial* in Tennessee in 1925. Media and intellectuals in the aftermath of the Scopes Trial had stereotyped Christian Fundamentalists as uneducated, rural, and relegated to the political fringe.

This episode, however, did not mark the final retreat of Christian fundamentalism from mainstream politics in North America. In the United States, scholars have turned their attention to examining the role of religion in explaining the rise of the "New Right," culminating in the election of President Ronald Reagan in the 1980s. Pivotal to the ascendance of the New Right was the "*Christian Right*," grassroots organizations, megachurches, and a robust Christian media. By the 1970s, Fundamentalist Protestant organizations such as the *Moral Majority* succeeded in making media a tool to popularize Christian conservative campaigns against abortion rights or the Equal Rights Amendment. Since the Reagan presidency, conservative Christians have played an outsized role in selecting Republican candidates for office while sanctifying ideas about limited government and tax cuts with spiritual legitimacy (McGirr 2001).

As religious broadcasting grew in the 1990s and 2000s, conservative Protestants and Roman Catholics allied to fight "culture wars," a term coined to describe how liberals and conservatives "warred" with each other over the values found in American homes, schools, and issues such as feminism, sexuality, and even entertainment. Talk

FIGURE 17.5 *President Barack Obama and Billy Graham.* Source: *Executive Office of the President of the United States / Wikimedia Commons.*

shows such as Pat Robertson's "The 700 Club" habitually covered current events from a decidedly conservative slant, casting mainstream media and liberal values as the cause behind crime, immorality, and even greed in the country. And since 9/11 the Christian Right has been linked to a rising nativism in the United States, supporting travel bans and restrictive immigration policies.

Often overlooked in the rise of Christian conservatism is the Mormon Church. Originating in the visions of Joseph Smith (1805–44), the *Church of Jesus Christ of Latter-day Saints* (LDS) was long seen as a political pariah. Prior to the 1970s, the Mormon Church was a marginal political force outside of Utah where LDS members often serve as state legislators. Since then the Mormon Church has found common ground with conservatives in the United States, Mexico, and Canada. Most prominently, the LDS has been able to put aside historical animosity and theological differences with institutions such as the Roman Catholic Church to forge a coalition opposed to same-sex marriage, transgender rights, and even hate crimes legislation. The most telling sign of the Mormon Church's integration into the mainstream of US political culture came with the Republican nomination of Mitt Romney (1947–) for president in 2012 (Campbell, Green, and Monson 2014).

The Christian Right in Canada is more marginal if still visible in the political arena. In 2019, an estimated 10 to 15 percent of Canadians identified as evangelical Christians with socially conservative viewpoints. Compared to their American counterparts, however, Canada's Christian Right is more supportive of public institutions and tolerant of liberal viewpoints. The modest influence of the Christian Right in Canada is best seen at the level of provincial government where campaigns led by Charles McVety, president of Canada Christian College, have altered sex education curriculum. Another example is the Ontario Progressive Conservative Party led by Doug Ford (1964–). Ford has cultivated enthusiastic support from Christian conservatives with a platform promising to strengthen the right of Christian doctors to refuse abortions. Still, the Christian Right is a minority and largely on the defensive against secularism and pluralism. As a result, the alliance of Canadian Catholics and Protestants in politics often aims to ensure broad religious freedom such as fighting attempts to revoke the charitable tax status of churches.

In Mexico, the dynamics between conservatism and Christianity are more nebulous. Polls reflect that nearly three-quarters of the populace think religion should be kept separate from politics. Yet the force of Christianity still compels politicians to ally with clergy and churches to win the hearts and minds of the Mexican people (Tuckman 2018).

Christianity in the Twenty-First Century

Has Christianity entered a period of decline in North America? Polling data from the past decade suggests that in the United States an increasing number of people, especially millennials, no longer identify with a religious affiliation. To the north, scholars and pundits have long discussed a longer, more gradual disappearance of

"Christian Canada" from public life. For example, historian Mark Noll has argued that in the aftermath of the Second World War, the idea of "Christian Canada" was as powerful as ever, as revivals led by evangelists such as Charles Templeton (1915–2001) equaled those for his American counterpart Billy Graham (1918–2018). By the 1960s, however, many Canadian churches failed to offer a compelling social and political vision to address a rapidly changing society. New parties and politicians drifted away from working closely with clergy and churches to secure a political base, as statistics showed a clear decline in church attendance (Noll 2002).

Certainly, one can argue that at least on the Left, Christianity has fallen into irrelevance in recent decades. On the one hand, this speaks to the success of the Right's attack on the idea that Americans, Canadians, and Mexicans can be authentically Christian and engage in leftist politics at the same time. On the other hand, political leftists are often unwilling to identify themselves by their faith (Malloy 2019). To do so beyond perfunctory prayer and attendance at churches in the United States and Canada seemingly runs the risk of alienating atheists and other allies on the Left. Unlike the numerous politicians, clergy, media, and institutions on the Christian Right, there is no political champion of a Christian Left and its values.

Surprisingly, though, data suggests that at least in the United States there has also been an abating Christian influence among white conservatives, too, most notably with the working class. Statistics from the Public Religion Research Institute record that white Republicans only nominally identify as Christians and attend church infrequently. A political consequence, some have suggested, is a hardening of political positions on issues such as gay rights, immigration, and even a turn toward more extremist, racially grounded nationalism. Paradoxically, critics of the Christian Right have typically held to the idea that Fundamentalist religion promotes intolerant views. Now it may prove that the waning influence of traditional Christianity on conservative politics has led to a more resentful agenda on the Right (Jones 2017).

It is unlikely, though, given the history of Christianity in North America and the wealth of financial resources, media, institutions, and cultural capital possessed by Christians, that religion will fade too far from the political scene. Christianity has been integral to North America's revolutions, campaigns for reform and rights, and the authority of politicians and groups seeking to make their mark on society. Rather, if history proves anything it is that the battle for the soul of Christianity in North America is a political contest of enormous consequence in the twenty-first century.

Further Reading and Online Resources

The American Yawp (2020), Available online: https://www.americanyawp.com/ (accessed August 8, 2019).

Pew Research Center (2020), "Religion and Public Life." Available online: https://www.pewforum.org/ (accessed August 19, 2019).

Pew-Templeton Global Religious Futures Project (2020), "Home." Available online: http://www.globalreligiousfutures.org/ (accessed July 7, 2019).

References

Agren D. (2016), "Separation of Catholics and State: Mexico's Divisive Religious History," *The Guardian*, February 12.

Butler M., ed. (2007), *Faith and Impiety in Revolutionary Mexico*, Studies of the Americas series, New York: Palgrave Macmillan.

Campbell D.E., J.C. Green, and J.Q. Monson (2014), *Seeking the Promised Land: Mormons and American Politics*, Cambridge Studies in Social Theory, Religion and Politics, Cambridge: Cambridge University Press.

Columbus C. (1893), *The Journal of Christopher Columbus (During His First Voyage), and Documents Relating to the Voyages of John Cabot and Gaspar Corte Real*, ed. and trans. C.R. Markham, London.

Cummings W. (2019), "'God's Used Imperfect People All Through History': Perry Shares Why He Thinks Trump Is the 'Chosen One'," *USA Today*, November 25.

Hamnett B.R.A. (2019), *Concise History of Mexico*, 3rd edn., Cambridge: Cambridge University Press.

Hollinger D.A. (2019), *Protestants Abroad: How Missionaries Tried to Change the World but Changed America*. Princeton, NJ: Princeton University Press.

Inboden W. (2008), *Religion and American Foreign Policy, 1945–1960: The Soul of Containment*, Cambridge: Cambridge University Press.

Jones R.P. (2017), "Trump Can't Reverse the Decline of White Christian America," *The Atlantic*, July 4.

Kidd T.S. (2010), *God of Liberty: A Religious History of the American Revolution*, New York: Basic Books.

La Croix International Staff (2019), "Pope Pledges $500,000 to Mexico-Stranded Migrants," *La Croix International*, April 29.

Las Casas, de B. (2007), "A Brief Account of the Destruction of the Indies," Project Gutenberg. Available online: http://www.gutenberg.org/ebooks/20321 (accessed November 14, 2020).

Malloy J. (2019), "Canada's Marginal 'Christian Right'," *The Conversation*, August 11.

Manning C. (1999), *God Gave Us the Right: Conservative Catholic, Evangelical Protestant, and Orthodox Jewish Women Grapple with Feminism*, New Brunswick, NJ: Rutgers University Press.

McGirr L. (2001), *Suburban Warriors: The Origins of the New American Right. Politics and Society in Twentieth-Century America*, Princeton, NJ: Princeton University Press.

Murphy T. and R. Perin (1996), *A Concise History of Christianity in Canada*, Oxford: Oxford University Press.

Noll M.A. (2002), *The Old Religion in a New World: The History of North American Christianity*, Grand Rapids, MI: Eerdmans.

Selby G.S. (2008), *Martin Luther King and the Rhetoric of Freedom: The Exodus Narrative in America's Struggle for Civil Rights. Studies in Rhetoric and Religion: 5*, Waco, TX: Baylor University Press.

Tuckman J. (2018), "Mexico's Leading Presidential Candidate Embraces Many Religions," *National Catholic Reporter*, June 13.

Turner N. (1831), *Confessions of Nat Turner*, Baltimore: Thomas R. Gray.

Tyrrell I. (2010), *Reforming the World: The Creation of America's Moral Empire*, Princeton, NJ: Princeton University Press.

West C. (1999), *The Cornel West Reader*, New York: Basic Civitas Books.

Glossary Terms

Christian Right This term refers to Christians—Catholics, Protestants, and Mormons—that are a major force in conservative politics in North America. Within each country these conservative Christians generally try to influence parties, candidates, and governmental policy on issues ranging from school prayer to contraception and intelligent design. As a movement, the Christian Right has a prominent force in political elections and campaigns since the 1940s to varying degrees in the United States, Canada, and Mexico.

Church of Latter-day Saints Founded by its prophet Joseph Smith in the nineteenth century, the Church of Latter-day Saints (LDS) or Mormon Church represents a distinct wing of Christianity from Protestantism and Catholicism. Long considered a pariah, the Mormon Church today has over 16 million members worldwide and mainstream acceptance in the United States, Canada, and Mexico.

Great Awakening This refers to widespread and prolonged religious revival that spanned North America and the Atlantic Ocean that first began in the 1730s and lasted into the 1750s. Subsequent "Awakenings," or periods of mass revival occurred later in the eighteenth century and again in the nineteenth and twentieth centuries. During the Great Awakening, Christianity became intensely personal and saw an outburst of activism by churches as well as the spread of new congregations and innovations in evangelism such as the use of the printing press and camp meetings.

Moral Majority This organization stood at the center of the alliance between the Christian Right and the Republican Party in the 1970s and 1980s. Formed by televangelist Jerry Falwell, the organization spoke to the belief that Fundamentalist Christians believed themselves to represent the "majority" of Americans and their values in campaigning for "traditional" family values and opposing the Equal Rights Amendment.

Scopes Monkey Trial In 1925, John T. Scopes was accused of violating Tennessee's Butler Act, a law making declaring the teaching of human evolution illegal in public schools. The trial became a media and national event as supporters of Fundamentalist Christianity, represented by the prosecuting attorney William Jennings Bryan, squared off against the defense, with famed attorney Clarence Darrow. Although Scopes was found guilty, national press and pundits would declare advocates of liberalism, modernism, and secular society the decisive winners of the theological and intellectual contest.

Social Gospel In the late nineteenth century, a number of theologians, preachers, and activists across the Atlantic World began to use Christian ethics and scripture to address modern problems related to economic inequality, the conditions of labor, agriculture, and substance abuse. Known as the "Social Gospel," the movement dominated progressive politics in many countries in the early twentieth century and shaped agenda of Christian missions in Asia and Africa toward work in the areas of education and medicine.

18

Conversion Therapy and the Fight over the First Amendment

Chris Babits

Nearly fifty years ago, lesbian and gay rights activists convinced the American Psychiatric Association (APA) to remove "homosexuality" from the list of mental disorders in the *Diagnostic and Statistical Manual* (*DSM*) (Bayer 1981: 101–54). Since the 1970s, the site of sexual orientation and gender identity change therapies has largely moved from the psychiatrist's couch to individual and group therapy sessions with religious counselors. There remain, however, a sizable number of professionally trained and licensed therapists who try to help patients with "unwanted same-sex attractions." Beginning in 2012, these therapists, many of whom identify as religious conservatives, have faced not only social but also legal pressures to halt sexual orientation change efforts with minors. In less than a decade, nonprofit organizations such as the Trevor Project and the Southern Poverty Law Center have helped lesbian, gay, bisexual, transgender, and queer/questioning (LGBTQ) activists usher in these bans on conversion therapy with minors in no fewer than twenty states. In their legal challenges to these state-wide bans, so-called conversion therapists have asserted that their First Amendment rights of free speech and religion have been violated.

The nature of the fight over conversion therapy offers an opportunity to assess how debates over religion, gender, and sexuality have shifted in recent history. In the late twentieth century, sexual orientation change therapists discussed how homosexuality was a freedom too far as they challenged the burgeoning LGBTQ rights movement. Additionally, many of these therapists and counselors discussed how their interventions provided freedom from homosexuality. By the early twenty-first century, things had changed. Landmark cases such as *Lawrence v. Texas* (2004) and *Obergefell v. Hodges* (2016) have transformed the political struggle between religious conservatives and LGBTQ activists. The language coming from sexual orientation change therapists

FIGURE 18.1 *Colorado Two LGBTQ bill signed into law.* Source: *Getty Images.*

reflects a new reality—large segments of the American public support gay rights and find efforts to change sexual orientation abhorrent (Moore 2014; Rodgers 2020). Facing down this challenge, proponents of sexual orientation change therapies have turned to the First Amendment to protect what they see as their freedom of speech and the free exercise of religion. In doing so, they have placed their hopes for the continued practice of conversion therapy in the hands of the conservative justices appointed across the federal judiciary by President Donald Trump.

Religion and Sexual Orientation Change Therapies in the Twentieth Century

The fusion of conservative understandings of religion, gender, and sexuality was an important part of the rise of psychoanalysis after the Second World War. In *Cold War Freud: Psychoanalysis in the Age of Catastrophe*, historian Dagmar Herzog (2016) argues that in the early Cold War, psychoanalysis became profoundly Christianized in the United States. Herzog's observation highlights two trends that are important for understanding the history of conversion therapy. First, the rise of sexual orientation change efforts in the postwar period depended on psychoanalysts incorporating Christian concepts into their writings and therapeutic interventions. Arguments in favor of gender complementarity as well as the male-female binary were two crucial ideas for this Christianization of psychoanalysis. And second, Herzog's work breaks down the artificial boundaries between religion and science. The brief overview of conversion therapy's history below demonstrates how religious influences shaped the beliefs and practices of psychoanalysts trained at one of the nation's most prestigious medical schools in the postwar period.

Creating a psychoanalytical tradition with gender complementarity at its center was an intellectual challenge in the early Cold War. Sigmund Freud (1856–1939), the founder of psychoanalysis and a well-known atheist, proposed that both men and women were constitutionally bisexual. Additionally, Freud stated that all humans, on their way to heterosexuality, passed through a homosexual phase (Bayer 1981: 21–3; Lewes 1988). Beginning in the late 1930s, however, psychoanalysts such as Sandor Rado (1890–1972) used the language of natural law and gender complementarity to argue that homosexuality was not only unnatural but that changing a patient's sexual orientation was possible. Notably, Rado had a functional understanding of sex. This meant that he saw sex for its reproductive capabilities and for little else. Moreover, Rado argued that there was a naturalness to the male-female design, effectively fusing

FIGURE 18.2 *Sigmund Freud (1856–1939): a conversion therapy skeptic.* Source: *Wikicommons.*

biology and psychology in a sexually conservative and moralistic way. He pointed to Darwinian notions of evolution to even argue that procreation between men and women determined the survival of the species (Tononoz 2017). Importantly, as a prominent professor at Columbia University's Psychoanalytic Training Institute, Rado also trained a number of the most prominent twentieth-century proponents of sexual orientation change therapies.

Charles Socarides (1922–2005) was one of Rado's proteges at Columbia, and from the 1950s into the twenty-first century, he strongly advocated for sexual orientation change therapies. To understand how Socarides helped foster the Christianization of psychoanalysis, it is important to "read against the grain," looking for a number of ways in which his work reflected conservative and religious ideas about gender, sexuality, and the family. In his earliest books and academic articles, he followed in the footsteps of Rado. Socarides proposed several psychobiological theories that not only incorporated ideas of gender complementariness but have also remained important parts of the contemporary movement for conversion therapy. In *The Overt Homosexual*, for instance, he contended that homosexuality resulted from a poor family upbringing. "The family of the homosexual is usually a female-dominated environment," he wrote, "wherein the father was absent, weak, detached or sadistic" (Socarides 1968: 38). Here, Socarides implied that homosexuality developed when sons and daughters were unable to learn traditional gender norms from their parents. He was much more forceful about gender complementarity in *Beyond Sexual Freedom*. There, Socarides expounded on the "immutable contrasts and complementarity between the sexes" and contended that complementariness could "be conceptualized as the *push-pull principle*" (Socarides 1975: 23). On this point, he contended that male sperm sought out the egg, whereas the woman's egg worked to attract the sperm. In making this argument, Socarides argued for the so-called naturalness of male aggression and female passivity, two core characteristics of traditional gender roles. He was using the biological basis of human reproduction to make a larger point about what was the supposed natural arrangement between men and women.

Socarides' tone became particularly polemical after the American Psychiatric Association removed homosexuality from the *Diagnostic and Statistical Manual* in 1973. He led a failed effort to have the APA reinsert homosexuality into the *DSM*, and he never shied from debating gay rights leaders (Bayer 1981). These experiences embittered Socarides. In *Beyond Sexual Freedom*, for example, he discussed the tyranny of women's equality and the damaging effects of group sex, and labeled pornography the rape of the senses (Socarides 1975). Twenty years later, in *Homosexuality: A Freedom Too Far* (1995), Socarides continued to rail against the redrawing of the male-female design, accusing the gay rights movement of trying to exempt humans from the supposed naturalness of sexual and gendered bipolarity. Yet by the 1990s, Socarides was fully ensconced in the nation's culture wars. He wrote *Homosexuality* for a general audience, espousing his hope to "offer an informed defense for good, old-fashioned sex between men and women, and for the old-fashioned loving family." He also accused the gay rights movement of subverting both heterosexuality and the traditional family. He further stated that labeling all forms of sexual relations as equal and indistinguishable was "a freedom that goes too far, because it undoes us all" (Socarides 1995: 13–14). On this point, he noted the importance of the nuclear family, which he contended was an institution that was part of human nature.

Socarides' views were ever-apparent by the early 1990s. In 1992, he founded the National Association for Research & Therapy of Homosexuality (NARTH) with Benjamin Kauffman and Joseph Nicolosi. NARTH's mission centered on disseminating information about the purported efficacy of sexual reorientation. Its membership was religiously diverse, attracting evangelical, Catholic, and Mormon adherents, and the organization earned the support of James Dobson's Focus on the Family. NARTH's position that sexual reorientation was possible helped it become a target of the LGBTQ rights movement. Many LGBTQ activists, for instance, observed how NARTH members not only fought against gay rights but also advocated for traditional gender roles, the male-female binary, and the nuclear family (Besen 2003).

Soon, Nicolosi became one of the most outspoken advocates for sexual reorientation, especially once his first book, *Reparative Therapy of Male Homosexuality* (1991), became the target of attack. Despite Nicolosi's protestations that he built a therapeutic routine on the basis of sound science, LGBTQ activists observed that religious beliefs were at the core of the therapy he offered. Most importantly, Nicolosi founded the Thomas Aquinas Psychological Clinic in the 1980s. By naming his clinic after Aquinas, a thirteenth-century Catholic theologian who argued for the complementarity of men's and women's reproductive organs, Nicolosi signaled his support for conservative understandings of religion, gender, and sexuality. The problem for Nicolosi and other members of NARTH, though, was that the postwar Christianization of psychoanalysis was no longer in vogue. In fact, the psychological establishment had started to frown on infusing religious values in the treatment of men and women with same-sex sexual desires.

The Contemporary Debate over Conversion Therapy and the First Amendment

Socarides, Nicolosi, and Kauffman founded NARTH in the early 1990s because they thought that the psychological establishment had abandoned the men and women who pursued sexual orientation change therapies. Subsequent events seemed to confirm their suspicions. In 1998, the American Psychiatric Association issued a formal denunciation of conversion therapy (APA Official Actions 2018), and around the turn of the twenty-first century, gay rights activists sought to discredit sexual orientation change efforts. Wayne Besen, a former spokesman for the Human Rights Campaign, for instance, caught John Paulk, a self-identified former homosexual and a Focus on the Family employee, at a gay bar in Washington, DC, in 2000. By this time, the ex-gay movement, comprised of professionally trained mental health professionals such as

Socarides and Nicolosi as well as a range of religious counselors and conservative political activists, faced increasing scrutiny. The US Supreme Court's ruling in *Lawrence v. Texas*, which overturned state laws prohibiting consensual same-sex sexual activity, highlighted one sea change in the struggle for gay equality. Most crucially, the law of the land no longer upheld previous court rulings that had relied on religious understandings that there were "ancient roots" against homosexuality and that granting the right to homosexual sex went against "millennia of moral teaching" (see *Bowers v. Hardwick* 1986). It was not until 2012, however, when LGBTQ activists helped push through the first bans on conversion therapy with minors.

California passed the first legislative ban on sexual orientation change efforts with clients under the age of eighteen. Introduced by Democratic State Senator Ted Lieu, the final version of the legislation called for licensed therapists who practiced sexual orientation change efforts to be disciplined by their respective state boards. Lieu argued that the legislation was necessary to protect children from their religiously conservative parents. Lieu also observed that multiple professional organizations contended that conversion therapy might do irreparable psychological harm to children. It is important to emphasize, though, that the bill, which passed the California State Senate 23–13 and the Assembly 52–22, targeted licensed mental health professionals. By exempting religious figures such as priests, pastors, and rabbis from the legislation, the bill's authors recognized how sexual orientation change therapists might be able to use the First Amendment's free exercise clause to overturn the ban. Instead, the legislation that Governor Jerry Brown signed into law on September 20, 2012, avoided the religious freedom challenges that would have likely resulted if the bill's focus had not been exclusively on licensed mental health officials.

The legislation's focus on licensed mental health professionals presented sexual orientation change therapists with unique challenges. Most importantly, since the law was not specifically focused on religious belief and practice, they had to find another legal justification for challenging the conversion therapy bans. David Pickup, one of Nicolosi's former patients and a practicing sexual orientation change therapist, filed a lawsuit in the Eastern District Court of California indicating that the signed legislation could be in violation of therapists' freedom of speech. Taking this approach not only challenged the proposed law on its own merits but also provided an opening for sexual orientation change therapists to insist that their therapeutic interventions were based on sound science. The California Supreme Court ultimately struck down these lines of reasoning, arguing that the state could protect the well-being of minors, as this is a legitimate state interest. On June 30, 2014, the US Supreme Court refused to hear the appeal of the California legislation, providing time for other states to pass their own versions of the bill to ban sexual orientation change efforts with minors.

The focus on how state and local bans violate freedom of speech has only been one part of the social and cultural challenge put forth by conservative supporters of sexual orientation change efforts. On the one hand, proponents of these counseling interventions argue that the bans violate parental rights. Although the California Supreme Court ruled that the state has an interest in protecting minors, advocates

CONVERSION THERAPY AND THE FIGHT OVER THE FIRST AMENDMENT

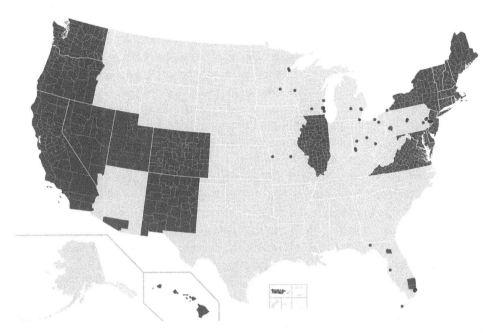

FIGURE 18.3 *US states and municipalities banning conversion therapy with minors (updated July 2020).* Source: *Wikicommons.*

for parental rights feel that their concerns and freedoms have been trampled on by an intrusive government. More specifically, these conservatives insist that it is the right of every parent to pass on religious doctrines about sexuality, including the conservative biblical argument that same-sex sexual activity is a prohibitive sin. The former Republican Governor of Maine, Paul LePage, noted this concern when he vetoed legislation in 2018 that would have banned conversion therapy with minors in his state. In his veto message, LePage wrote that "parents have the right to seek counsel and treatment for their children from professionals who do not oppose the parents' own religious beliefs" (LePage quoted in Kumar 2018).

Religious conservatives have also contended that these bans could start a war on Christianity. On the most basic level, they insist that conversion therapy bans on minors might prevent individuals with same-sex attractions from obtaining the kind of help that they want. Along these lines, religious conservatives believe that a significant number of youth and young adults want to satisfy what they view as the heavenly dictates of entering a heterosexual union and having children. These patients, this argument goes, would like to see a licensed mental health professional. Religious conservatives have been especially vocal about other legislative efforts, such as California's proposed legislation to label sexual orientation change efforts as consumer fraud. Tony Perkins, the arch-conservative president of the Family Research Council, praised the California legislation's inaction on the move to label conversion therapy consumer fraud, observing that (in his opinion) this "could have banned not just therapy but even the sale of books," including the Bible itself (Perkins 2018).

As a longtime participant in the nation's culture wars, Perkins is particularly adept at framing the fight over conversion therapy as another part of the purported war against Christianity. He is not the only one though. In *The Christian Post*, Christopher Doyle (2018), a licensed clinical professional counselor and the cofounder of the National Task Force for Therapy Equality, thought that there was hope in the fight for religious liberty. After revealing that he had been "distressed by unwanted attractions" and that he now "walk[s] in freedom with my beautiful wife," Doyle pointed to the US Supreme Court's ruling in *NIFLA v. Becerra* (2018), where the Court overturned California's Reproductive Freedom, Accountability, Comprehensive Care, and Transparency Act, as a sign of things to come. In the majority opinion, Justice Clarence Thomas wrote that the State of California could not compel pro-life crisis pregnancy centers to inform their patients about free or low-cost abortion services. Doyle, along with other proponents of sexual orientation change therapies, believes that *NIFLA v. Becerra* offers hope for overturning bans on conversion therapy with minors. Specifically, they have started arguing that state-wide bans on sexual orientation change therapies violate freedom of speech since the state is restricting and/or compelling a certain kind of speech.

Only time will tell if *NIFLA v. Becerra* will serve as precedent for overturning state laws banning conversion therapy with minors. Proponents of sexual orientation change therapies are hopeful, noticing that they have an opportunity to use the First Amendment's freedom of speech protections in a legal battle over these controversial interventions into same-sex desires. Despite the intense focus on free speech, though, there will be an opportunity for the sexual orientation change therapists to argue that bans on conversion therapy violate freedom of religion as well. If victorious, sexual orientation change therapists might have a new strategy for confronting the advancements of gay rights, and in doing so, prove to LGBTQ activists that their fight for equality continues to face significant challenges from religious conservatives. LGBTQ activists have beaten sexual orientation change therapists in previous battles. The question remains whether they can continue to do so in the nation's never-ending culture wars over religion, gender, and sexuality.

Further Reading and Online Resources

Erzen T. (2004), *Straight to Jesus: Sexual and Christian Conversions in the Ex-gay Movement*, Berkeley: University of California Press.

Gerber L. (2011), *Seeking the Straight and Narrow: Weight Loss and Sexual Reorientation in Evangelical America*, Chicago: University of Chicago Press.

Terry J. (1999), *An American Obsession: Science, Medicine, and Homosexuality in Modern Society*, Chicago: University of Chicago Press.

References

APA Official Actions (2018), "Position Statement on Conversion Therapy and LGBTQ Patients." Available online: https://www.psychiatry.org/File%20Library/About-APA/Organization-Documents-Policies/Policies/Position-Conversion-Therapy.pdf (accessed April 7, 2020).

Bayer R. (1981), *Homosexuality and American Psychiatry: The Politics of Diagnosis*, New York: Basic Books.

Besen W. (2003), *Anything but Straight: Unmasking the Scandals and Lies behind the Ex-Gay Myth*, Binghamton, NY: Harrington Park Press.

Doyle C. (2018), "Pro-Life Supreme Court Decision Good News for Religious Liberty, Sexual Freedom, and 'Gay Conversion Therapy' Bans," *The Christian Post*. Available online: https://www.christianpost.com/voice/pro-life-supreme-court-decision-is-good-news-for-religious-liberty-sexual-freedom-and-gay-conversion-therapy-bans.html (accessed April 5, 2020).

Herzog D. (2016), *Cold War Freud: Psychoanalysis in the Age of Catastrophes*, New York: Cambridge University Press.

Kumar A. (2018), "'Gay Conversion Therapy' Ban Vetoed by Maine Governor Citing Religious Freedom," *The Christian Post*. Available online: https://www.christianpost.com/news/gay-conversion-therapy-ban-vetoed-maine-governor-citing-religious-freedom-226022/ (accessed April 6, 2020).

Lewes K. (1988), *The Psychoanalytic Theory of Male Homosexuality*, New York: Simon and Schuster.

Moore P. (2014), "Only 8% of Americans Think Gay Conversion Therapy Works," *YouGov*, June 12. Available online: https://today.yougov.com/topics/lifestyle/articles-reports/2014/06/12/gay-conversion-therapy (accessed April 5, 2020).

Perkins T. (2018), "California Therapy Ban Posed an Unprecedented Threat to Freedom of Religion," *CNS News*. Available online: https://www.cnsnews.com/commentary/tony-perkins/tony-perkins-california-therapy-ban-posed-unprecedented-threat-freedom (accessed April 6, 2020).

Rodgers B. (2020), "Poll: 57% of Utahns Support Banning 'conversion therapy' for Minors," *The Salt Lake Tribune*, February 18. Available online: https://www.sltrib.com/news/politics/2020/02/18/poll-utahns-support/ (accessed April 5, 2020).

Socarides C.W. (1968), *The Overt Homosexual*, Northvale, NJ: Jason Aronson.

Socarides C.W. (1975), *Beyond Sexual Freedom*, New York: Quadrangle.

Socarides C.W. (1995), *Homosexuality: A Freedom Too Far*, Phoenix, AZ: Adam Margrave Books.

Tontonoz M. (2017), "Sandor Rado, American Psychoanalysis, and the Question of Bisexuality," *History of Psychology*, 20 (3): 263–89.

Name Index

Abbot, G. 234
Abzug, R. 56
Adam and Eve 93, 124
Adams, A. 239
Adams, J. 239
Agren, D. 42, 243
Ahlstrom, S. 67
Ahn, I. 153
Albanese, C. L. 84
Alfaro, S. 173
Alito, S. 31
Allen, R. 10, 52–4, 136–7, 139
Ammann, J. 106
Anderson, E. 50
Armstrong, A. 185
Asbury, F. 10
Avery, V. T. 85
Avery, V. Tippetts 85–6
Azuma, E. 146

Baer, H. A. 130, 135, 139
Baker, K. 207
Bakker, J. 61
Bakker, T. F. 61
Baldwin, D. 56
Balmer, R. 52, 58, 65–6, 74, 76–8, 226
Baltimore, Lord (Cecil Calvert) 6
Banker, M. T. 162
Baptista de Segura, J. 178
Barba, L. 170
Barnabas, St 16
Barton, P. 162
Baxter, R. 8–9
Bayer, R. 249, 251–2
Bederman, G. 206
Beecher, C. 56
Bell, L. A. 124
Bendroth, M. L. 57, 206
Benedict XVI (Pope) 43, 230

Beneke, C. 51
Bennet, D. J. 76
Berzon, T. 127
Besen, W. 253
Bibby, R. W. 58
Bickerton, W. 85
Biden, J. 31
Bieber, J. 23
Biencourt de Potrincourt, J. de 180
Bitton, D. 89
Blake, C. 23
Blankenship, A. M. 126, 149
Blum, E. 52, 56, 59, 207
Boles, J. 133
Bolin, C. J. 215
Bolz-Weber, N. 213
Bonomi, P. 49
Borja, M. 152
Bowler, K. 61
Bradley, A. B. 123
Brainerd, D. 182
Braude, A. 211
Brebeuf, J. de 178
Brekus, C. A. 68
Bringhurst, N. G. 98
Brown, J. 254
Bryan, W. J. 74
Buchanan, J. 88
Bueno, R. T. 171
Burke, K. 219
Burns, G. 223–7
Bushman, R. L. 85–6
Butler, A. 72
Butler, J. 52, 58
Butler, M. 242

Cabrillo, J. 4
Calderone, M. S. 216–17
Calhoun, D. B. 182
Calles, P. E. 242

NAME INDEX

Calvin, J. 208
Campbell, A. 13, 14
Campbell, D. E. 27, 245
Cannon, G. Q. 89–90
Carpenter, J. 57
Carpenter, J. A. 72
Carter, H. 52, 55
Carter, J. E. 188
Cartier, J. 5–6, 180
Cartwright, P. 68–9
Castillo-Ramos, T. 170
Cavenaugh, R. 190
Champlain, S. de 5, 241
Chang, G. H. 148
Charles I (King) 235
Chasteen, J. C. 159
Chavez, C. 173
Cheeshateaumuck, C. 182
Chen, K. H. 155
Cheng, A. A. 153
Child, L. M. 56
Chivington, J. 183–4
Choi, K. J. 153
Choy, C. C. 151
Clark, J. R. 86, 93–5
Clay, M. M. 67–8
Clement VII (Pope) 48
Cleveland, G. 90
Cody, W. F. 91
Cogley, R. W. 197
Colbert, S. 31
Collins, K. J. 11
Collinson, P. 47
Columbus, C. 4, 8, 130, 235
Conroy-Krutz, E. 200
Contreras-Flores, J. 165
Cortes, H. 160, 241
Cowdery, O. 187
Crane, R. 144
Criswell, W. A. 76
Cummings, W. 233

Dandelion, P. 49
Danielson, R. A. 171–2
Darby, J. N. 71
Darrow, C. 74
Daughrity, D. B. 125
Davidson, C. C. 167, 169
Davie, G. 33
Davis, R. L. 216

De la Torre, M. 167
de Smet, P.-J. 180
Deloria, V., Jr. 180, 186
Deming, J. C. 51
DeRogatis, A. 219
Desmond, M. 125
Deutsch, S. 162
Dias, E. 172
Diaz, L. 42
Díaz, P. 56
Dobson, J. 77, 253
Dolan, J. P. 164
Douglass, F. 131, 238
Dowland, S. 207, 226
Downie, J. 229
Doyle, C. 256
Driscoll, M. 208
Du Bois, W. E. B. 143
Duffy, J-. C. 96
Dugua De Monts, P. 180
Dulles, J. F. 237

Ecklund, E. H. 154
Eddy, M. B. 15–16, 211–12
Eden, J. 182
Edwards, J. 11, 67–8, 135, 182
Eliot, J. 182–3, 197
Elizondo, V. 161–2, 173
Emirbayer, M. 125
Erie, C. 48
Erzen, T. 219
Espín, O. 160
Espinosa, G. 161–3, 165, 173
Evans, R. L. 95

Falwell, J. 77, 78
Feeney, K. M. 188
Figueroa, A. M. 167, 169
Finkbine, S. C. 224
Finney, C. G. 14, 70
Firmage, E. B. 90
Fisher, L. 49
FitzGerald, F. 67
Flake, K. 54
Flanders, R. B. 85–6
Foote, J. 139
Ford, D. 245
Fowler, L. 183
Francis (Pope) 43, 243
Frazier, E. F. 130

NAME INDEX

Freud, S. 251
Frey, S. 49
Frey, S. R. 200
Fulop, T. 132, 133, 136

García, M. C. 168–9
García, M. T. 162
Gardner, C. J. 219
Garrett, M. 83
Gaustad, E. 52, 55
Gedge, K. E. 219
Gerber, L. 216
Geron, K. 146
Ginsburg, F. D. 226
Givens, T. 52
Glasson, T. 199
Glaude, E., Jr. 130, 140
Gleoge, T. E. W. 66, 71
Gómez, I. 171
Gompers, S. 147
González, J. L. 197
González, O. E. 197
Good, W. C. 239
Graham, B. 14, 21–2, 60, 75–6, 78, 244,
  246
Graham, F. 233
Grant, H. J. 93, 94
Gravely, W. 133
Green, J. C. 245
Greer, A. 197
Griffin, P. 123
Griffith, R. M. 213
Grimke, A. 56, 239
Grimke, S. 56, 239
Guarnieri, G. 98
Gutiérrez, D. G. 161
Gutstadt, H. 147

Hamer, F. L. 240
Hamer, J. C. 98
Hamilton, M. S. 51
Hamnett, B. R. A. 241–2
Han, J. H. J. 155
Harding, S. F. 219
Harding, V. 132
Harris, J. 219
Harrison, B. 90
Harvey, P. 52, 56, 59, 207
Hastings, A. 14
Hatch, N. O. 51–2, 199

Healey, J. F. 125
Hedstrom, M. 58
Henry VIII (King) 48
Herberg, W. 201
Herman, St 7
Herskovits, M. 130
Herzog, D. 250–1
Heyrman, C. 52
Hidalgo, M. 241
Hinojosa, F. 163
Hollinger, D. A. 201, 237
Hong, J. H. 148–9
Hostetler, J. A. 105
Howlett, D. J. 96
Hsu, M. Y. 146–50
Hutchinson, A. 212
Hutter, J. 106–7, 109

Inboden, W. 237
Inman, H. 91
Inveigh, A. 43
Irvine, J. M. 216
Isaac, R. 199

Jackson, A. 183
Jakes, T. D. 23, 61
James, St 16
Jeung, R. 143, 146
Joh, W. A. 154
John Paul II (Pope) 24–5, 43, 230
Johnson, J. 208
Jones, A. 136
Jones, J. M. 98
Jones, R. P. 246
Joseph III 85–6
Joshi, K. Y. 155
Juan Diego, St 160
Juarez, B. 242
Judd, W. 237

Kao, G. Y. 153
Kauffman, B. 253
Kennedy, A. 31
Kennedy, R. F. 163
Keppler, J. 92
Kidd, T. S. 66, 238
Kiemen, M. C. 178
Kim, H. J. 144
Kim, N. 154
Kim, R. Y. 202

NAME INDEX

Kimball, S. W. 187
Kirkby, M.-A. 108
Kleinsasser, J. 108
Knoll, B. R. 215
Koehlinger, A. 207
Koop, C. E. 217
Kraybill, D. B. 113–15
Krivulskaya, S. 219
Kulczycki, A. 229–30
Kumar, A. 255
Kurien, P.A. 154–5

LaHaye, B. 77
LaHaye, T. 77
Lai, T. A. M. 146
Landry, A. 187
Las Casas, B. de 178–80, 197, 235–6
Law, W. 85
Lee, A. 211
Lee, E. 146–7
Lee, H. B. 96
Lee, J. 52, 54, 138–9, 184, 212
Lentz, C. 23
Leonard, G. M. 88
LePage, P. 255
Lewes, K. 251
Lieu, T. 254
Liew, T. -s. 155
Lincoln, A. 89
Lincoln, C. E. 125, 131, 135
Lincoln, E. C. 52, 58
Little, W. 123
Liu, M. 146
Livermore, H. 68
Lomawaima, K. T. 182, 185
Long, C. 129, 130
Long, J. V. 87
Love, B. 123
Lowe, L. 151, 156
Lugo, J. 165
Luker, K. 225–6
Luther, M. 47
Luther King, M., Jr. 21–3, 59–60, 138, 153, 239
Lyman, E. L. 90

MacArthur, J. 208
Machado, D. L. 161–2
Maeda, D. 146

Malcolm X 153
Malloy, J. 246
Mamiya, L. H. 52, 58, 131, 135
Mangrum, R. C. 90
Manickam, J. A. 124
Mann, G. S. 202
Manning, C. 239
Marks, W. 85
Marquette, J. 5
Marsden, G. 57
Marsden, G. M. 71, 74
Martí, G. 160
Martin, L. 58
Martinez, J. 161–2
Martínez, J. 208
Martínez-Vázquez, H. 173
Masci, D. 140
Mason, C. H. 18
Mason, P. Q. 96
Matovina, T. 162
Mayhew, T. 182
McCartney, B. 207
McCorvey, N. 218, 225
McDaniel, E. A. 90–1
McGirr, L. 244
McKenzie, V. 23
McLaren, A. 223, 229
McLaren, A. T. 223, 229
McLoughlin, W. G. 67
McPherson, A. S. 21, 72–3, 211
McVety, C. 245
Medina, L. 162
Medina, N. 172, 173
Menard, R. 178
Menjívar, C. 171
Miki, R. 152
Miller, W. 15
Miranda, J. 162, 173
Mohamed, B. 140
Mohler, A. 208
Monson, J. Q. 245
Moody, D. L. 71
Moore, P. 250
Moore, R. 78
Moore, R. L. 74
Mora, A. 162
Morgentaler, H. 228–9
Moroni (Angel) 82
Mortimer, G. H. 95
Morton, F. L. 228

NAME INDEX

Moslener, S. 219
Mott, J. R. 205
Moultrie, M. N. 219
Mulder, M. 160
Murphy, T. 238, 241

Newell, L. K. 85–6
Nicolosi, J. 253–4
Niza, M. de 5
Noll, M. A. 13, 48, 50–2, 55–8, 65, 238–9, 246
Norman, W. V. 229
Numrich, P. D. 202

Obama, B. 98, 244
Occom, S. 198
Oikawa, M. 152
Okihiro, G. Y. 143, 146
Olivares, L. 162
Omatsu, G. 153
Osteen, J. 61
Ostler, J. 185

Parham, C. F. 17, 57
Park, B. E. 85
Paul, A. 184
Paul, St 16
Pelosi, N. 31
Pelotte, D. E. 180
Penn, W. 7, 49, 110
Pérez, L. 166, 167
Perin, R. 238, 241
Perkins, T. 255–6
Perry, R. 233–4
Peter, St 16
Petro, A. M. 217
Pickup, D. 254
Pinn, A. 140
Pon, G. 152
Porterfield, A. 52, 67
Pratt, R. 185
Prince, G. A. 98
Pruitt, N. T. 201
Putnam, R. D. 27
Putney, C. 205

Quinn, D. M. 84, 91, 93–6

Raboteau, A. 52, 132, 133, 136
Rado, S. 251–2
Raleigh, W. 5

Ramírez, D. 57, 163
Ramos, A. 160
Randolph, P. 132
Reagan, R. 22, 77, 78
Reedy Solano, J. 171
Reynolds, G. 89
Riedemann, P. 109
Riess, J. 96, 98
Rigdon, S. 85
Rivera-Pagán, L. N. 164, 179
Roach, D. 185
Roberts, B. H. 90
Roberts, J. 31
Robertson, P. 77
Rodgers, B. 250
Roland Sintos, C. 152
Romney, M. 54, 245
Roosevelt, F. D. 94
Roosevelt, T. 91, 205
Rosetti, C. 93–4

Sagarena, R. L. 162
Sánchez-Walsh, A. 163
Schaff, P. 87
Schlund-Vials, C. J. 156
Schultz, K. M. 58–9, 201
Scopes, J. 73
Sehat, D. 51
Selby, G. S. 239
Sernett, M. C. 131–2, 138
Serra, J. 4–5, 7
Seymour, W. J. 17, 57, 72
Shea, J. G. 177–8, 180, 185
Shields, S. 98
Shipps, J. 86
Silverman, D. J. 198
Simons, M. 114
Singer, M. 130, 135, 139
Slominski, K. L. 216
Smith, C. S. 186
Smith, E. H. 84, 85
Smith, G. A. 88, 140, 208
Smith, H. 85–6
Smith, J. 15, 23, 52–3, 55, 81–6, 98, 186–7, 245
Smith, J. F. 91, 95
Smith, S. 86
Smith, W. 86
Smoot, R. 91–3
Snow, J. C. 148
Socarides, C. W. 252–4

NAME INDEX

Sotomayor, S. 31
Spaulding, H. H. 184
Stanton, E. C. 239
Steinegger, H. 89
Stepnick, A. 125
Stone, B. 13–14
Strang, J. J. 85–6
Suárez, M. M. W. 167

Talbot, C. 54
Tarango, A. 185
Tatum, B. D. 124
Taylor, A. 4
Taylor, J. 90, 93
Taylor, S. M. 213
Tchen, J. K. W. 149
Tekakwitha, K. 180–1, 197
Templeton, C. 246
Tentler, L. W. 226
Teresa (Sister) 165
Thomas, C. 31, 256
Thornton, B. J. 160
Tierney, W. G. 182
Tijerina, R. L. 173
Todd, J. T. 95
Todorov, T. 159
Tontonoz, M. 252
Trudeau, J. 31
Trudeau, P. E. 26, 241
Trujillo, R. L. 167
Truman, H. S. 76
Trump, D. 76, 77, 97, 208–9, 233–4, 250
Truth, S. 55
Tseng, T. 126
Tuckman, J. 245
Turley, R. E., Jr. 88
Turner, J. G. 96
Turner, N. 238
Tweed, T. 167
Twiss, R. 186

Vásquez, M. A. 171–2
Veach, C. 23
Vidal, J. R. 164–5

Wacker, G. 52, 58, 71–2, 75
Wackerhausen, J. 126
Wadkins, T. H. 171
Wahlberg, M. 31

Walker, R. W. 88
Warren, R. 23
Washburn, A. W. 185
Watt, A. J. 162
Watt, G. D. 87
Weaver-Zercher, D. L 116
Wei, W. 146
Weis, R. 56
Weisenfeld, J. 139
Wellman, D. T. 124
Wells, I. 239
Wenger, T. 147
Wesley, C. 11
Wesley, J. 11–12, 67, 136–7
West, C. 90–1, 240
West, K. 23
Wheeler, R. 199
Wheelock, E. 198
White, E. G. 15
White, H. R. 216
White, P. 61
Whitefield, G. 11, 13, 50, 67–8, 134, 135
Whitman, M. 184–5
Whitman, N. 185
Wigger, J. 52, 61
Wijeysinghe, C. L. 123
Wilcox, M. M. 216
Wilkerson, R., Jr. 23
Williams, D. K. 218, 224–6
Williams, R. 134
Williams, R. B. 202
Wilmore, G. 131
Winiarski, D. 49
Winthrop, J. 235–6
Wolley, L. C. 93–4
Wong, K. S. 149
Wood, B. 49, 200
Woodruff, W. 90–1
Woolley, J. 93
Worthen, M. 72
Wright, B. 182
Wuthnow, R. 76

Yeats, D. 149
Yohn, S. M. 162
Yoo, D. 146
Yoo, W. 151
Young, B. 15, 53, 85–9, 91

Subject Index

abolitionism 70
abortion laws 76–7, 224–5
  abstinence-only education 227
  antiabortion movement 224, 226
  in Canada 228–9
  debates 218, 223
  liberalization of 224
  in Mexico 229–30
  restrictions, state level 227
  in the United States 224
abstinence-only education 217, 219
Act on Religious Associations and Public
  Worship 24
Act Prohibiting Importation of Slaves 10
Acts of the Apostles 16–17
African Americans
  Africanisms 130
  Black Baptists 134–6
  Black churches 125, 131–6, 140
  and Christian faith 131–3, 238
  interracial worship services 133
  Protestantism 48–9, 52, 56–9
  racial discrimination 125, 239
  religious identity formation 129–31, 140
  secret religious spaces 132–3
  slavery and enslavement system
    129–30, 238
African Methodist Episcopal (AME) Church
  10, 52
All Tribes Indian Assembly of God 185
altar call 14
American Board of Commissioners for
  Foreign Missions 200
American Civil War 8, 55–6, 125
American Colony: Meet the Hutterites
  television program 116
American Indian Religious Freedom Act
  (Public Law 95–341) 188
Americanism 201
American Revolution 51, 55, 199, 236, 238
Amish 106–7, 110–14

The Amish in the American Imagination
  (Weaver-Zercher) 116
Anabaptism 9, 105, 116–17
  Amish 106–7, 110–14
  Hutterites 106–10
  Mennonites 106–7, 114–16
  religious persecution 106
Angeles Temple 21
Anglican Church 24–5, 48, 67, 136
Anglicanism 48
antiabortion law 224–6
anti-polygamy laws 89–91
antislavery movement 239
anti-Vietnam War campaigns 145
apostles faith 16–17
Apostle to the Indians 182
Apostolicae Sedis 224
Apostolic United Brethren (AUB) 93
Arminianism 69
Asian American hypochondria 153
Asian American Political Alliance (AAPA)
  145
Asian Americans 125–6, 143
  Asian Christianities 147
  Chinese immigrants 147–9
  Christianities 143–4, 152–5
  educational reform 145–6
  evangelical Christianity 151
  Hmong Christians 152
  immigration histories/policies 147–52,
    155–6
  Japanese immigration 146, 149
  Korean immigration 146, 154
  migration of Asian 146–7, 202
  post-Second World War American
    challenge 143
  translational networks 155
  TWLF and 143
Assemblies of God church 18, 72, 76
assimilated Mennonites 114
Azusa Street Revival 15, 17–19, 57, 72, 163

SUBJECT INDEX

baptism 17, 48, 105
  Amish settlements 111–12
  The Dordrecht Confession of Faith
    document 112
  of the Holy Spirit 57, 71, 76
  Hutterite colony 108
  during the Second Great Awakening 69
Baptist movement 19, 48, 52, 56, 199
  Black Baptists 134–6
Battle of Peking 150
bend-and-break-the-rules Catholics 32
benevolent empire missionary 199–200
Bethel School of Supernatural Ministry 23
Beyond Sexual Freedom (Socarides) 252
Bible. *See also* Gospel
  dispensationalism 71
  Fundamentalists/modernists 57
  guidebook 219
  interpretation of 113
  plain reading of 71
  race and racism in 124
  stories 9–10
  studies 15, 56
  translation 182, 197
bishop
  Amish 111–12
  Hutterites 109
  Mennonites 115
Black Baptists 134–6, 140
Black Methodists 136–40
Black Power movement 145
Boarding School Movement 184–5
Book of Commandments 83
The Book of Mormon (Smith) 15, 52, 81–2,
  187
Burning Vision 152
by-the-rules Catholics 31–2

Calvinism 69, 208
Canada/Canadians 3, 5, 25
  abolishment of slavery in 238–9
  abortion laws in 228–9
  Boarding School Movement 184–5
  Catholics in 23–4
  Christian reformers in 239
  Christian Right 245
  education in 37
  immigrants to 58
  Latinx population 172
  mosaic 7
  political discourse in 233–4

Protestantism 24–5, 51, 58
  sexual abuse, document on 42
Cane Ridge Revival 13–14, 69
Carlisle Boarding School 185
Catholic Charities 39–40
Catholicism/Catholics 17, 31
  in Cuba 165–7
  culture and society 40, 44
  Dominicans as 169
  education 36–8
  health care 38–9
  in Mexico 160–3, 241–3
  parishes 35–6
  Pope Francis 43
  priests and nuns 41
  in Puerto Rico 164
  Salvadorans 169
  salvation 47
  secularism 40
  sexual abuse 41–2
  social services 39–40
  typology of 31–3
  in unity and nationalism 242
Catholic Maryknoll Missionary Society 149
celestial marriage 15, 93
Charismatic movement 76–7
chattel slavery 8
Chicano Movement 162, 173
Chinese
  Christians 126
  migrants 146, 148, 202
Chinese Exclusion Act 146–7
Christian Methodist Episcopal (CME) 137
Christian Right in Canada 245
Christians/Christianity
  African American and 129–41
  Asian Americans and 143–56
  denominations 2–3
  enslaved Africans and 8–10, 70, 131
  influence of 6–7
  Latinx Christianities 159–73
  masculinity and 205–9
  missionization and 197–202
  movements 14–15
  Native Americans and 177–90
  native leaders' concerns with 186
  Pentecostal 15–17, 71–2
  and politics 77, 233–45
  preaching 11–14, 67–8
  purity culture 219
  racism (*see* race/racism)

SUBJECT INDEX

revivalism 13–14, 17, 67–8
sexuality (*see* sex/sexuality)
in twenty-first century 245–6
in United States 1–3, 94–6
women and 185, 211–14
Christian Science today. *See* Church of
Christ, Scientist
churchly orientation 66
Church of Christ, Scientist 15, 212
Church of England (COE) 48, 136, 181,
199, 236
Church of God in Christ 18, 72, 76
Church of Jesus Christ of Latter-day Saints
(LDS) 15, 52–4, 83, 85, 93
Correlation Committee 96
Mormons in 96–7, 186–8
plural marriage 94
political force 245
restorationist movements 98
Church of Jesus Christ of the Children of
Zion 85
civilizing mission 235, 237–8
civil rights movement 59
*Cold War Freud: Psychoanalysis in the Age
of Catastrophe* (Herzog) 250–1
colonial missions 197–9
Colored Methodist Episcopal church 137
communal racism 124
complementarianism 213
confession 47, 105, 112
Congregational churches 48, 67
conservative movement 19–21, 243–5
conversion therapy 249
American Psychiatric Association 252–3
and First Amendment 254–6
homosexuality and 249
with minors 256
of religion, gender, and sexuality
249–51
Correlation Committee 96
*Critical Theology against US Militarism in
Asia* (Kim and Joh) 154
Cubans 165–8
culture and society, Catholics 40, 44

Dariusleut colony 108
denominationalism 12–15, 49
Protestant denomination 65
Disciples of Christ 13, 14
dispensationalism 71
Doctrine and Covenants 83

don't-know-the-rules Catholics 33
The Dordrecht Confession of Faith 112

Edinburgh Missionary Conference of 1910
205
Edmunds Act 90
Edmund-Tucker Act 90
education
Amish 113
Catholics 36–8
Hutterites 109
Mennonites 116
Eliot's mission 197–8
El Salvador 169–71
emancipation 10
England 7
Reformation in 48–9
English missionary society 197
European Protestant Reformation 66
Europe/European 7, 19
colonialization at Latin America 159
slavery 8–10
state churches in 1, 14
evangelicalism 11, 14, 24, 33, 60
abortion laws 224
Asian Americans 151
Charismatic movement 76–7
commitments 66
First Great Awakening 67–8
groups 65
history and beliefs 65–6
Korean American evangelicals 154
missionaries 200
muscular Christianity 207–8
neo-evangelicalism 74–6
postwar years 70–1
Protestant doctrinal orientations 66
religious Right 76–8
Second Great Awakening 68–70
sexuality behavior 219
Evangelical Lutheran Church of America
(ELCA) denomination 213
Exclusion Act 147

faith in Christianity 16–17, 19, 67
Federal Council of Churches (FCC), 147–8
Fellowship of Christian Athletes 207
Feminist Praxis Against U.S. Militarism
(Kim and Joh) 154
First Amendment 1–2, 14, 89
and conversion therapy 250, 253–6

SUBJECT INDEX

First Great Awakening 11, 12, 67–8, 134, 136, 238
First Nations. *See* Indigenous people
First Vision 84
First World War 58
Five Civilized Tribes 183
Five Solas of reformation 66
Foundation of Christian Doctrine 114
Foursquare Church 21
France 5
    Jesuit missionary 185
    Roman Catholics 180
Franciscan missionaries 197
Francis effect 162
Free African Society (FAS) 136–7
free agents 19
free population 147
Fundamentalist Church of Jesus Christ of Latter-Day Saints (FLDS) 93–4
Fundamentalist movement 19–21, 57, 72–4
    Fundamentalist Protestant organizations 244
    masculinity and 206
    Mormonism and 93–4, 96
    political and social issues 243–4
The Fundamentals: A Testimony to the Truth 57, 72

gathering 23, 70, 86
gay and lesbian Christians 215–16
Gebet (prayer) 109
gender complementarianism 213, 251–2
glossolalia 71, 76
the Gospel 9–11, 66
Green v. Connally religious Right case 77
Gütergemeinschaft 106

Hart Cellar Act 150
health care, Catholics 38–9
Hebrew Bible 52–3
Hispanic origin group 161
Hmong Christians 152
Holy Spirit 17
    baptism of 57, 71, 76
homosexual/homosexuality 216, 254
    conversion therapy 249
    gender complementarity 251–2
Homosexuality: A Freedom Too Far (Socarides) 252
hospitals, Catholics 38–9
House for All Sinners and Saints 213

Huffington Post 140
Hutterites 106–10

ignore-the-rules Catholics 33
Immigration Act 150, 201–2
immigration and missionization 201–2
Immigration and Nationality Act 201
Independent Black Church movement 133–4, 140
Indian missions 198
Indian Removal Act 183
Indians Christianity 197–9
Indigenous people 4. *See also* Native Americans
    and Asian American 152
    Catholics and 197
institutional racism 124
interdenominational organizations 186
invisible institution 131–2

Japanese
    Canadians 152
    Christians 126
    migration 143, 146–7
Jehovah's Witnesses 15
Jesuit missionaries 49
Jesus Christ 9–10
    curing sickness 38
    faith in 16–17, 22
    salvation 71
    on social services 39
    teachings 187
Jim Crow laws 17
Jones Act of 1917 164
Judeo-Christian 58

King Philip's War 182, 197, 199
Korean American evangelicals 154

La Luz del Mundo (Light of the World) 24
Lamanites 81–2, 187
La Matanza 169
Latino Reformation 172
Latinos 125
Latinx Christianities 159, 172–3
    Cubans 165–8
    Dominicans 168–9
    economies and political regimes 160
    Latin Americans 159–60
    Mexicans 160–3
    Popular Catholicism 160

268   SUBJECT INDEX

Puerto Ricans 163–5
Salvadorans 169–73
Lehrerleut colony 108
LGBTIQ
ordination 215–16
rights movement 253
liberal/conservative movement 20–1
Liberation Theology 242
Lord's Supper 48
Los Angeles Times 17
Louisiana Purchase of 1803 5

Macedonian call 184
Marielitos 167
Mar Thoma Syrian Christians 154
Martyrs Mirror 106
masculinity 205–6. *See also* muscular
Christians/Christianity
Mennonites 106–7, 114–16, 163
mestizaje 160–1
Methodist movement 11, 51–2, 56, 199
Black Methodists 136–9
Mexican Revolution 24, 56, 162
Mexico/Mexicans 5, 7, 24–6, 31
abortion laws 229–30
Catholicism in 31, 33, 160–2, 241–3
conservatism and 245
immigrants 202
labor reform 162
political discourse in 233–5
Protestantism in 56
racialization and missionization of 161–2
religiopolitical movements 162
sexual abuse 42
Misión Cristiana Elim (MCE) 171–2
missionaries 5, 7–8, 18, 160–3
missionization 197
in benevolent empire 199–200
Catholic and Jewish immigration and
201
colonial missions 197–9
evangelical missionaries 200
foreign missions from United States
200
Protestant missionary 199
reverse missionary 202
twentieth-century 201–2
Monkey Trial. *See* Scopes Trial
Montgomery Bus Boycott 59
Moor's Indian Charity School 198

Moral Majority religiopolitical organization
77, 244
Mormon Church 24, 187–8, 245
Mormonism 15, 54
American faith on 90–3
anti-polygamy laws 89–92
Christian nationalism 94–6
divisions 85–6
fundamentalism and 93–4
and Gospel 187
Lamanites and 187
Latter-Day Saint restorationist
movement 96–8, 186–8
missionaries and beliefs 83
Mormon Tabernacle Choir 90
polygamy and 93–4
restorationist movement 81
traditional narratives of 84
Utah and the Brighamites 86–7
Utah War 87–9
Morrill Anti-Bigamy Act 89
Mountain Meadows Massacre 87–9
muscular Christians/Christianity 205–6
evangelical supporters and 207–8
female leadership, resistance of 205–6
fundamentalists 206
Gospel of Christianity 205
Promise Keepers 207–8
racism of 207
Roman Catholics 207
sports 205, 207

National Association for Research &
Therapy of Homosexuality (NARTH)
253
National Association for the Repeal of
Abortion Laws (NARAL) 225
National Baptist Convention (NBC) 136,
138
nationalism 94–6
National Organization for Women 225
Native American Church of North America
(NACNA) 188–9
Native Americans 4, 82–3, 125
Boarding School Movement 184–5
Church of Jesus Christ of Latter-Day
Saints (Mormon) missionary 186–8
interdenominational organizations 186
leaders' concerns with Christianity 186
Native American Church 188–9

SUBJECT INDEX

Protestant missionary 181–4
religious orders 177
Roman Catholic missionary 177–80
Spanish missionaries 177–8, 180
women's contributions, spreading of
    Christianity 185
Nauvoo-era practices 85–6
neo-evangelicalism 74–6
Nephites 81–2, 187
New England Company 48, 197–8
New France 5
new light preachers 49
New Order Amish 110
New Testament 48, 105
    Amish reading of 112
    Hutterites reading of 109–10
New York City 6, 164–5
niche churches 19
NIFLA v. Becerra 256
nondenominational churches 3, 13, 65,
    154
nones 33–4, 40
North America 3, 24–6
    Catholics in 31–44
    Christianity (*see* Christians/Christianity)
    evangelical Christianity (*see*
        evangelicalism)
    immigrants 4–5
    Native Americans in (*see* Native
        Americans)

Old Order Amish 110, 114
Old Order Mennonites 114–16
Ontario Progressive Conservative Party
    245
Open Door policy 148
ordination 215
Ordnung (church rules) 113, 115
organization(s) of church 34–5
Our Lady of Peace 169
The Overt Homosexual 252

parishes 35–6, 41
    social services 39
Pennsylvania German 106, 112, 115
Pentecostal churches 18–19
Pentecostalism 14–15, 17–18, 21, 24, 57,
    71–2
    and Charismatic movement 76
    in El Salvador 171

Latinx Pentecostal denominations 163
    in Puerto Rica 165
Perpetual Emigrating Fund (PEF) Company
    86–7
personal racism 124
Pew Research Center 65, 77
    on African American Christians 140
    on Christian groups 125–6
    Christianity on politics 233
    on women and Christianity 211
Philippine-American Collegiate Endeavor
    (PACE) Philosophy and Goals 146
Pietism 66
pious paternalism 161
politics
    colonialism 235–7
    conservatism and culture wars 243–5
    influence of Christianity on 233, 235–7
    in Mexico, Canada, and the United
        States 233–4
    reform and progressivism 238–40
    slavery and 238–9
polygamy 85, 89–92
    Mormon Fundamentalism and 93–4
postmillennialism 69–71
premillennialism 70–1
Presbyterianism 13, 66
priests and nuns 41
progressive movement 19–21
Progressive National Baptist association
    138
Progressive National Baptist Convention,
    Inc., 136
Promise Keepers (PK) 207–8
prosperity gospel 60
Protecting Minors from Sexual Abuse:
    A Call to the Catholic Faithful in
    Canada for Healing, Reconciliation,
    and Transformation 42
Protestant-Catholic-Jew 201
Protestant German Christians 6
Protestantism 6–7, 11, 17, 24–6
    African Americans 48–9, 56–8
    American missionaries 148–9
    belief and biblical interpretation 57
    in Canada 57–8
    Charismatic movement and 76
    in Cuba 166
    denominations 49, 51
    enslaved African Americans 52

evangelical 60
Latinx Protestantism 163
methodism 51–2
in Mexico 56
new light preachers 49
Protestant Church 24, 47, 50
Reformation 47, 83
in Salvadorans 170
slavery 55–6
in the United States 55, 58
Protestant missionary 181–4, 199
Protestant Reformation (1517–1648) 105
Puerto Ricans 163–5, 202
Puritanism 6, 10, 48, 66
The Purpose Driven Life (Warren) 23

Quaker American Friends Service
        Committee 149
Quakers 7, 9, 49, 215, 238
Quebec 5, 24
    church and state 241–2

race/racism 123–4, 126–7
    African Americans 125
    Asian Americans 125–6, 147–54
    in biblical context 124
    and Christianity 123
    Latinos 125
    of muscular Christianity 207
    Native Americans 125
radical inclusivity 213
radical reformers 105
rapture 71
rationalism 17
rebaptizers 105
Reformation 47, 83. *See also*
        Protestantism
religiopolitical movements 162
religious conservatives 255
religious education 36–8
religious freedom 2, 14, 19, 24, 51
religious identification, Catholic family 33
Religious Landscape Survey 65
religious Right 76–8
Reorganized Church of Jesus Christ of
        Latter Day Saints (RLDS) 85
Reparative Therapy of Male Homosexuality
        (Nicolosi) 253
restorationism 81, 84, 96–8
reverse missionary 202

revivalism 13–14
    meetings 17–18
    preachers 67–8
Roe v. Wade case 76, 218, 223, 225
Roman Catholic Church 7, 23–6. *See also*
        Catholicism/Catholics
    organization(s) of church 34–5
    in Quebec 241
Roman Catholic missionary 177–80
rules-don't-pertain-to-me Catholics 33
R v. Morgentaler case 228

sacraments 47–8
Salem Witch Trials 10
Salvadorans 169–73
salvation 47–8, 69, 71
same-sex marriage 215–16
Sand Creek Massacre 183–4
Schmiedeleut colony 108
Scofield Reference Bible 71
Scopes Monkey Trial 20, 73–4, 244
Second Great Awakening 13–15, 17, 68–70,
        134, 136, 199
Second World War 58, 150, 201
sermons 11–13, 22, 67, 112, 135
Seventh-Day Adventists 15
Sex Information and Education Council of
        the United States 216
sex/sexuality
    abortion 218
    education about 216–17
    evangelical sexuality 219
    female ordination 215
    gender 215
    LGBTIQ ordination 215–16
    same-sex marriage 215–16
    sex scandals 219
    sexual abuse 41–2, 219
sexual orientation change therapies
        249–53
    First Amendment and 254–6
    licensed therapists 254
sins 13–14, 22, 47, 113, 124
slavery 8–10, 55–6, 70
    Methodism and 136
    politics of liberation 238
    religious communities worship 131–3
Slave Trade Act of 1794 10
Social Gospel 239
social services, Catholics 39–40

SUBJECT INDEX

Society for the Propagation of the Gospel
(SPG) 129, 199
Society in Scotland for Promoting Christian
Knowledge 198
Southwestern Assemblies of God
University 185
Spanish 4–5
Catholic missionaries 177–8, 180
Spanish-American War 164–5
speaking in tongues 57
state churches 1–2
St. Francis Xavier Church 32, 34, 36
St. George's Methodist Episcopal Church.
136
Strangites 86
Sub-Saharan Africa 18
syncretistic practices 189, 197

team Mennonites 114
technologies
Amish 114
Hutterites 110
Tennessee's Butler Act 73
Third World Liberation Front (TWLF) 143
Third World liberation movements 145–6
traditional Mennonites 114
Trail of Tears 183
transnationalism 169, 171
tribes 4, 8, 178, 187

United Church of Canada 24–5
United States 4–5, 19
Anabaptists groups in 9
Black churches in 134
Boarding School Movement 184–5
Catholics in 23–4
Christian nation 1, 3, 94–6
Christian reformers in 239
Christians/Christianity in 1–3, 10, 19, 23–5
church and state, separation of 241–2
church shop 19
conservative/progressive 19–20
Cubans in 166–7
denominationalism 12–14
dioceses in 41–2
Dominicans in 167–8
education in 36–7
Europeanization of 8, 130
evangelical Christians in 65–6
foreign missions from 200

freedom in worship 14
groups of Christians in 125–6
Hmong Christians 152
Hutterites 107–8
immigration in 201–2
metaphysical religion 84
Methodist churches in 14
Mormonism 90–3, 96–8
Pentecostal movement 21
politics in 7, 233–46
Protestantism 55, 58
revivalism 13–14
Salvadorans in 170
slavery in 130
state church in 2
younger people in 23
unlicensed preaching 67
Utah
and the Brighamites 86–7
Mountain Meadows Massacre 87–9
religious identity 95

*Varieties of African American Religious
Experience* (Pinn) 140
Vatican II 41–2
virgin birth 57
The Virgin of Guadalupe 160–1, 197

Whitefieldarians 49, 60
women and Christianity 185, 211–14
antislavery movement 239
female ordination 215
gender complementarianism 213
institutional and structural barriers 212–13
in leadership positions 205–6, 211
legalizing abortion 218
pastors and co-pastors 72
rights of 56, 68, 70, 76, 218, 225, 239
worship, freedom in 14, 19
worship services
Amish 113
Hutterites 109
Mennonites 115

Yellow Peril 149–50
Young Men's Christian Association (YMCA)
205–6

Zion (AME/AMEZ) denominations 137–9
Zoe Church 23

Printed in the USA
CPSIA information can be obtained
at www.ICGtesting.com
LVHW081940120524
779921LV00005B/530